Y0-AFJ-058

STRUCTURAL APPROACHES to SOUTH INDIA STUDIES

This volume is based on papers presented
at the Biennial Meeting of the
Society for South India Studies,
Wilson College, March 15-18, 1973.

Cover

Adapted from a watercolor painting
by Helen-Lee Jones

Frontispiece

Ink drawing, Martha Bush Ashton

STRUCTURAL APPROACHES to SOUTH INDIA STUDIES

Edited by
Harry M. Buck &
Glenn E. Yocum

WILSON BOOKS
1974

WILSON BOOKS, a collection for the liberal arts, are published by *Conococheague Associates, Inc.*, on the campus of Wilson College.

Composed in IBM Baskerville by Garnet W. Thrush
Printed by Kingsport Press, Kingsport, TN.
Composed and printed in the United States of America

Library of Congress Number 74-77412
ISBN: 0-89012-000-5

Contents

Photo Credits

Chapter Two. The Cage of Form

- I A. William Blake, The Ancient of Days, watercolor and print, 1794. Courtesy, Whitworth Art Gallery, University of Manchester.
- I B. Basohli painting, Hiraṇyagarbha (The Golden Egg), Late 18th century. Courtesy, Bharat Kala Bhavan, Banaras Hindu University.
- II A. Hildesheim Cathedral, The Accusation of Adam and Eve, bronze panel from the doorway of the Cathedral of Saint Michael, 12th century. Courtesy, Europe Verlag.
- II B. Kangra painting, Rādhā and Kṛṣṇa in the Grove, Raja of Lambagraon Collection, Late 18th century. Courtesy, Dr. M. S. Randhawa.
- III A. Gustave Dore, The Deluge, Engraving, 19th century.
- III B. Kangra painting, Kṛṣṇa and Gopīs Bathing, Late 18th century. Courtesy, Bharat Kala Bhavan, Banaras Hindu University.
- IV A. Peter Paul Rubens, Last Judgment: Fall of the Damned (Detail), oil, ca. 1620. Courtesy, Alte Pinacthek, Munich.
- IV B. Jaipur painting, Rāsamaṇḍala with Kṛṣṇa and Gopīs Dancing. Courtesy, Maharaja of Jaipur Museum, ca. 1880.
- V A. Auguste Rodin, The Thinker, bronze, ca. 1880. Courtesy, the Cleveland Museum of Art. Gift of Ralph King.
- V B. Sarnath sculpture, Buddha, stone, 5th century. Sarnath Museum, Sarnath. Courtesy, Sarnath Museum and American Institute of Indian Studies.
- VI A. Matthais Grunewald, Christ Crucified, Isenheim Altarpiece (Detail), oil on panel, ca. 1510-1515. Courtesy, Musée d'Unterlinden a Colmar.
- VI B. South Indian sculpture, Śiva as Nataraja, copper, 16th century. Marianne Brimmer Fund, 21.1829. Courtesy, Museum of Fine Arts, Boston.
- VII A. Pablo Picasso, Guernica, oil on canvas, 1937. On extended loan to The Museum of Modern Art, New York, from the artist. Courtesy, The Museum of Modern Art, New York.
- VII B. Kishangarh painting, Kṛṣṇa Holding up Mount Govardhana, ca. 1775. Courtesy, Bharat Kala Bhavan, Banaras Hindu University.
- VIII A. Paul Klee, Tightrope Walker, lithograph, 1923. Courtesy, The Museum of Modern Art, New York.
- VIII B. Prāṇāyāma (Subtle Centres and Channels of the Body), print, 20th century.
- X A. Auguste Rodin, The Prodigal Son, bronze, 1880-1882?. Musée Rodin, Paris. Courtesy, Press Ltd., London.
- X B. Mathura sculpture, Jain Votive Tablet, stone, ca. 1st. century A.D. State Museum, Lucknow. Courtesy, State Museum, Lucknow and American Institute of Indian Studies.
- XI A. Lunar Module, Apollo Nine. NASA Photo.
- XI B. Mewar painting, The Search for Kṛṣṇa in the Moonlight, ca. 1730. Raja of Udaipur Collection. Courtesy, Victoria and Albert Museum, Udaipur.

Chapter Seven. Paṇḍharpūr, The City of Saints

Viṣṇu Image, Courtesy, The American Academy of Benares

Sketches of the Paṇḍharpūr Kṣetra and the Viṭhobā Temple were prepared by the author, who made use of the two sketches found in G. Delury, Cult of Viṭhobā.

All photographs were supplied by the authors of the respective chapters.

Introduction

STRUCTURE, structural, and structuralism are terms which enjoy great popularity in academic circles today. They are also terms which are anything but univocal. To appreciate the diversity of meanings such words are capable of bearing one need only scan the essays which follow. It would be an understatement to say that all our contributors do not use structure in exactly the same way.

Fortunately, scholarly trends usually transcend their trendiness; for beneath the jargon there is more than fad. Willingness to re-examine received answers is always a sign of intellectual health – and one notes this willingness in several papers included here. Even those who refuse to imbibe at the well of structural terminology are well aware of the choices they have made.

In their original form, the papers in this volume were among those presented at the third biennial conference of the Society for South India Studies, held at Wilson College, Chambersburg, Pennsylvania, March, 1973. The conference theme was identical to the title of the present collection: *Structural Approaches to South India Studies.* As a perusal of the essays will readily show, our bonds as Indianists with particular interest in the southern regions of the subcontinent are far stronger than our ties as structuralists. However, at least some of the conference's success can be attributed to the fact that, although discussion was intense and prolonged, we never agreed or attempted to agree about what structure is or should be. Indeed, we did not even stage a final concluding session to weigh our various views. We did not come expecting to convert or to be converted.

To our mind, the value of associations like the SSIS (and publications such as this one) lies in its drawing together scholars of diverse disciplinary backgrounds who share common interest and, because of its small size, enabling them to interact in individually scheduled sessions. The cross-fertilization which occurs can only be beneficial to furthering our understanding of India.

If this volume seems dominated by linguists, anthropologists, art historians, and students of religion, it is not because political scientists, economists, and historians have no interest in South India. In fact, these latter disciplines are not unrepresented in the SSIS. Our 1973 conference, presumably because of its theme, simply attracted the above-mentioned types.

To introduce the studies which follow, we relate briefly some of the major ideas in our contributors' articles. The lead essay by Suzanne Hanchett discusses the general theme of structuralism and several of the methodological tendencies covered by that label. Basing her discussion mainly on the work of Lévi-Strauss, Dumont, and Piaget, she deals with the philosophical features of structuralism in a sensitive and lucid manner. Hanchett points out the structuralist emphases on ideological systems, totality, intuition, and the dialectical relationship between the subject-observer and his object of study. Her essay concludes with observations regarding the applicability of structuralist methods to the study of social organization.

Walter Spink juxtaposes carefully selected illustrations from the art traditions of India and the West as a springboard for grand-scale cultural comparison on the differences between eastern and western understandings of man, God, and the cosmos. While some of our more empirically oriented readers will doubtless have reservations about such broad generalizations, we recommend Spink's essay for its ingenuity of illustration and its overall provocativeness. From a structuralist perspective, one wonders if there are any categories mediating the oppositions between Indian and western thought outlined by Spink.

Although Kenneth A. David's essay on caste ranking in Jaffna, Sri Lanka focuses on a region which, strictly speaking, lies outside of South India, scholars have long recognized the many social and cultural continuities between the island and the Indian mainland. Add to this the fact that Jaffna is a Tamil-speaking, Hindu, caste-structured society and the reasons for including David's paper become all the more apparent. More directly than any of the other contributors, David comes to grips with the opposition (!) between social structural and structuralist (*à la* Louis Dumont) interpretations of caste. David claims that by attending the various "normative codes" of the caste society itself he is able to avoid the reductionist aspects of both the above approaches. His methodological self-consciousness makes his attempt at mediation between behaviorist (social structural) and symbolic (structuralist) points of view particularly valuable.

The two essays on sociolinguistics are in their separate ways concerned with the relationship between language form and the community of language users. In discussing code-switching – the alternation of different languages or dialects in the course of a single conversation – M. Shanmugam Pillai directs attention to the instances of such alternation in the dialogue found in a recent novel by the prominent contemporary Tamil writer Jayagandan. Shanmugam Pillai's detailed categorization and analysis of the examples of code-switching in the novel lead to some interesting observations about the status of the speakers and the occasions when shifts from one code to another occur. One might say that code-switching is a device whereby Jayagandan's characters – by extension multilingual Indians generally – are able to free themselves from some of the limitations of their own way of life. The remarkable diversity and richness of Indian society appears in this essay in a seldom noticed aspect.

Susan S. Bean deals with quite a different feature of the way in which language interconnects with social reality. Here the emphasis is on the dialectics of the communication process itself – in the spatial, social, and role distance encoded in the /i/-/a/ alternation in Kannada demonstratives, words signifying male and female human beings, and first and second person pronouns. Furthermore, Bean claims that this semantic structure is not limited to Kannada but may have been characteristic of proto-Dravidian. The socio-cultural implications of her treatment of the opposition between /i/ and /a/ are especially intriguing with regard to Indian attitudes toward pollution and the apparent concern with ritual purity evidenced in the archaeological remains of the Indus valley civilization, whose language is often speculated to have been a form of Dravidian.

The next essay returns to aesthetic phenomena, now in the narrow focus of a localized form. Yaksagana is a type of religious dance-drama largely neglected by western scholars, practiced on the Mysore coast. Martha Bush Ashton describes the colorful, often elaborate costumes and make-up of the Yaksagana performers. While structural considerations play little part in Ashton's paper, we are presented with a piece of ethnography fascinating to anyone interested in the study of South India. It should also be mentioned that Ashton herself is a skilled Yaksagana dancer and favored the SSIS conference with a performance that provided a pleasant and much appreciated change from the normal round of papers and discussion.

The historians of religion appear last with four papers, none of which evinces a strong interest in the kind of structuralism that concerns anthropologists and linguists. As students of religion ourselves, the editors are tempted to quip about our discipline's typical backward and contrary ways (or is it robust independence?).

Not all French scholars fly structuralist colors. Charlotte Vaudeville, whose presence added a welcome European dimension to the conference, contributes a richly detailed essay on Pandharpur, the focal point of the cult of Vithoba and important Mahārāstrian pilgrimage center. Again, we move outside the strict confines of South India (the Dravidian-speaking areas of the peninsula) to a border region which has combined cultural and religious elements from both North and South. This article on Mahārāstrian *bhakti* furnishes an interesting counterpoint to the concentration on Tamil devotionalism in the subsequent papers.

The Cittars are a far too little studied group of Tamil religious adepts. David Buck takes a step toward filling this gap with his article on Pāmpāṭṭi-Cittar. Buck draws our attention to the symbol of the snake in Pāmpāṭṭi's poetry, and we are impressed by the multivalent abundance of an apparently simple metaphor. The snake represents the soul, so claims Buck, and the intriguing associations which follow from this interpretation are numerous indeed.

Turning to Tamil *bhakti* per se, the essay by Glenn E. Yocum attempts to distinguish two patterns of relationship between devotee and deity. Yocum bases his argument on the hymns of the Tamil Śaiva and Vaiṣṇava poet-saints. In particular, he is concerned with the function of myth in their poetry and the difference between the role which myth plays for *bhaktas* of Śiva as contrasted with Vaiṣṇava devotees.

The final paper by M. Lucetta Mowry concentrates on the great Tamil Saiva devotional poet Māṇikkavācakar. She perceives in Māṇikkavācakar's *Tiruvacakam* a structure of devotion, a developing sense discernible in his poems of the full nature of his love for Śiva and Śiva's love for him. Thus, the devotee's life is seen as a pilgrimage with its definite path, stages, and goal.

While our editorial task has been a pleasant and, for the most part, a relatively uncomplicated one, there are certain difficulties inherent in editing a volume which has ten authors transliterating terms from four different Indic languages, some using a footnote style of documentation and others preferring a social science format for citing references. Our practice has been to regularize transliteration of the languages with which we are personally familiar – Sanskrit and Tamil – in accordance with accepted conventions. In the case of Tamil this means we have followed the system used in the *Tamil Lexicon* published by the University of Madras. Kannada and Marathi words we have let stand as we have received them. We have not changed documentation in the social science papers. Thus, some essays have bibliographies appended, whereas others do not.

There are many people to whom we are indebted in bringing together this collection. To Wilson College must go special recognition both for providing the conference with an ideal setting and for allowing us to initiate the series called Wilson Books with this publication. We thank Suzanne Hanchett for her conference notes, which were helpful in preparing the introduction. Helen-Lee Jones, resident artist at Wilson College, allowed the use of a detail from a watercolor she painted in South India. Rebecca Nisley carefully prepared copy and read proof.

–HMB
–GEY

ONE

Suzanne Hanchett

Reflections and Oppositions: On Structuralism

ONE YEAR AGO I had the privilege of meeting Professor Claude Lévi-Strauss while he was visiting Barnard College in the spring of 1972. At a small gathering of students and others, he spoke briefly and then invited questions. Wishing to receive *darshan* in as concentrated a form as possible, I inquired directly, "What is structuralism?" His answer was equally simple: "It is an epistemological method."

This brief but illuminating answer has led me over the past year to a series of reveries about its meaning for social anthropology. Although I do not find it necessary to accept a purely philosophical direction (which I am not trained to pursue), there are, nonetheless, significant issues – traditional concerns of both the social sciences and the humanities – which are confronted by this method of "knowing" phenomena. Regardless of their previous theoretical commitments, most observers of the human condition can find points worthy of consideration in this approach.

I shall argue that this approach to knowledge provides some challenging observations on the nature of human thought, the structure of human society, and the role of the human "scientist" as observer of these – challenging, that is, to some

---

I gratefully acknowledge the assistance of my student, Edward LiPuma, in providing some of the philosophical background necessary to this paper. I am, however, totally responsible for the theoretical arguments presented here. S.H.

basic assumptions of traditional empiricist and functionalist social science.

In the first place, structuralism in anthropology is explicitly opposed to the view that explanation consists in "reducing" human phenomena ultimately to physical factors. That is, if we view human social life as consisting of economic and psychological factors, social conditions, and ideologies or sign systems, structuralists are refusing to assign priority to any of these, especially refusing a priori to state that economic factors (being closer to physical "reality") are the underlying reality, and systems of thought, epiphenomena (cf. Tymieniecka 1962:xviii-xix).*

This position on symbolism and ideology seems to derive logically from the holistic orientation of structuralist method. This holism is, in turn, a basic premise of the related phenomenology of Husserl and Scheler, and gestalt psychology, schools of thought which see the human mind as organizing perception and thought in terms of wholes, configurations, or "patterns," which are logically prior to their parts. If we see human social life as a whole which includes thought as a major component, we are no longer obliged to assign priority to other components without serious consideration of the form of the whole as we understand it. Both within and outside of Indology, we find studies of symbolic processes (myths, rituals) increasing in respectability, as ideology becomes accepted as in some sense as being as real as other social institutions. We find a recent example of this attitude in South Indian studies. In *Homo hierarchicus,* Dumont has chosen to view the caste system primarily in its ideological aspect. He justifies this approach as "a faithful picture of the system as it appears" (1970:39) to him; and he also echoes the phenomenological credo when he speaks of the relations between ideology and political or economic components of the caste phenomenon: "It is only in relation to the totality thus reconstructed (from a combination

---

*In this and other essays prepared by social scientists for this volume, citations such as this refer to references at the end of the chapter.

of the indigenous Hindu view and our own) that the ideology takes on its true sociological significance" (1970:38).

The totality of human experience – or of any self-enclosed domain – is, then, an important assumption of structuralist analysis. In sociology and anthropology, this view is not original with structuralism. It was made explicit by Marcel Mauss in 1925, in his essay on *The Gift*, in which he stated that the goal of our study was to comprehend what he called "total social phenomena" (cf. Lévi-Strauss 1967). Throughout the twentieth century numerous thinkers have emphasized the importance of holism in anthropology and the other human sciences. Some of these would call themselves "structuralists," and some would not. (For example, Wolf 1964 would not.)

Within the range of structuralist studies, however, the concept of a totality is fundamental, to the extent that the value of each study depends on imaginative delineation of an enclosed domain. For without the assumption of wholeness or enclosure, it is difficult to claim that networks of relations are self-regulating, or that one has defined the laws of the composition of the whole. In the statement of Piaget (1970) structuralism depends on the conception of wholes or totalities. Sets are broken down into their constituent elements, but the whole has logical priority over its parts. The relations between parts and wholes are to be analyzed in terms of relations that exist between parts, and not the elements themselves. That is, the goal of structural analysis is to define a network of relationships that link and unite elements. A network is a series of relations between relations, in the words of the social anthropologist S. F. Nadel (1957); and Piaget, Lane and others employ a linguistic metaphor to say that structure resembles syntax more than anything else, in being a system of transformations in the networks of relationships which constitute the whole.

> As a first approximation, we may say that a structure is a system of transformations. Inasmuch as it is a system and not a mere collection of elements and their properties, these transformations involve laws: the structure is preserved or enriched by the interplay of its

transformation laws, which never yield results external to the system nor employ elements that are external to it.

(Piaget 1970:5; Cf. Lane 1970:14;35)

A second innovation represented by a structuralist methodology is the crosscutting of traditionally defined boundaries in our subject matter. Whereas nonstructuralist scholars generally delimit their studies in terms of certain traditional concepts (ecological *vs.* mythical *vs.* ritual domains; or definite groups, institutions, communities, cultures, culture-areas, or historical periods), one finds the structuralists carving human experience into unorthodox combinations of our traditionally separate categories. It is possible to define a structured totality according to a variety of criteria, and these criteria are not always made explicit. This creates an impression of magical force, or at least sleight of hand, in the eyes of some observers unsympathetic with the structuralist point of view. For example, among the structured totalities which structuralists define may be (1) a single myth or a single ritual (Jakobson and Lévi-Straus 1970), (2) one myth or one ritual plus select relevant features of the social organization within which it developed (Leach 1967),(3) one myth plus a ritual of a neighboring tribe in the same culture area (Lévi-Strauss 1963a), (4) a corpus of myths from a broadly defined culture area (Lévi-Strauss 1969), or (5) an institution in a distinct culture area viewed as a variation (or transformation) on an institution in another culture area (Lévi-Strauss 1963b). In this range of cases, we see the totality in question moving along a continuum from being a single ritual or narrative event, on the one hand, all the way to being the human mind itself, on the other hand. One is left at times with a feeling of awe at the cleverness of the analyst and at the intuitive recognition of relationships among domains where the onlooker might not have even thought to look; but one also experiences a feeling of discomfort that perhaps if the onlooker had taken on the analysis himself, it might have turned out differently. Intuition is a vital part of every scientific activity. Yet, having intuited relationships in an original way, the burden of proving their validity and usefulness still rests on the structuralist analyst.

This leads us to a third feature of the structuralist method: its dialectical framework. Regarding the question of "objectivity" (or perhaps even reproducibility of experiments), experience and perception are viewed in terms of relationships. This means that the observer becomes a part of the subject studied. In the interaction between the observer and the subject, the observer is able to form a model of the subject. The model thus conceived is the primary tool of structuralist research, a "theoretically constructed (pattern), conceived beforehand, which (serves) as a tool for enquiry. . . ." in the words of Anna-Teresa Tymieniecka (1962:186, n.13). According to Tymieniecka, phemonemology (and, we add, structuralism) has thus superseded the necessity to construct explanatory hypotheses, replacing them with models that have served to reveal complexities in various fields by "concentrating . . . on the direct analysis of the structure of phenomena. . ." (1962:19).

It is not only the observer (with model) that is viewed as being in a dialectical relationship of interaction with the subject of study; the nature of the models themselves can be understood only in dialectical terms. In the structure of the structuralists, systems are conceived as being in some sort of constant movement. The emphasis is on what anthropologists generally call *process*, and not on stasis. In fact, the dialectical position denies the possibility of the stability or fixity of forms which is a necessary part of many current models of social life.

The components of such structures are elements which are defined relationally. As Dumont stated it, a structure is a system of relations, not a system of elements (1970:40). Generally speaking, these relations are ones in which elements (defined dialectically) generate each other, cut against each other, clash, pass into each other in processes of transformation, and are necessary to each other. The elements are not the complementary items, fixed and definite, a structural-functionalist model of society, for example. The things of a structuralist-dialectical model exist only in their relationships to other things. And these relationships are in a constant state of flux.

The system being in constant motion, a structuralist model attempts to move to a deep level, beneath the surface motion, to determine the principles governing the flux itself, to ascertain regularities in the observed processes. Using analogies from deSaussure, a model is found in the distinction between *parole* ("speech") and *langue* ("language," as a system of grammatical principles, never in itself audible). Other metaphors are found in the concepts of *deep structure* and *surface structure* as used in generative grammar (cf. Lane 1970:15), or in the distinction between a message and the code by which it is communicated.

The goal, then, is to identify structures which underlie the chaos which presents itself to our senses. In this effort, the well-known techniques of structural analysis are introduced. This consists of determining the nature of relations between basic elements of a given system and determining the ways in which relations affect each other in some sort of network. Ultimately, in the case of a myth or a sociological analysis, the relations (and elements) themselves will be transformed by dialectical interaction. Rejecting the traditional notion of causality, the structuralist replaces it with laws of transformation (Lane 1970:17; Piaget 1970). Speaking of the long-standing discussion of the relationship between myth and ritual, Lévi-Strauss says,

> The reconstruction of the correspondence [between myths and rituals of a large geographical region] requires a series of preliminary operations—that is, permutations or transformations which may furnish the key to the correspondence. If this hypothesis is correct, *we shall have to give up mechanical causality as an explanation*, and, instead, conceive of the relationship between myth and ritual as dialectical, accessible only if both have first been reduced to their structural elements.
>
> (Lévi-Strauss 1963a:233 *italics added*)

In constructing models (of myth structure or of kinship relations, for example) Lévi-Strauss and others draw heavily on the concept of fundamental oppositions among distinctive features, as these were defined in the structural linguistics of the Prague School (Trubetskoy 1957; Jakobson and Halle 1956), and in American descriptive linguistics. Just as the sound system of a language can be seen or ordered as a set of fundamental sound principles (mostly deriving from articulatory principles, but also defined by distributional criteria), so also a myth can be seen as the manipulation of a set of fundamental conceptual distinctions. But note that the relations between elements, as in phonology, are viewed in terms of distinction or opposition. A sound unit in language forms its identity as it participates in a system of opposed principles: if it is a high-front vowel /i/, it is also *not* a low-front vowel /e/; *nor* is it a high-back vowel /ɨ/. Further, if it is a vowel, it is *not* a consonant. Similarly, the characters and events of mythology or ritual are defined as much by what they are *not*, as by what they are: left is not right; clockwise is not counterclockwise; red is not white; male is not female; the sun is not the moon. The significance of this cannot be over stated: opposites define each other in the linguistic and dialectical models alike. The use of a code – in speech, myth, or other social institutions – consists in the manipulation of these deep principles of opposition to produce meaningful messages.

If items in a mythical (or social) structure are opposed to each other, on the linguistic analogy, the opposition is not conceived as a static arrangement of parts. Rather, it is a state of tension and movement – a state tending toward change. Thus, myth is seen as developing out of an intellectual impulse to overcome a particular contradiction:

> Since the purpose of myth is to provide a logical model capable of overcoming a contradiction (an impossible achievement if, as it happens, the contradiction is real), a theoretically infinite number of slates will be generated, each one slightly different from the others. Thus, myth grows spiral-wise until the intellectual impulse which has originated it is exhausted. . . . If this is the case we should consider that it closely corresponds, in the realm of the spoken word, to the kind of being a crystal is in realm of physical matter.
>
> (Lévi-Strauss 1963a:229)

The concept of *mediation* or *mediator* is the device by which contradictions or dialectical tensions are transcended in a structuralist model. The mediator is the agent of transformation in a particular structure, in that it is ambiguous and equivocal, partaking of the characteristics of both parties to an opposition and serving to resolve oppositions by transforming the terms themselves. As a popular mythological figure, the trickster is generally cast in the role of a mediating device in structuralist models.

In regard to social organization, as traditionally studied, one finds more difficulty in describing a structuralist approach. Many students of human social relationships, groups, and institutions would not identify themselves as structuralists, even though they do use (and have for sometime used) a concept of structure. A key term linking different positions, in my view, is the word *principle* in anthropological studies of social structure. In the domain of social relationships, we can see the manipulation of such principles as lineality *vs.* affinal ties, alliance, reciprocity, confrontation (e.g., in F. G. Bailey 1968), rivalry, conflict, contradiction. These and other organizing principles of social life are often basic to processual models, which have produced significant insights. Though not dialectical in their basic inspiration, the "structures" of social anthropologists are sometimes similar to those of the structuralist. It is interesting to note that in his *The Theory of Social Structure* Nadel chose to discard *status* as a central concept and to use only *role*, defined *relationally*, and not in isolation from a network of obligations. Thus the action-process dimension of a social position was merged with its item identity as a marked category.

Although neither Lévi-Strauss nor Dumont has built a reputation on social change studies of the American or British variety, I wish to emphasize that the structuralist approach they represent is dynamic and processual, and thus compatible with that of other students of history or structure who deal with different types of subject matter than they ordinarily handle.

Discussing the phenomenon of spread of related myths or rituals over a region, Lévi-Strauss suggests that he is contributing to theories of historical spread and change by his type of dialectical analysis:

> Structural dialectics does not contradict historical determinism, but rather promotes it by giving it a new tool. . . . The phenomena of reciprocal influence between geographically related linguistic areas. . . can be seen not only in the diffusion of certain structural properties outside their area of origin or in their rejection. . . . The affinity (between regions) may also be demonstrated by anththesis, which generates structures presenting the character of answers, cures, excuses, or even remorse.
> (Lévi-Strauss 1963a:240-241)

In handling of symbolic and ideational material, I feel that the structuralist approach is liberating us from the need to see art as reflecting life in any simple sense. In fact, following Marx and Freud, we can confidently assert that "The relationship between 'ideas' and their sustaining social processes is [also] a dialectical one," as Berger and Luckmann expressed it. Although this view of ideas has been prominent in philosophy, psychology, and Marxist sociology during the past century, anthropologists have been limited by the American and Durkhemian functionalist approach. This approach suggests that in the organic integration of all social institutions myth, ritual, and other symbolic forms serve mainly to reinforce this integration by expressing the basic values or mores to communicants. Although there is some proven merit in the reflection-reinforcement hypothesis, it is refreshing to hear Marriott (1966) remind us that the *Holī* ceremony has to be read in a mirror before we can find a reflection of any ordinary reality in it (cf. Turner 1969). In my own work on festivals in South India, I have found conflict and contradictions incorporated into ceremonies, an observation made intelligible within a structuralist-dialectical framework.

Insofar as myths, rites, and art forms serve to "say" something about life – i.e., to present a model, as it were, of reality – this statement may be correct, or it may very well distort reality to varying degrees. In fact, if Freud is correct in his work on dreams and fantasy, and if Marx is correct in his views on ideology, it is safe to assume that ideas, though developed in relation to social action, tend to present a distorted (re-organized, or even reversed) model of that action. As Murphy has suggested, in accordance with Freud's and Simmel's views, the very distortedness of human images of reality may be what makes social life possible (Murphy 1971). But anthropology has been unable until now to develop an adequate theory of the relationships between symbolic or ideational structures and social institutions, because of the limitations of the functionalist framework. I am suggesting that the techniques and the dialectical nature of the structuralist approach will serve to make this development possible.

In conclusion, I have attempted to discuss certain ways in which structuralism, as an approach to knowledge, science, and human social life, offers significant challenges to other schools of thought. The areas I have mentioned include: (a) the definition of our subject matter, especially the relations of sign systems to other social institutions in a non-reductionist scheme; (b) the methods delineating structured domains, and of analyzing networks of relationships within those domains or totalities; and (c) the dialectical view of both the subject matter itself and of the observer's relation to the phenomena which are objects of study.

In these, and in other ways, structuralism confronts the social sciences with a distinct challenge. Although I have discussed the significance of this challenge primarily in terms of anthropology, the force of structuralism as an intellectual movement is felt in other disciplines as well. Literary criticism, psychology, and mathematics have also been profoundly influenced by this movement. It may be that in facing the challenge we (structuralist and non-structuralist alike) can all learn something about our fields of interest, and about the ways our minds handle these fields. It is possible that the fields themselves, and our views of our own observer roles, could be changed in the process of confrontation.

REFERENCES

Bailey, F. G.
1968 "Parapolitical systems." In *Local Level Politics: Social and Cultural Perspectives.* Marc. J. Swartz, ed. Chapter 13. (Chicago: Aldine Publishing Co., pp. 281-294).

Berger, Peter L., and Thomas Luckmann
1966 *The Social Construction of Reality: A Treatise in the Sociology of Knowledge.* (Garden City, N. Y.: Doubleday and Co., Anchor Books, 1967 edition).

Dumont, Louis
1957 *Hierarchy and Marriage Alliance in South Indian Kinship.* Occasional Papers of the Royal Anthropological Institute. . . . No. 12.

1970 *Homo Hierarchicus.* (Chicago: University of Chicago Press).

Durkheim, Émile
1915 *The Elementary Forms of the Religious Life.* (London: George Allen and Unwin Ltd.).

Freud, Sigmund
1961 *The Interpretation of Dreams.* James Strachey, trans. (New York: Science Editions, Inc.).

Hanchett, Suzanne
1972 "Festivals and social relations in a Mysore Village: Mechanics of two processions." *Economic and Political Weekly* 7:31-33: 1517-1522.

n.d. "The festival interlude: some anthropological observations," In *Interludes; Religious Festivals in South India and Ceylon.* (forthcoming. Guy Welbon, ed.

Jakobson, Roman, and Morris Halle
1956 *Fundamentals of Language.* (The Hague: Mouton & Co.).

Jakobson, Roman, and Claude Lévi-Strauss
1970 "Charles Baudelaire's 'Les Chats'." In *Structuralism: A Reader.* Michael Lane, ed., Katie Furness-Lane, trans. (London: Jonathan Cape, pp. 202-221).

Lane, Michael, editor and introducer
1970 *Structuralism: A Reader.* (London, Jonathan Cape). (recent edition: *Introduction to Structuralism.* New York: Basic Books).

Leach, E. R.
1967 "Virgin birth. . . ." *Proceedings of the Royal Anthropological Institute . . . for 1966.* pp. 39-49.

Lefebvre, Henri

1968 *The Sociology of Marx.* Norbert Guterman, trans. (New York: Random House, Vintage Books).

Lévi-Strauss, Claude

1963a. "Structure and dialectics," Chapter XII, in *Structural Anthropology.* Claire Jacobson and Brooke Grundfest Schoepf, trans. (New York: Basic Books, pp. 232-241).

1963b. "The bear and the barber." *Royal Anthropological Institute, Journal* 93:1:1-11.

1967 *The Scope of Anthropology.* Sherry Ortner Paul and Robert A. Paul, translators. (London: Jonathan Cape). (Also in *Current Anthropology*, Vol 7, No. 2).

1969 *The Raw and the Cooked: Introduction to a Science of Mythology: I*, trans. John and Doreen Weightman (New York: Harper and Row).

Marriott, McKim

1966 "The feast of love." In *Krishna; Myths, Rites, Attitudes* Milton Singer, ed., Honolulu: East-West Center Press. pp. 200-212.

Mauss, Marcel

1954 *The Gift: Forms and Functions of Exchange in Archaic Societies.* Ian Cunnison, trans. (Glencoe, Ill.: The Free Press).

Murphy, Robert

1971 *The Dialectics of Social Life.* (New York: Basic Books).

Nadel, S. F.

1957 *The Theory of Social Structure.* (Glencoe, Ill.: The Free Press).

Piaget, Jean

1970 *Structuralism.* (New York: Basic Books).

Ramanujan, A. K.

1973 *Speaking of Siva.* (Middlesex, England: Penguin Books).

Trubetzkoy, N. S.

1957 *Principes de phonologie.* J. Catineau, trans. (Paris: Klinchsiek).

Turner, Victor Witter

1969 *The Ritual Process; Structure and Anti-structure.* (Chicago: Aldine Publishing Co.).

Tymieniecka, Anna-Teresa

1962 *Phenomenology and Science in Contemporary European Thought.* (New York: The Noonday Press, Farrar, Straus, and Cudahy).

Wolf, Eric R.

1964 *Anthropology.* (Englewood Cliffs, N. J.: Prentice-Hall).

TWO

The Cage of Form: A Comparison of Religious Imagery in the Western World and in India

Walter Spink

"We trap heaven and earth in the cage of form."

Lu Chi

"WE BECOME," SAID BLAKE, "what we behold." What man depicts records both what he is and what he is to be. Our imagery not only describes our history but by revealing our attitudes toward time and death and salvation it equally defines our destiny. Or to put it another way, it exposes our connections with divinity.

The following essay is a brief pictorial introduction to the traditional beliefs of India, on the one hand, and to those of the biblical (most particularly the Christian) West, on the other. In a loose sense the fundamental comparisons we make hold true for western and eastern attitudes as a whole, since the essential manner in which man approaches his gods – or faces the phenomena of time – divides in this general way. Western man tends to seek for deity beyond the self and the world; for the man in the East, on the other hand, the search for divinity is ultimately a search within. "The only Buddha," the Buddhists can say, "is the Buddha which is found within one's own heart."

We shall not attempt to analyze what has caused the divergence of the modes of thought in India and the West. We shall instead center our discussion around a *description* of these modes – which could be considered their *effects*. The fascinating question must remain: why did one culture develop

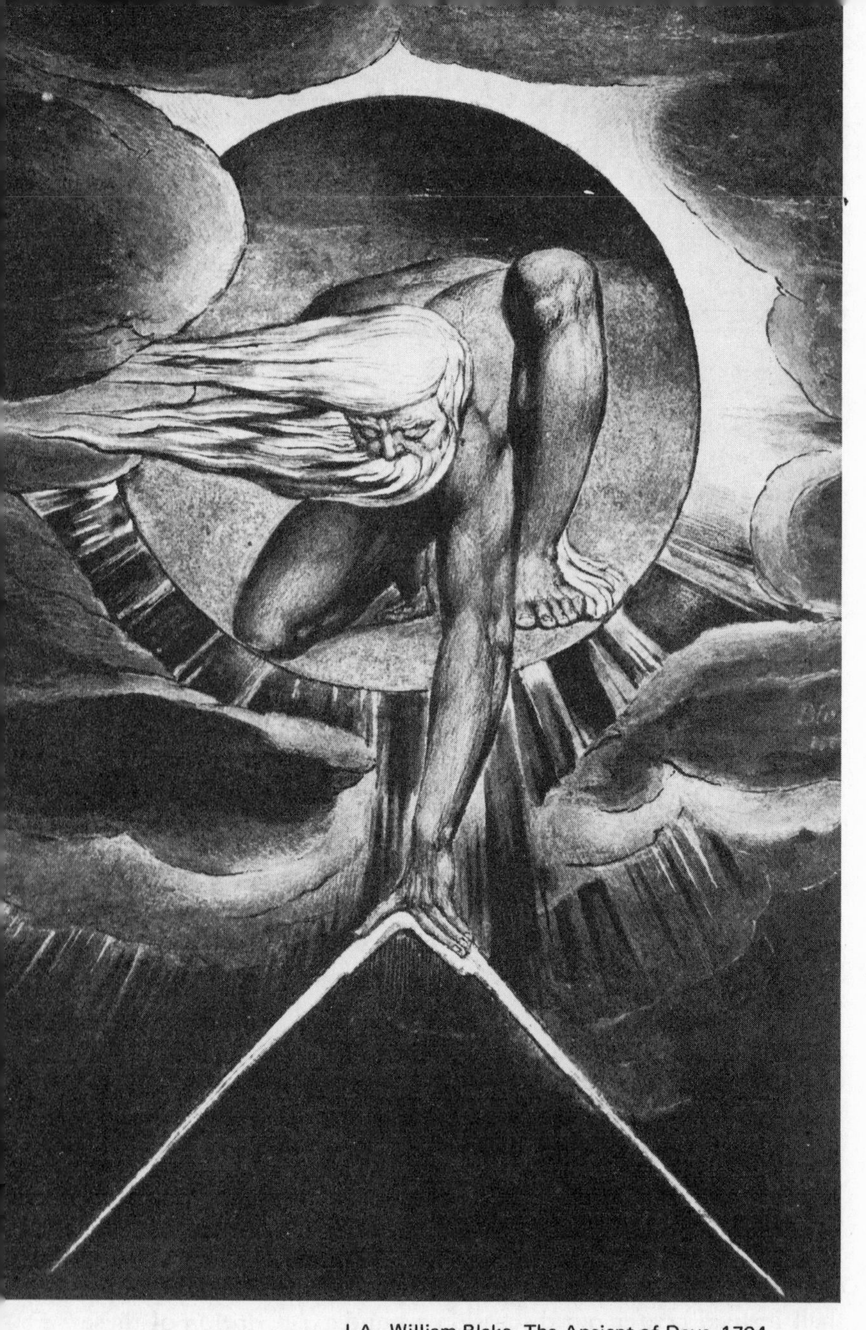

I-A William Blake, The Ancient of Days, 1794

I-B Basohli painting, Hiraṇyagarbha (The Golden Egg), Late 18th century

an essentially protective view of time wherein the individual sees himself eternally involved in a cyclical cosmic play, while the other culture developed an essentially threatening conception in which the individual, filled with what has been called "the terror of time," moves inexorably toward an absolutely final and therefore fearful goal. The one tradition developed the concept of inevitable salvation and absorption; the other developed the concept of necessary assertion and ultimate judgment. The one view leads to an underlying calm, to an assumption of innocence and a rejection of notions of "responsibility"; the other leads to anxiety, to concepts of freedom, concern, and guilt. The one world, reflecting protective (maternal?) psycho-spiritual norms, insists upon the validity of an inward journey; the other, with an aggressive (paternal?) bent, insists upon the validity of thrust and outer conquest. The "meeting of East and West" is an ideal which may be valid as a guide to action; but it is still inconceivable on the profounder levels of belief.

I

In their separate creation legends the difference between the basic religious conceptions of India and the West is immediately made clear. In Blake's characteristically western description, the Ancient of Days with his oppressing calipers exists completely

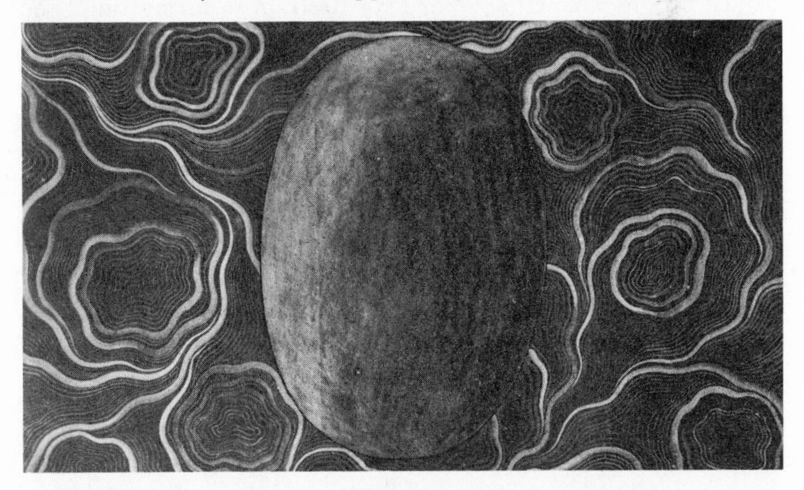

apart from and unaffected by the thing he makes. God is beyond time; but man is completely bound by it. Perfection, immortality (the condition of God), lies far beyond our reach; despair remains our destiny. Therefore we must either choose the pathway of expiation – crying out in anguish, "I despise myself and repent in dust and ashes" and trusting God to draw us to himself across that primal gap – or we must strive in our helpless but heroic determination to complete ourselves, to become like God or to become God, in a final self-ordained transcendence.

The Indian creation story – one version of which is incorporated into the descriptions of the *hiraṇyagarbha* or the Golden Egg – provides a diametrically opposed definition of man's place within the cosmic scheme. In that world of creation without a creator one cannot speak of creation *by* but only of creation *from*. God is not a distant source, but the very substance of the world we know.

> In the beginning this was non-existent. It became existent; it grew. It turned into an egg. The egg lay for the time of a year. The egg broke open. The two halves were, one of silver, one of gold. . . ."
>
> (Chāndogya Upaniṣad)

In this and other variants of the Indian origin myth, the whole world, breathing in and breathing out, emerges inexorably from that empty yet overflowing vessel called the Void. The inexhaustible exhausts itself into form; time and space and history, men and animals and gods, appear, disappear, and reappear. In India, as Gandhi declared, "There is no death, no separation from the substance." There is nothing of that traumatic cleavage of form from Form which, for western man, defines the "Fall" and denies such a filling.

II

> And now, God said, lest he put forth his hand, and take also of the Tree of Life, and eat, and live forever . . . the Lord God sent him forth from the garden of Eden to till the ground from whence he was taken.
>
> (Gen. 3:22-23)

"The key to mythology" Freud declared, "lies concealed in the study of neurosis." One can see the whole biblical account,

II-A Hildesheim Cathedral, The Accusation of Adam and Eve, 12th century

from its descriptions of rejection to its formulae for salvation, as developing from western man's sense of alienation from God and from his terrifying conviction of his own mortality. Thus, man immediately established himself in the biblical account as unworthy, as already guilty; for only by declaring a causative guilt could he explain (even if he could never conquer) his sense of oppression by death and time, and only by recognizing the absoluteness of death and time – for thus is his distinctness and his isolation confirmed – could man be convinced of his self-identity. Thus the expulsion from Eden is ultimately man's own doing, not his God's. Western man never was destined to live within that perfect and eternal realm. His true home was "east of Eden" in the land of wandering, in the cold and threatening and demanding world outside.

By contrast, the environment of belief in India is essentially protective; the motif is one of invitation rather than accusation, of a joyful fusion of devotee and deity rather than of a threat of judgment. Here, in the garden of the world, which is the manifested body of God, divinity can always be found. In this world, where existence is conceived in ever-recurring cycles

II-B Kangra painting, Rādhā and Kṛṣṇa in the Grove, Late 18th century

rather than in a single linear thrust, death can have no final sting, nor grave a final victory; the one certainty is the certainty of eventual salvation. Such a world is ultimately equivalent to Paradise – a paradise from which, even if man would, he could not escape; for the world within forever circumscribes the world without.

III

The events described throughout the mythologies of the West continually emphasize conflict: conflict between the deity and the devotee, between the king and the subject, between the parent and the child. The biblical story of the flood provides a characteristic example. Western sacred history is a sequence of traumas, of demands and payments, in which man's underlying guilt – his debt for the freedom which his conceptions have imposed upon him – is repeatedly exposed and his ultimate dependency upon a just and wrathful god is repeatedly proved. Salvation must come from beyond and above – it is not of this world; and it must come from God – it is not to be found within the self. "He that believeth on him is not condemned" is the comforting message of the Gospel. However, the message of hope is typically balanced by a threat: "but he that believeth not is condemned already." Firmly set forth in the Old Testament, the message is furiously confirmed in the New.

By contrast, the Indian account of the bathing of Kṛṣṇa and the maidens in the moonlit stream ("that enchanting river which reflects the form of the formless one") is an equally telling expression of Hindu belief. The whole of nature is suffused with the beauty and the presence of a divine power which has become revealed. The cooling waters, the blossoming trees, the radiant sky, the central figure of Lord Kṛṣṇa, the tantalizing maidens – all partake of the substance of divinity. The stream of love, so all-encompassing that "it has no other shore" is the ocean of salvation, the very body of God, as fully engulfing as that sea of judgment which swept the contemporaries of Noah away.

III-A Gustav Dore, The Deluge, 19th century

III-B Kangra painting, Kṛṣṇa and Gopīs Bathing, Late 18th century

IV

The ecstatic agonies of the Apocalypse, acted out in miniature over and over again in western history, assert in the most final terms the absolute distinction between an established divinity and a needful humanity, between that immortal realm which is beyond Time, and mortals, who are afflicted and inevitably defeated by it. That ocean of death which Noah saw was only a foretaste of the deluge of doom which is destined to flood across the western world at the final day. At that moment the linear thread of temporality so tautly spanning the western tradition, shall finally be cut. Western man inexorably moves toward that decisive cartharsis, that awe-ful completion, when his conflict with that "absolute paternal power, which will not leave us, but prevents us everywhere" shall finally be resolved. Then those who have fallen upon their knees, admitting that an undeserved redemption can come only from God, shall rise upward in streams of glory; while those who, in a desperate pride, have stood in dignity upon their own two feet, shall be rewarded with eternal death.

The ultimate meeting of the Indian devotee with God, which eternally happens within a cosmos where time is dissolved by its own recurrence, is an ultimately static rather than an *ec*static and imbalanced event. The whole of creation, symbolized by the gathering of the radiant dancers crowded together upon the Yāmuna's moonlit sands, is an ever-renewed lotus which blossoms, is absorbed, and blossoms ever again. The manifest world, and the unmanifest source from which divinity and

IV-A Peter Paul Rubens, Last Judgment: Fall of the Damned, ca. 1620

IV-B Jaipur painting Rasamaṇḍala with Kṛṣṇa and Gopīs Dancing, ca. 1880

humanity alike are brought forth into form, alternate in a grand and mysterious cosmic play.

> This vast universe is a wheel. Upon it are all creatures that are subject to birth, death, and rebirth. Round and round it turns, and never stops. It is the wheel of Brahman. . . .
>
> (Śvetāśvatara Upaniṣad)

V

Rodin's *The Thinker* could well qualify as a paradigm of western man's image of the self, fusing as it does suggestions of dignity of mind with force of body, of nobility with a suppressed savage fury, and of high pride with a deep inner suffering. It is an illustration of a tragic and heroic concept, of man filled with a determination to retain his pride and his integrity in the face of those implacable forces which in the end must inevitably defeat him. It is a picture of man isolated and exposed, divorced from a paradise which he himself rejected from the start. It is a picture of man pondering his place in a universe which (whether viewed from a Christian or an existential standpoint) must end in a denial rather than a discovery of the power of the self. Deriving in part from the representation of a damned soul in

V-A Auguste Rodin, The Thinker, ca. 1880

Michelangelo's *Last Judgment* and carrying much of that same burden of meaning, it was originally conceived as the central motif for Rodin's apocalyptic *Gates of Hell*, over the brink of which it was to sit in dark and brooding meditation.

V-B Sarnath sculpture, Buddha, 5th century

One might say that if Rodin's *Thinker* is meditating upon the obliteration of man by time, then the famous image of the Buddha from Sarnath – characteristic of a diametrically opposed tradition – is meditating upon the obliteration of time by man. The Buddha (the "Enlightened One") might well be called the "Thinker" of the Indian tradition, but his mind is suffused by calm rather than afflicted by concern. The purified

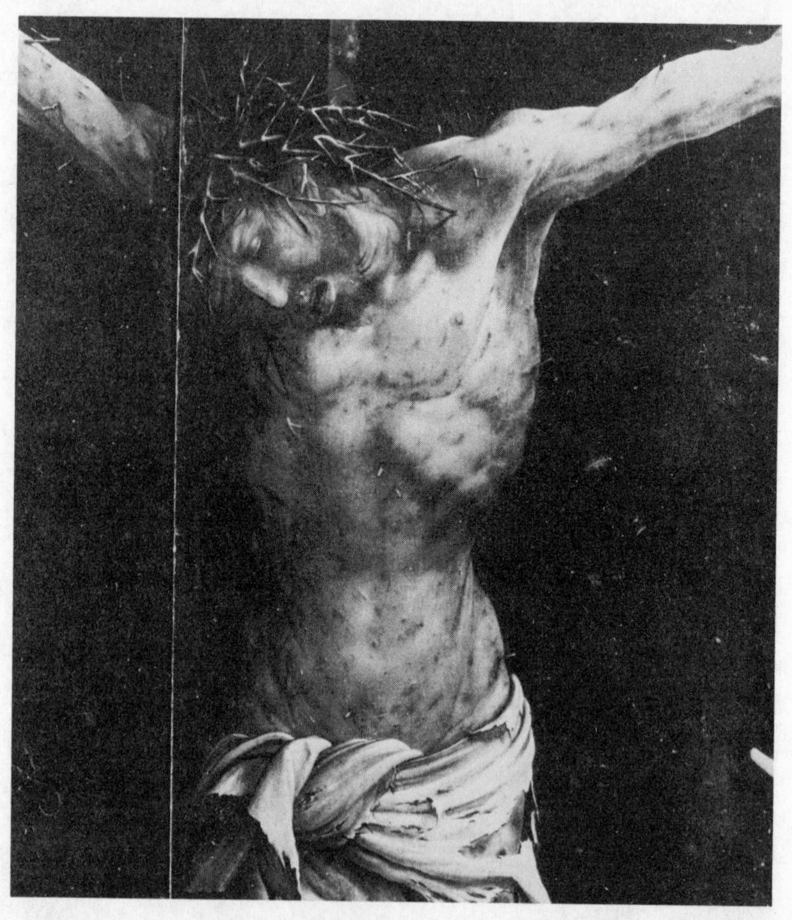

VI-A Matthais Grunewald, Christ Crucified, ca. 1510-1515

volumes of his form equally suggest his escape from the trammels of the ephemeral. The radiant centrality of the image tellingly communicates the Buddha's message of the essential connectedness of the cosmos and the self, where ultimate truths are revealed not by any sudden outer "vision," but by a constantly intensified insight.

VI-B South Indian sculpture, Śiva as Nataraja, 16th century

VI

The blossoming tree beneath which the meditating Buddha sits has certain analogies with the cut and the broken tree upon which Christ was crucified. But the way to the *arbor vitae* under which the Buddha sits is the path of absolute identification, and it ends in the discovery that there is no distinction between the Enlightened One who is found there and the soul who seeks him out. The way to the cross, on the other hand, is not the way of identification but the way of expiation. Christ, as scapegoat for mankind, is the receptacle for all of the sins of the fallen world. But since Christ must be ritually destroyed before becoming established once again in his paternal role, his shame-filled sacrifice becomes but one more burden of guilt which man must bear; for man's only hope of salvation is from the very Christ – the symbolic Son who is also the Father – whose blood man spilled upon that cruel tree.

The Indian devotee approaches deity in an entirely different way. Instead of demanding contrition, the divine power, in descent, offers involvement. The image of Śiva provides a visual metaphor for the whirling dance of the cosmic order itself, of which both God and worshipper are part. The Lord's dancing figure, at once frozen and dynamic, at once disciplined and urgent, with its taut central core and its flailing arms invites the worshipper into the contexts of its perpetual movement. "How can we know the dancer from the dance?" asks Yeats. For the seeker after the truth the goal has been achieved when it is clear that the question and the answer are identical; when he sees the god – and finally sees himself – as actor and as audience as well.

VII-B Kishangarh painting, Krsna Holding up Mount Govardhana, ca. 1775

VII

Even today the crucifixion, with its purgative symbolism and its denial of any inner relationship between man and God, is the most significant model of western man's psychological and spiritual conceptions. Playing grotesquely upon this theme, the broken horse in Picasso's *Guernica*, the innocent beast which has become the focus of the holocaust and is the very vessel of man's need and suffering, screams in despair and defiance at the fierce power above. Its gesture, reflected over and over again in the composition, is both a plea and an accusation – an agonized "Why?" And if, in earlier times, western man might have believed in a responsive deity, now in our increasingly secular and increasingly anxious age, no answer comes from on high. Overseeing the anguished scene, there is nothing more than the

VII-A Pablo Picasso, Guernica, 1937

cutting and ironic glare of a harsh mechanical eye. And the light which it projects, a light which is by no means a cure, and is perhaps a cause, only exposes and reveals. It no longer illumines.

By contrast, when a cataclysm of destruction comparable to that rain of bombs which fell upon the people of Guernica poured down upon the village of Gokula, Kṛṣṇa responded as always and sheltered his devotees from the raving storm. Taking his position as *axis mundi*, as the very trunk of the all-encompassing tree of immortality to which all men may freely come, he raised the great Mount Govardhana as an umbrella of protection and even as a canopy of honor above their heads. Instead of appearing in some Jehovic or Jovian fury above the holocaust, he appeared within it. And if he was ultimately its cause (for the operations of the divine are full of mystery) he was also its defeater. There is no fundamental separation. Kṛṣṇa; his devotees; the apparently separate powers which caused the storm: all are, in the end, part of a single statement, or a song, which all eventually shall come to understand.

VIII

Paul Klee's *Man on a Tightrope* plays upon the same crucifixion theme as Picasso's *Guernica*, and upon the same underlying sense of anxiety and isolation. Heroically and absurdly balanced upon his shifting world of ropes and wires, the tightrope walker, "that struts and frets his hour upon the stage" moves toward that fragile structure's unstable center, toward final full exposure against the crossing circus lights. Existentially conceived, tragic because the dangerous path he treads will lead only to death, it is a picture of action without resolution, of self-assertion with no final self-assurance, "full of sound and fury, signifying nothing." Indeed the whole quixotic edifice is finally unattached. It is a lonely cage which hangs upon itself, a neurotic interior landscape, in which the subtle

VIII-A Paul Klee, Tightrope Walker, 1923

contours of a half-seen human head (wired for *son et lumière*) are fitfully revealed.

The taut lines of history which support the fool or saint or hero of the West are woven in a different and concentric pattern in India, where the individual's spiritual quest leads not to an assertive ecstasy, not to a cry of bliss or a scream of pain, but to a centripetal calm which dissolves external concepts of divinity. "An invisible and subtle essence is the Spirit of the whole universe. That is reality. That is truth. That art thou *(tat tvam asi).*" says the Chāndogya Upaniṣad. The cosmic power, whether it be described in the form of deity or defined in purely abstract "higher" terms, by no means afflicts the seeker after truth, but rather is ultimately absorbed within him. Microcosm and macrocosm coincide; self and Self, the seed and the Sphere, are one.

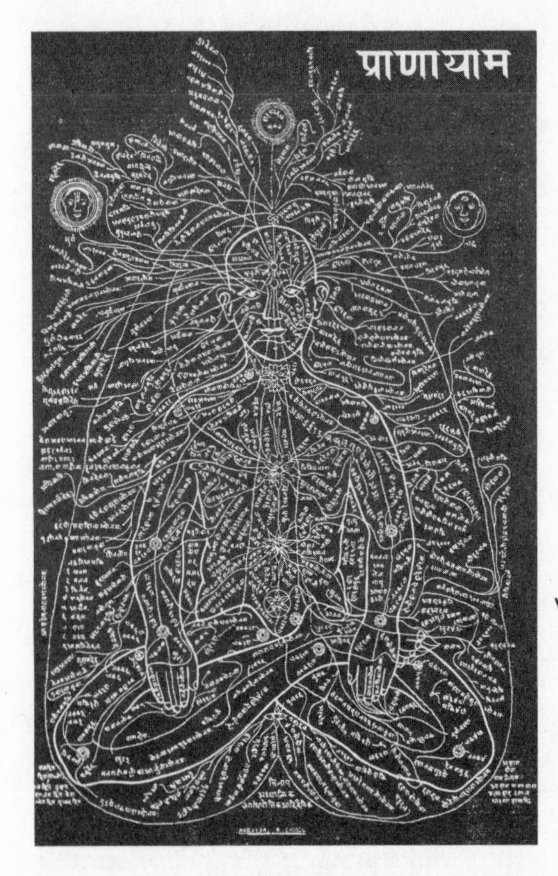

VIII-B Prāṇāyama (Subtle Centres and Channels of the Body, 20th century

IX

If Picasso's *Guernica* and Klee's *Man on a Tightrope* insist upon man's alienation from any saving power which is congruent with the self, the same "truth" is expressed in that most western of all games, Monopoly. Disregarding the offensive sociological implications of the board – where Mediterranean, Baltic, Oriental, and even Vermont Avenues are relegated to the cheapest sections, ominously close to the Reading Railroad, the Community Chest, and the Jail – one can rather point out how it emphasizes the isolation of the player, whose only hope lies in a materiality which he aggressively compounds. Moving from triumph to trauma and from trauma to triumph in a world cohering around urban and individualistic ideals, all participants are ultimately called to account when the finite resources of the "bank" are divided, judgment is due, and the game is done.

In the old Indian game of Parcheesi, by way of contrast, the movement is not centrifugal – outward toward ego-expression – but constantly inward, along a static and oriented course. Actually, in its present form the game represents the secularization and consequent loss of signification of ancient spiritual rites; but in its diagrammatic arrangement one can still discover the configurations of the *maṇḍala* and the *terra sacra* of the Indian temple plan. In such cosmicized territory, as the worshipper proceeds back toward the sacred womb (the *garbha-gṛha* or womb-home) the peripheral structures of experience (time and space and action) are seen to fall away, while the expanding center realizes itself at a circumference which is in the end no different from the core. "Between saṃsāra and nirvāṇa," says the sage, "there is not the slightest difference."

X

As we have seen, the teachings of India emphasize a centripetal focussing upon the powers within the self, a contraction of outer phenomena in response to an inner expansion of the mind. By contrast, the western seeker must forever reach upward and outward; he must be caught up in a spiralling response of belief which denies his own ultimate significance and which asserts the separateness and the supremacy of divinity – "whose only care is not to please, but to remind of our and Adam's curse." He is, and is expected to be, a Prodigal. Only as such, in hope and guilt, can he return to his paternal home.

By contrast, the world in the Indian view is not a separate and doomed entity existing apart from God and needing only completion, but rather it is a continuum, a reflection of an inevitable urgency to become continuous. The sphere of time and space, in this view, is not something down below (and in this sense debased); it is rather a diagram of the cosmic expression in which both men and gods participate and coalesce. And because the gods of India are ultimately coterminous with man, because they are only more ideally ordered aspects of the ultimate mysterious power, when they participate in the actions of the world they do so neither with wrath nor satisfaction nor concern – with none of the self-aggrandizing compulsions of divinities such as Jahweh or Marduk or Baal. Their work is not work but play; and this play – this *līlā* – is an eternal and recurring drama, forever revolving not *into* time but *as* time; and constantly returning to that silent center – that still point – where the dance is.

X-A Auguste Rodin, The Prodigal Son, 1880-1882

X-B Mathura sculpture, Jain Votive Tablet, ca. 1st century

XI

As our illustrations have suggested, the spiritual search of western man is infused with ambivalence. On the one hand, it is a plea for the assertiveness of deity; encumbered by fears of time and death, western man seeks help from a power which he has defined as beyond the tragic nature of the self. On the other hand, it is a search for self-assertion; for western man, in his primal conflict, rejects as much as he yields to the conception

XI-A Lunar Module, Apollo Nine

of a saving power beyond. Therefore, to the degree that he feels this isolation, he strives to destroy his boundaries and to reach forever outward. The need to conquer the moon – to create a moon-conquering culture – is symbolic of this heroic search, this continual striving to render the unknown known. Seeking always for further mysteries, he refuses to accept as mysterious anything which he fails to understand. That is to say, he rejects God, or at least intends to do so, in his desperate resolve to achieve his own divinity.

To the devotee in India, on the other hand, to one who is uninterested in "conquering" celestial bodies and all that that implies, the moon is not of importance because of its material character, but for quite the opposite reason – its very elusiveness. Ever-changing, darkly illumined, it can be seen and finally known only as metaphor. Its radiance, which both draws forth and guides the moonstruck maidens through the fearfully

XI-B Mewar painting, The Search for Kṛṣṇa in the Moonlight, ca. 1730

enclosing night is none other than the radiance of Kṛṣṇa himself – Śri Candra, the Silver One. He is the goal – the light – which encloses and invades his devotees. And ultimately, "the moon is surrounded by moons." The identification of the seeker and the sought develops in an oscillating interplay where boundaries are dissolved within the edgeless confines of the soul.

Oppositions: Western and Indian

These lists are arranged as a series of contrasting concepts which we have arbitrarily related to the two different cultures which we have been discussing. Perhaps these verbal oppositions will elucidate and play upon the polarizations which we have set forth in our pairs of illustrations. How each item is conceived and whether or not the different sets of "opposites" reveal a meaningful dichotomy will of course depend upon the imagery each word elicits in any reader's mind. In any case, the listing is only proffered as food for thought – all the more palatable, one will find, if it is taken with a grain of salt.

Western	*Indian*	*Western*	*Indian*
Agent	Source	Horizon	Center
Apocalypse	Resolution	Hot	Cool
Centrifugal	Centripetal	Judgment	Nirvana
Chicken	Egg	Labyrinth	Maṇḍala
Circumcision	Virginity	Linear	Circular
Disclosure	Enclosure	Non-returnable	Recycled
Dust	Mud	Orgasm	Coitus reservatus
Ecstasy	Stasis	Phallus	Womb
Expiation	Integration	Projection	Introspection
Faith	Works	Race	Dance
Fall	Filling	Sin	Karma
Father	Mother	Sperm	Semen
Gin	Grass	Sprout	Seed
Good/evil	Order/chaos	Time	Eden

... Then the Lord rained upon Sodom and upon Gomorrah brimstone and fire from the Lord out of heaven;

And he overthrew those cities, and all the plain, and all the inhabitants of the cities, and that which grew upon the ground.

But his wife looked back from behind him, and she became a pillar of salt.

(Genesis 19:17, 24-26)

As a lump of salt when thrown into water melts away and the lump cannot be taken out, but wherever we taste the water it is salty, even so, O Maitreyī, the individual self, dissolved, is the Eternal – pure consciousness, infinite and transcendent.

(Bṛhadāraṇyaka Upaniṣad)

THREE

Kenneth David

And Never the Twain Shall Meet? Mediating the Structural Approaches to Caste Ranking

IN A VOLUME on structural approaches, it seems appropriate to attempt to bridge the analytic gap between social structural (Bailey) and structuralist (Dumont) explanations of caste ranking. Bailey stresses hard facts of control of economic resources and power; differential control of resources results in a summation of stratified relations between pairs of castes which is reflected in relative religious ranking (Bailey 1964: 266-7). Dumont emphasizes the pervasive influence of the hierarchical ideology of purity/impurity, an implicit opposition on the level of thought by means of which caste society appears rational and coherent to those who live in it (Dumont 1966). These accounts are in complementary relation: they are mutually reductionist. Similarly, each account successfully deals with complementary levels of a local caste hierarchy. The social structural account clarifies the middle ranges of the hierarchy, where socio-economic ranks mirror religious ranks. And the structuralist account explains the extremes of the hierarchy, where Brahmin and Untouchable, the most and the least pure of castes, retain the highest and lowest religious ranks irrespective of socio-economic rank. Having debated the issue, Bailey finally wondered whether the disagreement lay beyond the pale of academic discourse (Bailey 1959:88).

I reject that proposition. This article, first, attempts to mediate the opposition between social structural and structuralist analyses. To do this, I shall define explicit normative schemes not as "things in themselves," but in relation to observable patterns of behavior, the object of social structural analysis, and in relation to ideational features, the object of structuralist analysis. The *relation* between normative schemes and actual behavior is a reciprocal relation: normative schemes are both *codes for* actual behavior and *codes of* actual behavior (see Figures 2 and 3). The *relation* between explicit normative schemes and implicit ideational features is also a reciprocal relation: an ideational feature is the *conceptual focus* of each normative scheme (see Figures 1 and 2). In this, I draw on Piaget's notion of the *relativity of form and content* (Piaget 1970). Normative schemes are form with respect to behavior and content with respect to ideational features.[1]

Second, this article attempts to mediate the substantive opposition of extremes/middle ranges of a local hierarchy. To analyze the regional caste hierarchy of the Jaffna peninsula, northern Ceylon (Sri Lanka), I shall argue for the dichotomy, bound mode/nonbound mode intercaste relations, a dichotomy which builds from previous distinctions such as castes who serve some other castes, castes who serve all other castes (Wiser 1936), and castes whose occupation is/is not a direct reflection of the pure/impure ideology (Pocock 1962). Bound mode relations, which resemble jajmāni style relations, occur between castes in the agricultural sector: between the dominant landowners and their serving castes such as domestics, barbers, washermen, and laborers. Nonbound mode relations occur in the rural entrepreneurial sector, between artisans and fishing castes and every other caste with which they trade.

Initially to focus the discussion, I turn to one part of my social structural account, caste ranking data from the Jaffna peninsula, to show that this latter distinction, bound/nonbound intercaste relations, is quite as relevant as the distinction extremes/middle ranges of the hierarchy.

---

[1] This analytic strategy has been dealt with more extensively in David 1974. See below for further definition of ideational feature (p. 6), normative scheme (pp. 5-7), behavioral mode (p. 11), Ideology, and ideology (p. 28 and footnote 8).

gure 1 Ideational analysis: ideational features

commanded/ being commanded	purity/impurity	*mutual satisfaction*

gure 2 Normative analysis: normative schemes

	Aristocratic scheme	Priestly scheme	*Mercantile scheme*
Glosses of symbols prescribing general code for intercaste conduct	work diffuse aid non-negotiable rights to service and remuneration command, honor, respect	purity, pollution, natural substance, spirit substance	*business* *specifically constracted job* *fairness, profit,* *the clever one/the fool* *mutual satisfaction*
Glosses of ranking transactional symbols	seating behavior; giving with one or two hands; rising when alter enters; removal of shawl and turban; second person pronoun usage	permission to enter verandah, use well, touch cooking pot; giving and taking food and water	*none*
Code for conduct	hierarchical amity	hierarchical separation	*equivalent instrumentality*

igure 3 Social structural analysis: modes of intercaste relations

ttern riables	Bound mode relationships (kaṭṭuppaṭu = bound; kōṇṭāṭṭam = connection)	*Nonbound mode relationships (iṣṭamāṇa = free willing; koṇṭaṭṭam illai = no connection)*
Recruitment	ascribed relationship between individuals qua members of caste categories	*voluntary contract between individuals*
Time	long lasting, often hereditary	*no set duration*
Space	restricted and defined in locality	*not restricted nor defined in locality: alocal*
Clientele	restricted to certain categories of people (those who serve some)	*client's ability to pay for the commodity is the only criterion (those who trade with all)*
Pricing mechanism	"traditional" fixed pricing, periodic payments with ceremony	*supply and demand pricing; payment on delivery; no ceremony*
Context	multicontextual: roles played in ritual, economic, and political contexts	*mainly unicontextual: economic roles only*
Vector	stratified, asymmetrical exchanges within each context	*nonstratified, symmetrical exchange in the economic context*

igure 4 Value-orientation analysis: behavioral strategies

Pattern of exchange	asymmetrical reciprocity: giving and not taking	asymmetrical reciprocity: not giving and taking	*symmetrical reciprocity: giving & taking*	*symmetrical nonreciprocity: neither giving nor taking*
Allocation choice	net expenditure	net profit	*neither net expenditure nor profit: requires resources to remain autonomous*	

igure 5 Ranking analysis

enotation/ ondenotation f relative nk	stratified: superior	stratified: inferior	*nonstratified: equivalent*	*nonstratified equivalent*
xample	Landowner caste	Barber caste	*Fisher caste*	*Goldsmith caste*

The following data on the Jaffna rank-opinion hierarchy and commensal hierarchy is presented according to the conventions of Marriott (Marriott 1968). A rank-opinion hierarchy (Figure 6) presents the results of fifty-six informants' rank-orders of the twenty-four castes of Jaffna. Each informant ranked each caste as superior, equivalent, or inferior to every other caste. The boxes summarize the collective opinion. Castes whose number appears alone in a box are ranked distinctly from every other caste, while castes sharing one or more boxes with other castes are not ranked dinstinctly, that is, not distinguished as superior or inferior to the other castes in the box. The bound mode castes are given gothic numbers and the nonbound mode castes are written in italic script. Note that the castes occupying the extremes of the hierarchy are all bound mode castes, while the castes in the middle ranges are, excepting two, nonbound mode.

Following Marriott, various studies have shown that the collective rank-opinion hierarchy closely resembles hierarchies of stratified interaction between castes. One such hierarchy is the commensal hierarchy (Figure 7). The caste rank order in the matrix on giving and taking of cooked food between castes does approximate the rank-opinion order. Castes are listed on the vertical axis as potential givers of food; they are listed on the horizontal axis as potential receivers of food. Again I use the box notation (set inclusion/exclusion notation) to indicate distinct/indistinct caste ranking. This matrix is more explicit in that the observer knows why castes are distinctly or indistinctly ranked. Two castes are ranked if there is asymmetrical reciprocity: caste A gives food to caste B but refuses to take food from caste B. Two castes are not ranked if, first, there is symmetrical reciprocity: caste A and caste B accept food from each other (giving and taking), and second, two castes are not ranked if there is symmetrical nonreciprocity: caste A neither gives nor takes food from caste B. To summarize this data, bound mode castes are distinctly ranked because they are involved in patterns of asymmetrical reciprocity, while nonbound mode castes are not distinctly ranked because they engage in patterns of either symmetrical reciprocity or symmetrical nonreciprocity with other castes (see Figures 4 and 5, Appendix A and Appendix B).

FIGURE 6:

RANK OPINION HIERARCHY, JAFFNA PENINSULA, CEYLON

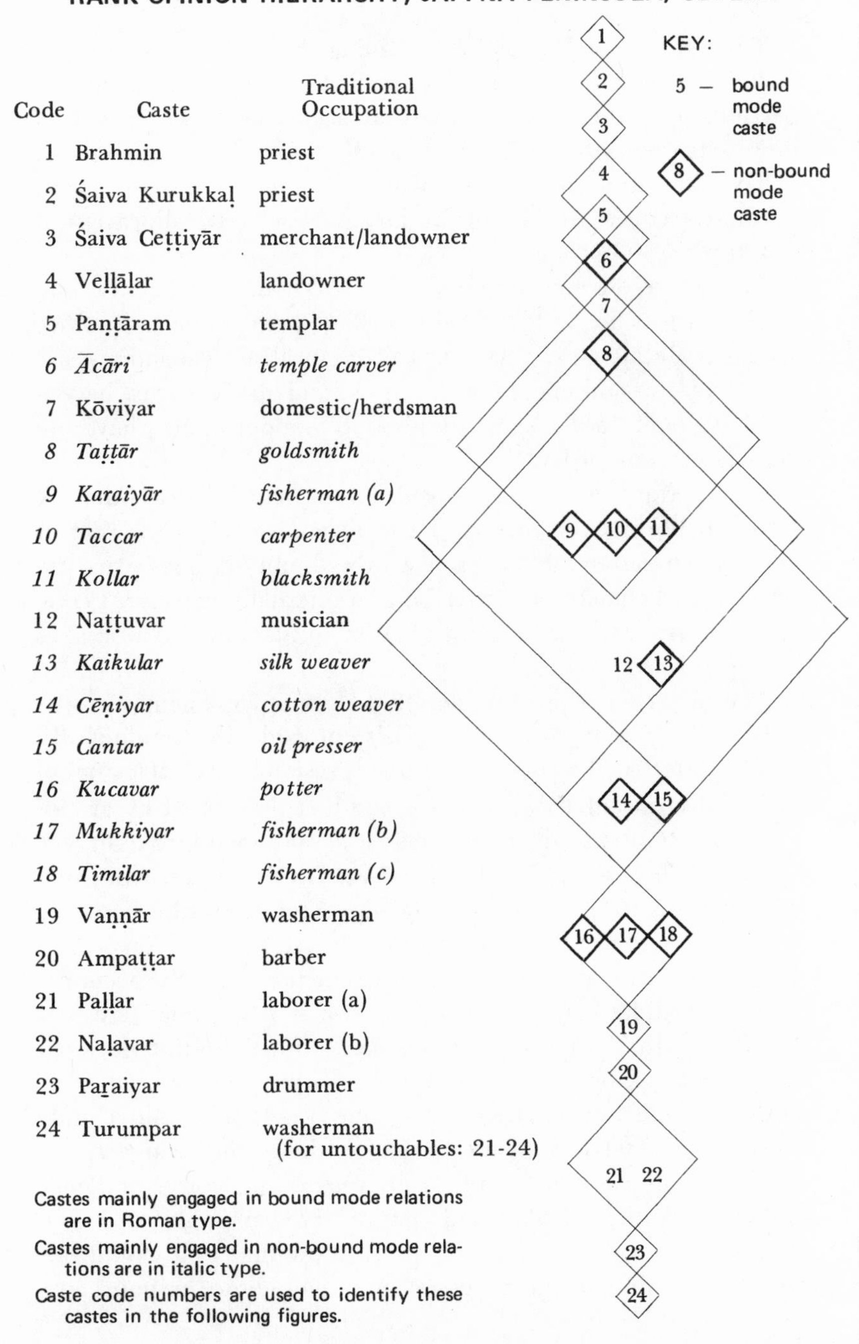

There are several steps in explaining this correlation. First, a normative account of explicit codes for intercaste conduct. Second, a further social structural account of the modes of intercaste behavior. And third, a value-orientation analysis of behavioral strategies with which natives translate their normative codes into action by means of selective allocation of economic resources.

The general conclusion will be that bound and nonbound mode castes are differentially oriented to three normative schemes. Because they translate different ideas into action, that is, intercaste ranking transactions, bound mode castes have a distinct rank order and nonbound mode castes have an ambiguous rank order.

I now want to specify the different sets of ideas, that is, different normative schemes. Each normative scheme is a set of explicit, shared symbols. Each will be doubly defined: first, in relation to behavior, as prescribing an internally consistent code for conduct, and, second, in relation to ideational features, as having a conceptual focus.

The first criterion for defining normative schemes is the prescription of an internally consistent code for conduct. By this I mean that the code for conduct prescribed by each symbol does not contradict the code for conduct prescribed by any of the other symbols which the analyst has grouped into a set (for a similar view, see Wagner 1972: 7-9). On the other hand, two of the normative schemes to be disucssed prescribe contrary codes for conduct: both cannot be followed simultaneously.

Presence of contrary normative schemes partially accounts for the well-known difference "between what they say and what they do." Another reason is the fictional relation between norms and action. Although cultural norms provide a guide to evaluate social action (they are a code of conduct) and a guide to plan activity (they are a code for conduct), the term *fictional relation* implies that there is no one-to-one correspondence between explicit norms and action. For example, if I say, "Make yourself at home!", we both know that you would not proceed to do all the activities you would do at your own

FIGURE 7:

COMMENSAL HIERARCHY – JAFFNA PENINSULA

Castes as Potential Receivers of Cooked Food

1	2	3	4	6	9	7	13	8	5	14	15	10	11	17	18	16	12	19	20	21	22	24	23	Total Given	Total Received	Net Score
	1	1	1	1	1	1	1	1	1	1	1	1	1	1	1	1	1	1[a]	1[a]	1	1	1	1	23	0	23
0		1	1	1	1	1	1	1	1	1	1	1	1	1	1	1	1	1[a]	1[a]	1	1	1	1	22	1	21
0	0		1	0	1	1	0	0	1	0	0	0	0	0	0	1	1	1[a]	1[a]	1	1	1	1	12	2½	9½
0	0	X		0	1	1	1	0	1	/X/	/X/	0	0	1	1	1	1	1[a]	1[a]	1	1	1	1	15½	6	9½
0	0	0	0		0	0	0	/1/	/1/	0	0	/1/	/1/	0	0	X	1	X[b]	X[b]	X	X	X	1	9	2	7
0	0	0	X	0		1	0	0	1	0	0	0	0	1	1	1	1	1[b]	1[b]	1	1	1	1	12½	6	6½
0	0	0	1	0	1		0	0	1	0	0	0	0	0	0	1	1	1[b]	1[b]	1	1	1	1	11	6	5
0	0	0	X	0	0	0		0	1	1	0	0	0	0	0	0	1	1[b]	1[b]	1	1	1	1	9½	5	4½
0	0	0	0	/0/	0	0	0		/1/	0	0	/1/	/1/	0	0	0	1	X[b]	X[b]	X	X	X	1	7½	3	4½
0	0	0	1	/0/	1	1	1	/0/		1	1	1	1	1	1	1	1	1[a]	1[a]	1	1	1	1	18	7	1
0	0	0	/0/	0	0	0	1	0	1		0	0	0	0	0	0	X	X[b]	X[b]	X	X	X	1	6	5	1
0	0	0	/0/	0	0	0	0	0	1	0		0	0	0	0	0	X	X[b]	X[b]	X	X	X	1	5	4	1
0	0	0	0	/0/	0	0	0	/0/	1	0	0		1	0	0	X	X	X[b]	X[b]	X	X	X	1	6½	6	½
0	0	0	0	/0/	0	0	0	/0/	1	0	0	1		0	0	X	X	X[b]	X[b]	X	X	X	1	6½	6	½
0	0	0	0	0	0	0	0	0	1	0	0	0	0		1	0	X	X[b]	X[b]	X	X	X	1	6	6½	-½
0	0	0	0	0	0	0	0	0	1	0	0	0	0	1		0	X	X[b]	X[b]	X	X	X	1	6	6½	-½
0	0	0	0	0	0	0	0	0	1	0	0	0	0	0	0		X	X[b]	X[b]	X	X	X	1	5	9	-4
0	0	0	0	0	0	0	0	0	1	X	X	X	0	X	X	X		1[a]	1[a]	1	1	1	1	9½	13½	-4
0	0	0	0	0	0	0	0	0	0	0	0	0	0	0	0	0	0		1	1	1	X	1	3½	13½	-10
0	0	0	0	0	0	0	0	0	0	0	0	0	0	0	0	0	0	1		1	1	X	1	3½	13½	-10
0	0	0	0	0	0	0	0	0	0	0	0	0	0	0	0	0	0	0	0		1	1	1	3	16½	-13½
0	0	0	0	0	0	0	0	0	0	0	0	0	0	0	0	0	0	0	1	1		1	1	3	16½	-13½
0	0	0	0	0	0	0	0	0	0	0	0	0	0	0	0	0	0	0	0	0	0		0	0	17½	-17½
0	0	0	0	0	0	0	0	0	0	0	0	0	0	0	0	0	0	0	0	0	0	1		1	22	-21

NOTE: Caste code number is the same as in Figure 6

Superscripts /a and b/ – Washermen and Barbers as potential receivers – denote two separate grades of the washerman caste and of the barber caste.

SCORING NOTATION IN MATRIX:

/1/ = transaction occurs = 1 in score columns
/0/ = transaction does not occur = 0 in score columns
/X/ = transaction sometimes occurs; subject to regional, situational, or idiosyncratic variation = ½ in score columns

home. There is a shared cultural fiction involved in the cultural utterance, "Make yourself at home!" It is in this fictional sense, then, that cultural norms provide form to the content of actual behavior.

The second criterion for defining a normative scheme, conceptual focus, speaks to the form/content relation between implicit ideational features and explicit norms. Most symbols have several associated meanings. American natives could probably list diverse meanings for each of the following symbols: 1776, the Liberty Bell, Valley Forge, the vandalism in Boston Harbor. These and other related symbols might be labeled a normative scheme prescribing patriotism. Whatever other meanings are associated with each of these symbols, I would guess that a certain meaning might have reappeared in each of the definitions, probably independence. Though conscious of each of the definitions, Americans would probably be unaware of the recurring meaning, that which gives a conceptual focus to this set of symbols. In this example, then, the ideational feature independence is the conceptual focus for this small set of polysemic symbols. I call it an ideational feature because it is the anthropologist's abstraction from native definitions of symbols. The relation of an ideational feature to a set of symbols is that of form to content in that an implicit ideational feature is the conceptual focus for a set of symbols which the anthropologist has grouped into a normative scheme.

In short, the notion of normative scheme is the analyst's grouping of a set of symbols. The symbols are grouped by two criteria: in relation to actual behavior, the scheme provides an internally consistent code for conduct; in relation to ideational feature, the symbols have a conceptual focus. This double relational definition of the normative scheme intends to operationalize Piaget's notion of the relativity of form and content.

Jaffna villagers have three normative schemes with which they evaluate transactions between castes: the arisocratic, the mercantile, and the priestly schemes.

Castes engaged in bound mode relations show a strong orientation to the aristocratic scheme, a set of symbols (listed in

Figure 2a) including *vēlai,* work; *ātaram,* the mutual right to aid in times of stress; *urimai*, the non-negotiable right to service and to remuneration; *anumati*, command; *kauravam*, honor; and *maraiyātai*, respect. As shown in Figure 2b, I also include in the aristocratic scheme certain transactional ranking symbols which prescribe asymmetrical exchanges between superiors and inferiors. The superior has an honorific seating arrangement; he gives an object to the inferior with one hand who accepts the object with two hands; he expects the inferior to rise when he passes by or enters a room, to remove his shawl and turban; and he uses derogatory second person pronouns to address the inferior.

I shall now define this scheme with the two criteria, code and conceptual focus. This set of symbols prescribes a code of hierarchical amity in intercaste relations. For example, a barber once tripped and fell in front of his master, who tumbled over him. The master became enraged, beat the barber and announced he was not going to pay him his annual distribution from the harvest. The village council – composed mainly of the master's caste – convened and decided that the high-born offender must apologize to the barber and pay him his due. When the offender refused, the council decided that *all* the serving castes should dishonor him, that is, they should not obey his commands nor serve him until he complied. He did so several months later. Note that the judgment touches on most of the symbols I list together as the aristocratic scheme. This scheme prescribes a code of hierarchical amity between castes; as the above example shows, stratified relations between castes does not preclude a strong sense of solidarity and mutuality of interests.

The conceptual focus of the aristocratic scheme is commanding/being commanded. In defining symbols such as work, non-negotiable rights, and honor, villagers made recurrent reference to this ideational feature. For example, "Work is demeaning because when you work for someone you are commanded by him"; "The master does not have unlimited command over his servants because he must heed their non-negotiable rights to remuneration"; "The most important sign of a master's honor is his relations with his servants in which he commands them." Similarly, the various ranking symbols mentioned above are defined as denoting the commanding/being commanded relation, as one person showing honor and respect to the person who commands him.

Castes engaged in nonbound mode relations show a strong orientation to the mercantile scheme, a set of symbols including *viyāpāram*, business; *upakāram*, specifically contrasted assistance, *nītam*, fairness; *kettikkārar/mūtal*, the clever one/the fool, and *cantōcam*, mutual satisfaction (Figure 2a). Unlike the aristocratic scheme, there are no ranking transactional symbols (Figure 2b) identified with the mercantile scheme.

Now to define the mercantile scheme with the criteria of code and focus. The mercantile scheme prescribes a code of equivalence and instrumentality, the opposite of hierarchical amity. When Tamils trade with an artisan or buy goods from a fisherman or merchant, they arrive, with talented and frequently angry bargaining, at what is *then* proclaimed a fair *(nītamāṉa)* price. When the transaction is finished, there is a ritual of mutual satisfaction. For example, a taxi driver and I agreed to a fare of one rupee. I gave him one rupee and twenty-five cents at the end of the ride. I was surprised when he held out his hand and said, "*Cantōcamā?*" My Jaffna friend explained the driver knew I had already given him a gratuity and wanted to verify that I was not being deceived and that the whole transaction was acceptable *(cantōcam)* to both of us. The driver had asked for one more cent to acknowledge these facts, which I then gave him. The driver appeared quite content. Equivalent relations risk antagonism and manipulation and are resolved with a ritual of mutual satisfaction.

The conceptual focus of the mercantile scheme is the term mutual satisfaction, a meaning which re-appears in the exegesis of these symbols. For example, fairness was defined as follows: "Buyer and seller must both try to know what price the other wants and settle for a price which is *cantōcam* to both. But there are no rules for this kind of exchange and they must often get very angry with each other before they are mutually satisfied." They defined *keṭṭikkārar* as "someone who is skillful and clever and proves it to you each time you trade with him. His fish are not rotten. His jewelry does not crack when you put it on. So you return to him because you are *cantōcam* with the deal. A fool, *mūtal*, is just the opposite; he proves he is a fool each time he tries to deceive you – gives you a rotten fish that looks fresh – and fails to deceive you. Of course, if he successfully deceives you, then he is the clever one and you are the fool."

The priestly scheme is a set of symbols, which include *ācāram*, purity, *tiṭṭu*, pollution, and *uṭampu* and *uyir*, natural and spiritual substance. These symbols prescribe a code of hierarchical separation between beings defined as different in natural and spiritual substance. Contrary to Dumont's assertion that this hierarchical ideology does not exist outside mainland India (Dumont 1966: 271-273), this code is alive and well in Jaffna, prescribing rules of separation between castes and between grades of a caste. For example, if a woman from a priestly descent unit identified as hearing only two initiations *(tītcai*, Skt., *dīkṣā)* marries into a descent unit known as hearing three initiations, she is forbidden to dine with her parents since their substance is less pure.

The conceptual focus of these symbols for general intercaste conduct and of those I list as ranking transactional symbols is the ideational feature purity/impurity. Commensal behavior, for example, is defined with reference to purity/impurity: villagers say that particles of food become particles of your body. You are what you eat. And the purity of the substance of the person who cooks the food becomes part of the food. Therefore you may not accept cooked food from someone whose substance is less pure than your own.

In summary, Jaffna villagers orient their action by three contrasting normative schemes, each of which has a different conceptual focus and each of which prescribes a distinct code for intercaste conduct.[2] Note that there are ranking

[2]Sylvia Thrupp suggested that these schemes could be modified to describe the guiding principles of the three estates of the ancient regimes of western Europe – personal communication.

transactional symbols associated with both hierarchical schemes – the priestly and the aristocratic schemes – while the scheme prescribing equivalence – the mercantile scheme – has no associated ranking transactional symbols. The code for intercaste conduct prescribed by the aristocratic scheme is logically contrary to the code prescribed by the mercantile scheme. Two persons cannot, for example, simultaneously exchange with both a traditional fixed price and with a bargained fair price. Command and mutual satisfaction are likewise antithetical. However, a third normative scheme, the priestly scheme, prescribes a code of hierarchical separation between castes; this code is complementary to both of the above codes.

I move now to the social structural analysis to describe two modes of intercaste relations which are behaviorally contrary. As the lines connecting the boxes in Figures 2 and 3 indicate, castes oriented to the aristocratic and to the priestly normative schemes are those engaged in bound mode relations, while castes oriented to the mercantile and priestly normative schemes are those engaged in nonbound mode relations.

Seven pattern variables – recruitment, time, space, clientele, pricing mechanism, context, and vector of relationship – contrast the social relations of a bound mode caste such as the Barber from those of a nonbound mode caste such as the Goldsmith.

Recruitment: The relationship between the Barber and his master exists due to the caste categories assigned to the two persons at birth. Recruitment between the Goldsmith and his client, on the contrary, is voluntarily contracted.

Time: The Barber's relations are long-lasting, frequently hereditary. The Goldsmith's relations are of no set duration.

Space: The Barber's relations are categorically restricted and defined by locality. The Goldsmith's relations are alocal.

Clientele: The Barber's clientele are categorically defined. He serves only some castes – those of equivalent or higher purity.

The Goldsmith's clientele is not categorically restricted. He trades with anyone able to pay him.

Pricing mechanism: The pricing mechanism for the Barber's services is traditional, redistributed, periodic, ceremonialized compensation. This mode of payment occurs irrespective of the media – cash or produce – of the payment. Commodity transactions with the Goldsmith are governed by supply, demand, skill, and bargaining talent, again, irrespective of the media of payment.

Context: Interaction between the Barber and his master occurs in social contexts which we label economic, ritual, and political. Villagers do not distinguish such contexts but define such a multicontextual relationship as "connection," *kontāttam*. The Goldsmith trades only economically with clients. He may be hired to participate in a gold melting ceremony as part of the job of making the wedding badge, *tāli*, but is neither asked nor commanded to attend the wedding – as is the Barber. Informants define such a unicontextual relationship as just a "matter of money," *paṇa viṣayam*, and as "no connection," *kontattam illai.*

Vector: The Barber's relationships with his master are stratified in each context: client/patron, servant/master, ritual inferior/superior. Note that not all bound mode relationships have such a constant direction or vector, of asymmetrical stratification. The Brahmin, for example, is the ritual superior of the Landowner but is inferior in other contexts. In contrast with both of these cases, the Goldsmith does not have stratified relations. Market exchanges between buyer and seller are not stratified.

This brief description of two contrary modes of intercaste relations must be modified with the statement that the actual relations of several castes such as Carpenter, Blacksmith, and Potter, must be described as a mixture of the above two modes. Their relations are more long-lasting and localized, in an agricultural village, than that of the Goldsmith; but, like the Goldsmith, these relations are voluntarily contracted, the pricing mechanism is by supply, demand, etc.; they are unicontextual and nonstratified.

Also, my choice of descriptive terminology foreshadows a conclusion. I use the terms *context* and *vector* in place of Bailey's, Barth's, and Béteille's usage of *status summation.* Status summation requires a multicontextual relationship in which the vector of stratified relations is constant – as it is in the case of the Barber/Landowner relations. This is not so in the Brahmin priest/Landowner relations., where they are client/patron, servant/master, and *ritual superior/inferior*. Their relations are multicontextual. There is a vector of stratified relations in each context. But the vector of stratified relations is not constant; hence, there is no status summation. This must be pointed out since the notion of status summation is central to these authors' explanation of caste ranking.

Having separated two aspects of action, observable modes of intercaste behavior and indigenous codes for intercaste behavior, I now turn to a value-orientation analysis to bridge the gap between ideas and action, that is, to show how these different analyses map together. Bound mode castes are committed to the aristocratic and priestly normative schemes; and nonbound mode castes are committed to the mercantile and priestly normative schemes. As I have written elsewhere, these orientations are independently confirmed by several kinds of data: incorporation of normative symbols into caste origin myths, into spatial symbolism of caste residence, and in data on disputes (David 1972, 1974). These kinds of data are all, in the anthropological terminology, value-orientations. A value-orientation is the translation of ideas into purposive action by means of selective allocation of material resources and power.

We now can return to the ranking transactions in terms of conscious value-orientations. As noted in Figure 4, exchanges between castes mutually stratify the transacting units when the exchanges are asymmetrically reciprocal (for example, giving and not receiving food); exchanges between castes do not relatively rank the transacting units when the exchanges are either symmetrically reciprocal (giving and taking food) or symmetrically nonreciprocal (neither giving nor taking food). Since this data is the result of observation and questioning – with hypothetical questions excluded – ranking exchanges can further be designated as categorical or noncategorical. As informants said, the Landowner caste gives but refuses to accept food from the Barber caste by rule, *muṟaimai*: a categorical exchange. On the contrary, exchanges are noncategorical when the occurrence is idiosyncratic, sporadic, and subject to regional variation; no consistent pattern of exchange occurs between such caste categories. For example, I saw an Oil Presser at the wedding of a Landowner. Both men agreed there was no rule *(muṟai illai)* that all Oil Pressers come to Landowner weddings and eat at the wedding feast. This Oil Presser was invited and accepted food from the Landowner because the Landowner's brother's shop adjoined the Oil Presser's shop. Ranking exchanges are then coded as asymmetrical/symmetrical, reciprocal/nonreciprocal, and categorical/noncategorical.

Kenneth Burke writes that symbols imply strategies. A caste's choice out of the four possible patterns of exchange listed in Figure 4a is what I label its behavioral strategy; that is, its way of translating ranking symbols into action.

The behavioral strategies of bound and nonbound mode castes differ markedly, as is seen in the comparison of the Landowner and Goldsmith castes. I first consider a transactional ranking symbol, second person pronoun usage, which is related by informants to ideas of command and respect. As shown in Figures 8 and 9, Jaffna Tamils use five pronouns. Two persons relating to each other with extreme respect and disrespect code such asymmetrically reciprocal behavior with the pronouns *nām/nītā*. The inferior says *nām*; the superior says *nītā*. Less extreme respect and disrespect (not only between castes, but between an elder and a younger man of the same caste) is coded with the pronouns *nīnkaḷ/nī*. In addition, there is one pronoun used symmetrically to denote equivalence (not equality): *nīr*.

As shown in Figure 8, the Landowner makes extensive use of pronouns of honor and disrespect but only limited use of the equivalence pronoun. On the contrary, the Goldsmith infrequently uses pronouns of honor and disrespect and uses the equivalence pronoun when addressing clients from a wide range of castes, castes ranked both higher and lower than the Goldsmith in the rank opinion hierarchy. The Landowner's strategy of assymmetrical reciprocity thus maximizes rank discrimination with pronoun usage, while the Goldsmith's stretegy of symmetrical reciprocity tends to nullify ranking denotation.

In food exchanges, a purity related symbol (see Figures 7 and 10), the Landowner mainly has asymmetrical reciprocal exchanges, that is, stratified transactions. Of eighteen stratified transactions, ten are categorical and eight are noncategorical. He has but four categorical nonstratified transactions. In contrast, the Goldsmith mainly has symmetrically nonreciprocal, that is, nonstratified transactions. He has ten stratified exchanges, that is, with priests and other Kammāḷan artisan castes. Only five are categorical, the other five noncategorical stratified exchanges are with hired, nonhereditary servants. He has twelve categorical nonstratified exchanges with his client castes. The Landowner clearly engages in more stratified exchanges than the Goldsmith. But the Goldsmith is slightly more strict, more purity conscious; he refuses to accept food from the Merchant caste, a caste from whom Landowners accept food.

The total scores of stratified/nonstratified transactions permit us to relate these different behavioral strategies (ways of translating ideas into action) to the facts of differential control of resources and allocations of resources (see Figure 4b). The Landowner, a superordinate in his bound mode relations, gives out much more food than he receives, to enhance his status. Conversely, the Barber, a subordinate in his bound mode relations, receives much more food than he gives and thus accepts inferior status. With a strategy of asymmetrical reciprocity, superior religious status is gained at definable cost while the acceptance of inferior status is profitable. On the contrary, the Goldsmith, who is engaged in nonbound mode relations, neither gives nor receives much food and thus maintains equivalence in religious status. With a strategy of symmetrical nonreciprocity, the Goldsmith neither expends nor profits but must possess enough resources to maintain his

FIGURE 8:

BEHAVIORAL STRATEGY OF A CASTE ENGAGED IN BOUND MODE RELATIONS IN SECOND PERSON PRONOUN USAGE WITH OTHER CASTES

Castes:	Pronoun Used by Landowner Caste:				
	nām	nīṅkaḷ	nīr	nī	nītā
Brahmin	+	+	–	–	–
Non-brahmin priest	+	+	–	–	–
Merchant	–	+	–	–	–
Landowner	–	+	+	+	–
Templar	–	–	–	+	–
Temple carver	–	–	+	+	–
Domestic	–	–	+	+	–
Goldsmith	–	–	+	+	–
Fisherman A	–	–	+	+	–
Carpenter	–	–	–	+	–
Blacksmith	–	–	–	+	–
Musician	–	–	–	+	–
Silk weaver	–	–	–	+	–
Cotton weaver	–	–	–	+	–
Oil presser	–	–	–	+	–
Potter	–	–	–	+	–
Fisherman B	–	–	–	+	–
Fisherman C	–	–	–	+	–
Washerman	–	–	–	+	+
Barber	–	–	–	+	+
Laborer A	–	–	–	+	+
Laborer B	–	–	–	+	+
Drummer	–	–	–	+	+
Washerman for untouchables	–	–	–	+	+

autonomy; that is, he sacrifices income by not accepting food from the Landowner.

Thus these different behavioral strategies – which require different budgets – show commitment to different normative schemes. The Landowner expends his resources to maximize rank discrimination and thus to translate into action the hierarchical norms of the aristocratic and priestly schemes. The Goldsmith conserves his resources; his abstinence nullifies the ranking denotations of food exchanges. He does not violate but simply obviates the purity dictates of the priestly scheme. In his permissiveness with pronoun usage, the Goldsmith nullifies the ranking denotations of this symbolism. In both cases, he maintains an ambivalent equivalence with other castes with which he wishes to trade. Thus he translates into action the norms of equivalence and instrumentality of the mercantile scheme.[3]

With these last comments, I can claim an analytic strategy which is less reductionist than previous accounts. I have shown who translates which ideas into action by means of which kinds of allocations of resources and with which results regarding ranking. Bound mode castes show commitment to aristocratic and priestly codes by engaging in stratifying ranking transactions. To do so they either expend resources or profit in the transactions. The result is that they are distinctly ranked. On the contrary nonbound mode castes express their orientation to mercantile and priestly codes by engaging in nonstratifying ranking transactions. Their allocation regime is self-sufficiency and the result is ambiguous ranks. The main point is that such value orientation analysis grants analytic

---

[3]After this article was completed, I received a draft of McKim Marriott's "Hindu Transactions: Rank without Dualisms," Association of Social Anthropologists, Oxford, July 9, 1973. Combining empirical studies of ranking transactions and an ethnosociological account of transfers of gross and subtle substances, Marriott proposes four strategies of ranking transactions which illustrate the "systematic, ranked relations among the Indian analogues of status, power, and asceticism," (p. 7). These strategies replicate my behavioral strategies of asymmetrical reciprocity, symmetrical reciprocity, and symmetrical nonreciprocity (see Figure 4a).

FIGURE 9:

BEHAVIORAL STRATEGY OF A CASTE ENGAGED IN NON-BOUND MODE RELATIONS IN SECOND PERSON PRONOUN USAGE WITH OTHER CASTES

Castes:	Pronoun used by Goldsmith caste:				
	nām	nīṅkaḷ	nīr	nī	nītā
Brahmin	+	+	–	–	–
Non-brahmin priest	+	+	–	–	–
Merchant	–	+	–	–	–
Landowner	–	+	+	–	–
Templar	–	–	+	–	–
Temple carver	–	+	+	–	–
Domestic	–	–	+	+	–
Goldsmith	–	+	+	+	–
Fisherman A	–	–	+	–	–
Carpenter	–	–	+	+	–
Blacksmith	–	–	+	+	–
Musician	–	–	+	–	–
Silk weaver	–	–	+	–	–
Cotton weaver	–	–	+	–	–
Oil presser	–	–	+	–	–
Potter	–	–	+	–	–
Fisherman B	–	–	+	–	–
Fisherman C	–	–	+	–	–
Washerman	–	–	–	+	–
Barber	–	–	–	+	–
Laborer A	–	–	–	+	+
Laborer B	–	–	–	+	+
Drummer	–	–	–	+	+
Washerman for untouchables	–	–	–	+	+

FIGURE 10

BEHAVIORAL STRATEGIES OF A CASTE ENGAGED IN BOUND MODE RELATIONS (LANDOWNER) AND A CASTE ENGAGED IN NONBOUND MODE RELATIONS (GOLDSMITH) WITH RESPECT TO COMMENSAL TRANSACTIONS

1. Landowner

	Categorical "by rule" *(mur̲ai)*		Noncategorical some do; some don't "no rule" *(mur̲ai illai)*	
	asymmetrical	symmetrical	asymmetrical	symmetrical
reciprocal (Landowner as inferior) ---------------- (Landowner as superior)	Br. priest non-Br. priest Merchant ---------------- Musician Washerman Potter Barber Laborer A Laborer B Drummer	Temple Cook Domestic	---------------- *Fisherman A* *Silk weaver* *Carpenter* *Blacksmith* *Cotton weaver* *Oil presser* *Fisherman B* *Fisherman C*	
nonreciprocal		*Temple Carver* *Goldsmith*		
Totals	10	4	8	0

18 (10 + 4 + 8)

Stratified exchanges = 18
Nonstratified exchanges = 4

2. Goldsmith

	Categorical		Noncategorical	
	asymmetrical	symmetrical	asymmetrical	symmetrical
reciprocal (Goldsmith as inferior) ---------------- (Goldsmith as superior)	Br. priest non-Br. priest *Temple Carver** ---------------- *Carpenter** *Blacksmith** **Kammāḷan̲ artisans*	Temple Cook	---------------- Washerman Barber Laborer A Laborer B Drummer (all hired servants; therefore not categorical)	
nonreciprocal		Merchant Landowner *Fisherman A* *Silk weaver* Domestic Musician *Cotton weaver* *Oil presser* *Fisherman B* *Fisherman C* *Potter*		
Totals	5	12	5	

10 (5 + 5)

Stratified exchanges = 12
Nonstratified exchanges = 10

Note: Names of castes engaging in bound mode relations are written in gothic type.
Names of castes engaging in nonbound mode relations are written in italic type.

parity of status to ideas and material resources; neither is reduced to epiphenomenal status.[4]

Now I shall return to the previous accounts of local caste ranking and state partial revisions of the opposed explanations of Bailey and Dumont.

Bailey's social structural analysis reduces cultural ideas to epiphenomena of the hard facts of control of resources and power. He (I cite also Barth and Bétille) explains ranking with Nadel's notion of status-summation.[5] Differential control of resources yields status summation; that is, two castes have a constant direction of stratified relations in different contexts. One caste is master, patron, and ritual superior; the other caste is servant, client, and ritual inferior. This constant direction of stratified relations yields a consensual relative ranking of the two castes. Bailey recognizes one problem with his position. Control of resources is irrelevant at the extremes of the hierarchy. A poor, powerless Brahmin caste is still the ritual superior of the dominant Landowner caste; a rich Untouchable is still considered polluting. When he dismisses such data as "a peculiar rigidity at the extremes of the hierarchy," he incurs Dumont's charge of reducing the religious ideology of purity to an epiphenomenon.

There is another problem with the status summation explanation of caste ranking. Castes fully engaged in nonbound mode relations have no summation of status. Their intercaste relations, in my term, are unicontextual; in Bailey's terms, they involve but a single status: seller/buyer. Summation of a single status is logically absurd. His explanation does not apply to nonbound mode castes. In this case I cannot charge Bailey with

---

[4] No study is complete. Limits of space prevent me from describing ecological and economic systems which complement the above analysis. Patterns of allocation of resources can only be understood in relation to the system of land tenure, the system of ownership and distribution in fishing communities, and the system of distribution of artisans' commodities. I expect to do this in a later study.

[5] For a review and critique of status summation and related terms, see Lynch 1969: 10-13.

reducing ideas to epiphenomenal position since the nonhierarchical mercantile scheme has not previously been reported as a systematic structure of symbols used by villagers. South Asianists are familiar with the idea of *artha*, and have related it to town and urban data, but have not reported how it is systematically relevant to village life.

The status summation position can also be modified when describing changes in relative religious rank between castes: positional change. Briefly put, changes in the politico-economic order are translated into changes in relative ranking. A caste gets richer and more powerful and forces or bribes a caste formerly considered superior to accept a reversal in relative ranks. Such a shift occurred in Jaffna (it was recorded by my predecessor, Michael Banks). Early in the 1950's, the Washerman caste opened laundries in market towns and became wealthier. Within several years, their contributions to temple funds persuaded the managers to admit them into the temples. Formerly, the Barber caste – who were not, and are still not permitted temple entry – were ranked superior to the Washermen. Now, as the rank-opinion study shows, they are somewhat inferior to the Washermen. In some villages, Barbers accept food from Washermen while in other villages, there is a stand-off: neither accepts food from the other (Banks 1960). Bailey's position is tenable in this case, which involves castes engaged in the bound mode of intercaste relations, castes who play the ranking game for profit.

But I must limit the applicability of this thesis by stating that castes involved in nonbound mode relations cannot easily be coerced to trade rank for profit. While I was in Jaffna, a locally dominant caste of Silk Weavers approached various Kammāḷaṉ artisans – the poorer ones first – in hopes of getting them to accept cooked food. An informal meeting of various artisan castes convened and rejected this proposal. "How can we bargain with someone," said an artisan, "if we must take account of his high rank?" Bailey's thesis that changing control of resources is translatable into shifts in rank – for castes in the middle ranges of a local hierarchy – is a necessary but not a sufficient condition. Another necessary condition is that both parties whose relative economic fortunes have changed be interested in playing the game. Commitment to the equivalence code of the mercantile normative scheme militates against playing the ranking game and calculating increase/decrease in relative rank in return for expenditure/profit.

Then I argue that stratificatory grading of castes is not simply a reflex of status summation, status summation being maintained by differential control of resources. This argument is reductionist in that cultural structure is made an epiphenomenon of social structure. Rather, I hold that implementation of ideas is as relevant as the implementation of material resources in determining caste ranking in any community. The ability to affect the course of interaction with other castes by means of material expenditure is a necessary condition in the determination of rank order of castes in a local hierarchy. But another necessary condition is the commitment to an hierarchic *vs.* a nonhierarchic normative scheme. Such commitment conditions the way in which material resources will be spent and received and thus affects patterns of ranking/nonranking in the local hierarchy.

Dumont's structuralist definition of caste ranking is on the level of unconscious structures of thought. Unlike Bailey, he has no trouble with the peculiar rigidity at the extremes of the hierarchy because the irrelevance of power and economics to the rank position of Brahmin and Untouchable directly reflects the hierarchical ideology of purity/impurity. To Dumont, the middle ranges are problematic. Faced with data (for example, in Ramkheri, Mayer 1960) in which the powerful meat-eating Landowner caste ranks superior to less powerful, less wealthy vegetarian castes, he must admit that the rank gradation of purity does not reign supreme but is contradicted by facts of power and economic differences.

Dumont's reply to the problematic middle ranges is to make an analytic precedent out of Hindu scriptural lore. In *śāstra*, the priest encompasses the king ("The brahman being the source, or rather the womb, from which the ksatra [the king] springs, is superior.") and the spiritual principle of purity encompasses the temporal principle of power (Dumont 1962: 50). Then Dumont reduces facts of economics and power to an epiphenomenon of the purity/impurity ideology in a novel way: he assigns these empirical factors, economics and power, to an "encompassed" position relative to the "encompassing" position of the purity ideology (Dumont 1966: 28).

My response has been not to limit my analysis to this hierarchical ideology stressed in *śāstra* and other esoteric writings. To better represent Hindu village mentality, I have argued that we must consider not only facts of power but also hierarchical ideas about command and power (aristocratic scheme), not only facts of differential control of resources but also nonhierarchical ideas about entrepreneurial activity (mercantile scheme). In secular exchanges, it is difficult to decide which of these ideas are encompassing and which are encompassed.[6] Villagers explicitly refer to these contrasting

---

[6] In the context of relations between all men or all castes, as I have written elsewhere, the opposition of hierarchical vs. non-hierarchical ideational features (pure/impure and commanding/being commanded vs. mutual satisfaction), normative schemes (priestly and aristocratic vs. mercantile) and behavioral modes (bound vs. nonbound mode relations) is present. In another context, relations between all men and God, this opposition is neutralized: only the hierarchical features appear (pure/impure and commanding/being commanded; priestly and aristocratic; bound mode) (David 1974a). That is, for the ordinary villager in ritual and temple festival activity, the relation with God is that of a servant to a lord. But even this picture of consistency, of neutralization of contraries, must be amended if we consider the cases of the *bhakta* and the *saṃnyāsin*. In these cases, the relation between men and God is imaged as that of the relation between wife and husband, a relation which, as I have written elsewhere, has the connotation of equivalence (as well as hierarchy) in the sense that the wife's body is thought to become identical in natural substance with that of her husband during the wedding ceremony (David 1973). *Bhaktas* and *saṃnyāsins* assured me that it was no coincidence that the term *cantōcam*, which means equivalence or mutual satisfaction, the ideational feature underlying the mercantile scheme, resembles in sound and meaning the term *cāntam*, which means the peace, equilibrium, or tranquility felt by the *bhakta* or *saṃnyāsin* on uniting with God. After the work of V. Turner, it seems foolish to reject indigenous etymology (Turner 1967: 50ff.). In sum, even the religious context of relations between men and God is defined by natives as guided by

codes for intercaste conduct in evaluating their activities. Villagers selectively allocate their resources not only in terms of the priestly scheme (stressed by Dumont) but also in terms of the aristocratic and mercantile schemes. And different value-orientations to these schemes affect the outcome of ranking transactions and hence relative ranking.

In summary, two brands of analytic reductionism, social structural and structuralist accounts, each leave different ranges of the local caste hierarchy unexplained. Attention to a third level of data which is treated tangentially in the above accounts, alternative normative codes, yields greater specificity in explaining the whole range of relative caste ranking in the village while maintaining parity of analytic status for both the ideational and material determinants of human action.

This substantive problem has been a vehicle for the more general theoretical question of resolving differences between symbolic analyses and behaviorist analyses. The tack I have taken here is to propose a differentiated analytic scaffolding whose purpose is to reduce reductionism. Reductionism can be reduced, as I proposed in another paper, if normative codes are recognized as a cognitive mediator. That is, I described the relations between the levels of ideational features and norms and between the levels of norms and behavior with Piaget's notion of the relativity of form and content, implicit ideational features being form with respect to explicit normative codes and normative codes being form with respect to actual behavior (David 1974a).

To conclude this article, I wish to discuss several points raised about this model by discussants at a recent conference. For this, thanks are due to Professors Fürer-Haimendorf, Marriott, Khare, Lynch, Barnett, and Morrison.[7]

---

hierarchical (master/servant relation) and by equivalence (husband/wife) features. Given such ethnosociological detail, it is indeed difficult to decide that certain ideas unequivocally encompass other ideas.

[7] The conference "Changing Identities in South Asia" convened at Michigan State University, East Lansing, Michigan, August 29-30, 1973, in preparation for a session of the IXth International Congress of Anthropological and Ethnological Sciences.

The first problem is whether or not ideational features are in the mind of the analyst or in the culture, a problem addressed to all symbolic or structuralist anthropologists who posit some sort of unconscious structure in the integration of cultural symbols. Nicholas has recently reviewed some aspects of this problem and states that "it now appears that cultural systems are integrated in two ways: 'horizontally' with respect to discrete meanings, and 'hierarchically' with respect to the ultimate ground of authority of a culture." "Horizontal" integration subsists in a coherence of meanings. Discrepant interpretations of the same phenomena and inconsistent or contradictory meanings given to related phenomena tend not to persist within a single system (Nicholas 1973:74). Nicholas summarizes the approaches of Schneider (central symbols), Turner (dominant ritual symbols), and Geertz (synoptic paradigm) and continues, "Whichever approach is taken, the hierarchical pattern of cultural integration appears as a relation between a small number of semantically complex symbols, which often have a 'sacred' quality and are frequently used in rituals and myths, and a relatively large number of dependent symbols which are semantically simpler and are used in ordinary contexts" (p. 75). In other words, some cultural symbols are more equal than other symbols in that an ideational feature (or central or dominant symbol or whatever) is structurally dominant either in a taxonomic sense, a marked/unmarked category sense, or as I have proposed here, in the sense of providing a conceptual focus to symbols in a normative scheme. Then I can restate the problem as follows: are natives aware of this hierarchical ordering of the symbols in their culture (as is the analyst)?

Use of the dichotomy of analyst's unconscious model/native's conscious model tends to shroud this question. This is why I prefer the dichotomy of implicit/explicit awareness. I take it as an empirical question to be determined whether or not different sectors of the population are aware of the hierarchical ordering of symbols in their culture (that is, aware of the hierarchical relation between ideational features and the dependent symbols in normative schemes or in ideologies).

In this article, I have offered one discovery procedure to distinguish implicit from explicit awareness: collection of definitions of polysemic normative symbols and the charting of reappearing meanings in different sets of symbols. Informants' ability to define their symbols is explicit awareness of shared meanings; ability to apply these symbols to purposive social action enacts explicit reference to symbols. On the other hand, lack of ability to recognize hierarchical ordering of symbols in use can be interpreted as implicit reference to the ideational feature underlying the set of symbols.

It should be argued that the ideational feature is sometimes explicitly known and referred to by people in society. For instance, not only the writers of the Indian Constitution but also some of the urban constituencies of India can explicitly tell you that egalitarianism is one of the ideational features giving a conceptual focus to the specific normative statutes – such as the abolition of Untouchability – elaborated in the Constitution. Similarly, many Tamils know that the political ideologies[8] of the DMK and Anna-DMK parties stress a notion of Dravidian unity and that this ideational feature is elaborated into a number of specific normative codes for conduct such as resistance to the imposition of Hindi as the national Indian language.

Normative schemes and ideologies are then similar in that the analyst can discern stratified relations between an ideational feature and the dependent symbols. It remains an empirical question whether or not the stressed position of the ideational feature is explicitly known to natives. I would suggest that this is more typically the case with recently emerging ideologies than with previously established ones, particularly when the ideational feature and its associated codes directly contradict previously established features and codes. For example, I saw the customary barrier which prohibits Untouchables in front of a temple and asked an upper caste man why it was there since

[8]This usage of *ideology* follows Geertz 1964 and Nicholas 1973: the thought scheme of a specific sector of the population. Below I refer to Dumont's usage of *Ideology*: the thought scheme of the entire (Hindu) population.

the courts had ruled that Untouchables were now permitted entry. "They can get into the courts," he said, "but not into the temples." The distinction of implicit/explicit reference is then more flexible than the distinction of the analyst's unconscious model/the native conscious mode. Pointing out an ideational feature does not imply that the feature is only in the mind of the anthropologist.

A second problem can be stated as what is the utility of viewing explicit norms as mediator between implicit ideational features and actual behavior when observers continually spot discrepancies between these levels of action? By positing a tripartite model I am open not only to the old conundrum about the difference between what they say and what they do but also to the conundrum about the difference between what they don't say (implicit reference) and what they say (explicit reference). A partial answer to these puzzles – the fact of discrepancies between different levels of human action – is possible in the light of the study I have presented here. We note that an endogenous sociocultural structure includes contrary features at different levels of action. Then we can recognize that the inappropriate matching, by actors in the society, of features at different levels, leads to observable discrepancies between levels. Mismatching of, let us say, a normative code with a mode of behavior yields a discrepancy between what they say and what they do.

Some analysts, whether studying symbolic or behavioral structure, argue for endogenous consistency structures. In the previous quotation from Nicholas, we are told that, "Discrepant interpretations of the same phenomena and inconsistent or contradictory meanings given to related phenomena tend not to persist within a single system." Similarly, in the analysis of disputes, Bailey holds that "conflicts" can be settled within the rules of the endogenous system while "contradictions" are disputes which cannot be so settled. The presence of contradictions results from a confrontation between an endogenous system of rules and an exogenous system of rules and is "symptomatic of social change" (Bailey 1960: 7, 239).

Other analysts, again, whether studying symbolic or social

structure, argue for the co-existence of contrary or contradictory structures within a single system. Wagner, for example, holds that,

> Every meaning in a culture is generated through metaphorical opposition, but not all the meaningful relationships in a culture are those of opposition. The metaphors that combine to make up a set of consistent meanings do not oppose each other; such metaphors exist in a complementary relationship to one another. I will call such a set of complementary metaphors an ideology . . . meaning is created by the formation of metaphors involving the formal elements of a culture. The relationship among specific metaphors within a culture can be either one of complementarity (consistency) or of innovation (contradiction). A set of complementary metaphors, whose meanings are consistent, constitutes an ideology, but the distinct ideologies of a culture stand in an innovative relationship to one another, that is, they achieve their meaning by metaphorizing, and hence contradicting, one another.
>
> (Wagner 1972: 7-9)

(We need not be detained by Wagner's special use of the terms metaphor and metaphorizing, since they are related to his argument concerning the innovation of meaning.[9] His usage of metaphor and of ideology and the relation between metaphor and ideology is strikingly similar to my usage of normative symbol and normative scheme or ideology – as opposed to Ideology, see below.) Similarly, Moore, criticizing the uniformity assumption of equilibrium theory, notes that the predominant institutionalization of one ideal type of behavior does not dispel nor dismiss the alternative ideal type of behavior (Moore 1960: 815). (Note that my usage of modes of behavior resembles ideal types, but differs in that I do not wish to be bound by the ideal type stricture that ideal types correspond to no empirical cases.)

This study has helped me decide between a view that an endogenous system is a consistency structure and the view that an endogenous system includes contrary features, each feature being internally consistent. I call the strategy of opting for the

[9] Wagner wishes to distinguish between lexical signification/metaphorical signification as tautologous/nontautologous meaning and as an arbitrary/nonarbitrary or determinant relation between signifier and signified (Wagner 1972:5).

latter view the opening of the field. In the context of intercaste relations, contrary features can be specified at the levels of, first, ideational features, second, normative schemes, and, third, behavioral modes.

First, Dumont holds that at the encompassing or global level, a hierarchical, holistic Ideology makes caste society appear rational and coherent. In opening the field of inquiry, I have replied that the Ideology or the set of ideational features [10] includes not only the opposition emphasized by Dumont, purity and impurity, but also the features commanding/being commanded and mutual satisfaction. Various recent works have dealt with other ideational features such as left/right (Beck 1973), good/bad sacred (Das and Uberoi 1971), power (Wadley 1973), the nondivisibility of natural substance and code for conduct (Marriott and Inden 1974), etc. Various authors thus have rejected the notion that South Asian Ideology can be defined with reference to a single ideational feature. Each has proposed his own feature. The job of ordering the various features has hardly begun. One starting point for that exercise might be the assumption that these features must be defined in reference to the explicit representations of the ordinary villager or the ordinary city dweller, and not only in relation to the representations of writers of *śāstra* (several writers have criticized Dumont on this point; see Berreman 1971).

Second, writers have already called attention to various normative orders such as Sanskritization, Kṣatriyaization, etc., in which upper caste lifestyles are imitated by lower castes seeking mobility. Thus I do not criticize the literature as maintaining a monolithic structure on the normative level, but add that I have tried to specify contrary normative schemes which include not only the Priestly and Aristocratic schemes but also the Mercantile scheme for intercaste conduct. The first two schemes are not wholly different from the import of Sanskritization and Kṣatriyaization except in that they specify codes for intercaste conduct while the latter terms specify non-relational lifestyles which are or are not imitated. Third, much

---

[10] See footnote 8.

of the literature on rural South Asia is prey to a collective methodological bias. That is, the stereotype of intercaste behavior in rural South Asia derives from the study of agricultural villages; this has yielded the stereotype of jajmāni style intercaste relations as the established, dominant form of relations. Consideration of fishing and artisan villages has led me to note the presence of a sub-dominant form of relations in Jaffna, the nonbound mode of relations. In short, when I say the opening of the field, I mean that we must leave open for further research and analysis the set of ideational features, the set of normative schemes, and the set of behavioral modes relevant to intercaste conduct.

How, then, does recognition of contrary features relevant to a single system of action, such as intercaste relations, aid in partially answering the puzzle of discrepancies between implicit and explicit levels of thought, or between thought and observable action? Whatever their primary value-orientation, Jaffna villagers are aware of both the hierarchical and non-hierarchical normative schemes and behavioral modes. Such knowledge, as I witnessed at various points in my field research, led to a mismatching of code with behavior. One talented Goldsmith had the reputation of being rather imperious with his customers. Customers had to suffer his caprices if they wished the benefit of his skill. On several occasions, I saw him turn down the invitation to perform a gold-melting ceremony even if his schedule was not crowded; "Those people are parvenus. They spoil my appetite," he said. Both his kin and his clients told me he was acting more like a landlord than like a goldsmith; he was applying aristocratic norms to what should have been nonbound mode relations governed by mercantile norms. Though they disapproved of this inappropriate behavior, they did not reprove him. For, after all, he made exquisite jewelry! And, in another sense, his inappropriate behavior was not incomprehensible to them. It was not random deviance but behavior recognizable in terms of a code for conduct which was thoroughly familiar to them. Then the puzzle of the difference between what they say and what they do is partially clarified when we recognize that what they say includes contrary codes for conduct, each code being internally consistent. It is only when a consistency structure is posited that a difference between what they say and what they do is explicable as random deviance or deviance driven by material or power interests.

There are, doubtless, other problems with this tripartite model which, as Marriott recently said in a discussion of this work, ". . . the metaphysic of western science can tear apart." It should be remembered, however, that I am not proposing frozen, watertight levels of analysis to be considered as things in themselves. I have set up these levels, first, in order to delineate relations between levels, and second, to reduce reductionism. I do not feel bound by the necessity to choose either thought or action as the real starting point for analyzing human action systems. In this way, we might have a reply to students who tell us, "Dumont is Dumont and Bailey is Bailey. And never the twain shall meet."

APPENDIX A: Rank opinion data from which the rank opinion hierarchy (Figure 6) was derived.

In this study, the discovery methods and the scoring techniques follow the conventions of Marriott (1968).

Fifty-seven informants from fifteen castes and one Muslim were asked to rank the twenty-four castes resident in the Jaffna peninsula, north Ceylon. Thirty-one informants reside in four agricultural and fishing villages along the north coast of the peninsula, the coastal region. Twenty-six informants reside in three inland villages around Nallur, villages in which a number of artisans live. This doubly stratified sample reflects regional diversity and decreases the bias of individual informants. A list of informants by caste and by region follows:

Caste	*Coastal region*	*Inland region*
Brahmin priest	–	1
Śaiva Cetti merchant	–	1
Paṇtāram templar	2	–
Veḷḷāḷa landowner	7	12
Karaiyār fisherman	13	–
Naṭṭuvar musician	–	3
Kaikular silk weaver	–	2
Kollar blacksmith	1	1
Taccar carpenter	1	–
Kōviyar domestic	1	–
Kucavar potter	–	1
Vaṇṇār washerman	1	1
Paḷḷar laborer	–	2
Naḷavar laborer	5	–
Paraiyar drummer	–	1
Muslim	–	1
Totals	31	26

Separate rank opinion matrices were constructed for the coastal and inland regions. These are available in David 1972. The following rank opinion matrix (Figure 11) combines the data from both regions. In the matrix, three figures appear at the intersection of a column of one caste (A) and the row of another caste (B). These are to be read as follows:

A is higher than B / A and B cannot be ranked as unequal / A is lower than B.

To derive the rank opinion hierarchy from the above rank opinion matrix, the following steps were taken:

First, divide the number of opinions "A and B cannot be ranked as unequal" by two.

Second, add half of this figure to the number of opinions stating, "A is higher than B"; add the other half of this figure to the opinions stating "A is lower than B," and thus arrive at a corrected ratio.

Third, if the corrected ratio is 2:1 or better, caste A is noted as being higher than caste B and assigned a separate box in the rank opinion hierarchy. If the corrected ratio is less than 2:1, these castes are noted as not being distinguished in rank and are both placed in the same box in the rank opinion hierarchy.

	Brahmin	Śaiva Kurukkaḷ	Śaiva Ceṭṭiyār	Veḷḷāḷar	Panṭāram	Ācāri	Kōviyan	Taṭṭār	Karaiyār	Taccar	Kollar	Naṭṭuvar
Śaiva Kurukkaḷ	45/7/5											
Śaiva Ceṭṭiyār	54/1/2	48/6/3										
Veḷḷāḷar	55/0/2	52/4/1	35/10/12									
Panṭāram	55/0/2	53/2/2	46/ 3/ 8	36/3/18								
Ācāri	55/1/1	52/2/3	46/ 1/10	45/1/11	30/12/15							
Kōviyan	57/0/0	57/0/0	53/ 1/ 3	57/0/ 0	42/ 4/11	32/ 3/22						
Taṭṭār	56/0/1	56/0/1	55/ 0/ 2	55/0/ 2	47/ 1/ 9	35/17/ 5	35/3/19					
Karaiyār	56/0/1	56/0/1	51/ 1/ 5	46/7/ 4	44/ 1/12	39/ 0/18	35/3/19	30/ 1/26				
Taccar	56/0/1	56/0/1	55/ 0/ 2	56/0/ 1	50/ 2/ 5	37/18/ 2	35/3/19	19/34/ 4	28/ 1/28			
Kollar	56/0/1	56/0/1	55/ 0/ 2	56/0/ 1	50/ 2/ 5	38/17/ 2	35/3/19	21/34/ 2	29/ 1/27	10/46/ 1		
Naṭṭuvar	57/0/0	56/0/1	56/ 0/ 1	53/2/ 2	50/ 3/ 4	41/ 6/10	37/5/15	28/11/18	25/ 2/30	27/ 8/22	26/9/22	
Kaikular	57/0/0	57/0/0	52/ 0/ 5	54/0/ 3	49/ 1/ 7	41/ 5/11	38/2/17	30/ 8/19	31/ 1/25	27/ 6/24	26/6/25	26/6/25
Cēṇiyar	57/0/0	57/0/0	57/ 0/ 0	57/0/ 0	52/ 1/ 4	46/ 4/ 7	41/2/14	39/ 4/14	31/ 1/25	32/ 7/18	29/7/21	32/4/21
Cantar	57/0/0	57/0/0	57/ 0/ 0	57/0/ 0	49/ 3/ 5	46/ 3/ 8	43/4/10	35/ 5/15	33/ 1/23	34/ 6/17	33/6/18	32/3/22
Kucavar	57/0/0	57/0/0	56/ 0/ 1	56/0/ 1	54/ 0/ 3	53/ 3/ 1	47/1/ 9	49/ 5/ 3	38/ 2/17	46/ 6/ 5	44/7/ 6	45/3/ 9
Mukkiyar	57/0/0	57/0/0	54/ 0/ 3	57/0/ 0	51/ 0/ 6	51/ 0/ 6	46/1/10	42/ 6/ 9	39/14/ 4	44/ 4/ 9	43/4/10	48/1/ 8
Timilar	57/0/0	57/0/0	57/ 0/ 0	57/0/ 0	49/ 0/ 8	56/ 1/ 0	45/2/10	45/ 1/11	36/19/ 2	45/ 1/11	43/2/12	47/1/ 9
Vaṇṇār	57/0/0	57/0/0	57/ 0/ 0	57/0/ 0	57/ 0/ 0	56/ 1/ 0	56/1/ 0	56/ 0/ 1	49/ 0/ 8	56/ 1/ 0	56/0/ 1	57/0/ 0
Ampaṭṭar	57/0/0	57/0/0	57/ 0/ 0	57/0/ 0	57/ 0/ 0	56/ 1/ 0	56/0/ 1	56/ 0/ 1	49/ 0/ 8	56/ 0/ 1	56/0/ 1	57/0/ 0
Paḷḷar	57/0/0	57/0/0	57/ 0/ 0	57/0/ 0	57/ 0/ 0	55/ 0/ 2	56/1/ 0	56/ 0/ 1	55/ 1/ 1	56/ 0/ 1	56/0/ 1	56/0/ 1
Naḷavar	57/0/0	57/0/0	57/ 0/ 0	57/0/ 0	56/ 0/ 1	57/ 0/ 0	57/0/ 0	55/ 0/ 2	54/ 1/ 2	55/ 0/ 2	55/0/ 2	56/0/ 1
Paṟaiyar	57/0/0	57/0/0	57/ 0/ 0	57/0/ 0	57/ 0/ 0	57/ 0/ 0	57/0/ 0	57/ 0/ 0	56/ 0/ 1	57/ 0/ 0	57/0/ 0	57/0/ 0
Turumpar	57/0/0	57/0/0	57/ 0/ 0	57/0/ 0	57/ 0/ 0	57/ 0/ 0	57/0/ 0	57/ 0/ 0	57/ 0/ 0	57/ 0/ 0	57/0/ 0	57/0/ 0

	Kaikular	Cēṇiyar	Cantar	Kucavar	Mukkiyar	Timilar	Vaṇṇār	Ampaṭṭar	Paḷḷar	Naḷavar	Paṟaiyar
Cēṇiyar	24/26/ 7										
Cantar	33/ 3/21	27/4/26									
Kucavar	41/ 4/12	39/7/11	37/6/14								
Mukkiyar	40/ 3/14	35/4/18	34/5/18	30/2/25							
Timilar	41/ 2/14	38/3/16	35/4/18	29/1/27	29/14/14						
Vaṇṇār	53/ 0/ 4	51/0/ 6	52/1/ 4	44/2/11	43/ 3/11	42/1/15					
Ampaṭṭar	56/ 0/ 1	54/0/ 3	55/0/ 2	50/2/ 5	47/ 1/ 9	45/0/12	32/18/7				
Paḷḷar	55/ 0/ 2	54/0/ 3	56/0/ 1	53/0/ 4	54/ 1/ 3	53/1/ 3	51/ 0/6	50/0/7			
Naḷavar	55/ 0/ 2	54/0/ 3	55/0/ 2	51/0/ 6	52/ 1/ 4	53/1/ 3	50/ 0/7	50/0/7	25/20/12		
Paṟaiyar	57/ 0/ 0	56/0/ 1	57/0/ 0	54/1/ 2	54/ 1/ 2	56/0/ 1	54/ 3/0	53/3/1	39/ 3/15	40/4/13	
Turumpar	57/ 0/ 0	57/0/ 0	57/0/ 0	56/0/ 1	57/ 0/ 0	57/0/ 0	57/ 0/0	57/0/0	52/ 2/ 3	53/2/ 2	41/3/13

FIGURE 11 RANK OPINION MATRIX:

JAFFNA COASTAL REGION AND INLAND REGION COMBINED

APPENDIX B: Commensal Hierarchy Sub-Matrices

To underline the point that it is castes engaged in bound mode relations with other castes which have asymmetrical exchanges and castes engaged in nonbound mode relations with other castes which have symmetrical exchanges, I have broken down the commensal hierarchy matrix (Figure 7) which includes all castes in two sub-matrices. The first sub-matrix (Figure 12) includes only castes engaged in bound mode relations, the second sub-matrix (Figure 13) includes only castes engaged in nonbound mode relations.

FIGURE 12

COMMENSAL HIERARCHY (FOOD-GIVING AND FOOD-TAKING OF CASTES ENGAGED IN BOUND RELATIONSHIPS

	Receiver Castes										Net
	1	4	7	19	20	21	22	23	Given	Received	Score
Giver Castes 1		1	1	1	1	1	1	1	7	0	7
4	0		1	1	1	1	1	1	6	2	4
7	0	1		1	1	1	1	1	6	2	4
19	0	0	0		0	1	1	1	3	3	0
20	0	0	0	0		1	1	1	3	3	0
21	0	0	0	0	0		1	1	2	6	-4
22	0	0	0	0	0	1		1	2	6	-4
23	0	0	0	0	0	0	0		0	7	-7
	0	2	2	4	4	6	6	7			

FIGURE 13

COMMENSAL HIERARCHY OF CASTES ENGAGED IN NONBOUND RELATIONSHIPS

	Receiver Castes										Net
	6	9	11	12	13	15	16	17	Given	Received	Score
Giver Castes 6		∅	1	X	∅	∅	∅	∅	1½	0	1½
9	∅		1	1	∅	∅	∅	1	3	½	2½
11	0	0		X	∅	∅	∅	X	1	3	-2
12	0	X	X		X	X	X	X	3	4	-1
13	∅	∅	∅	X		∅	∅	∅	½	½	0
15	∅	∅	∅	X	∅		∅	∅	½	½	0
16	∅	∅	∅	X	∅	∅		∅	½	½	0
17	∅	0	X	X	∅	∅	∅		1	2	-1
	0	½	3	4	½	½	½	2			

When a food transaction is known to occur, the digit /1/ is written. When a transfer of food occurs irregularly, subject to regional, idiosyncratic, or situational variation, the letter /X/, (or "sometimes") is written. When no transfer of food occurs, a zero /0/ is written. Whenever there is a case where the food transfer symbolism yields no decision because neither caste gives food nor takes food from a given other caste, the null set indicator /∅/ is written.

I am following Marriott's system of scoring for determining the ranks of single castes: "The total number of encounters . . . in which a caste dominates or 'wins' over other castes is the total number of digits in its row. The total of the encounters . . . in which a caste is dominated or 'loses' is the total number of digits in its column." (Marriott 1968:155).

In addition, partial "wins" or losses are indicated by "X" and scored as 1/2. Null set "∅" is scored as zero.

These matrices represent actual transaction. Hypothetical data is not included. I have asked, for example, five different weavers (caste /13/) whether or not they *would* receive food from other castes if the occasion arose. I received five different (overlapping) lists. And asking whether you *would* give food to another is a hopeless question. Most mercantile castes (weaver, oil presser, etc.) told me they would give food to every other caste – with the exception of the high (*uyrnda*) castes such as Brahmin, Śaiva Kurukkaḷ, Śaiva Ceṭṭiyār, and Veḷḷāḷa.

Comparison of Figures 12 and 13 yields two conclusions. First, many more paired asymmetrical transactions occur between castes primarily involved in bound relationships than between castes primarily involved in nonbound relationships. Second, the rank-opinion hierarchy corresponds to the commensal hierarchy for castes involved in bound relationships. Caste /1/ has the highest net score (7); caste /4/ has the next highest net score (4), etc. But there is no correspondence for castes involved in nonbound relationships. Caste /6/ has a net score (1½) which is lower than the net score (2½) of caste /9/ which was ranked lower in the opinion ranking than caste /6/.

REFERENCES

Bailey, F. G.

1959 "For a Sociology of India?" In *Contributions to Indian Sociology*, No. III.

1964 *Caste and the Economic Frontier.* (Manchester: Manchester University Press).

Banks, Michael

1960 "Caste in Jaffna." In *Aspects of Caste in South India, Ceylon, and North-West Pakistan*, E. R. Leach, ed. Cambridge Papers in Social Anthropology, No. 2. (Cambridge: Cambridge University Press).

Beck, Brenda

1973 *Peasant Society in Konku.* (Vancouver: University of British Columbia Press).

Berreman, Gerald

1971 "The Brahmanical View of Caste." In *Contributions to Indian Sociology*, N.S. 5.

Das, Veena, and Jit Singh Uberoi,

1971 "The Elementary Structure of Caste." In *Contributions to Indian Sociology*, N.S. 5.

David, Kenneth

1972 *The Bound and the Nonbound: Variations in Social and Cultural Structure in Rural Jaffna, Ceylon.* Unpublished Ph.D. dissertation, Department of Anthropology, University of Chicago.

1973 "Until marriage do us part: A cultural account of Jaffna Tamil categories for kinsmen," In *Man*, Vol. 8.

"Hierarchy and Equivalence in Jaffna, North Ceylon." To appear in *Changing Identities in South Asia,* Proceedings of the IXth International Congress of Anthropological and Ethnological Sciences, Kenneth David, ed. (The Hague: Mouton).

1974b. "Spatial Organization and Contrary Normative Schemes in Jaffna, North Ceylon. In *Modern Ceylon Studies*. (In press).

Dumont, Louis

1962 "The conception of kingship in Ancient India." In *Contributions to Indian Sociology*, No. VI.

1966 *Homo Hierarchicus.* (Paris: Gallimard).

Geertz, Clifford

1964 "Ideology as a Cultural System." In *Ideology and Discontent*, D. E. Apter, ed. (New York: Free Press).

Lynch, Owen M
1969 *The Politics of Untouchability*. (New York: Columbia University Press).

Marriott, McKim
1968 "Caste Ranking and Food Transactions: a Matrix Analysis." In *Structure and Change in Indian Society*, M. Singer and B. S. Cohn, eds. (Viking Fund Publications in Anthropology Number 47. Chicago: Aldine).

1974 An Ethnosociology of South Asian Caste Systems. To appear in *Changing Identities in South Asia*, proceedings of the IXth International Congress of Anthropological and Ethnological Sciences, Kenneth David, editor. (The Hague: Mouton).

Mayer, Adrian C.
1960 *Caste and Kinship in Central India: a Village and Its Region*. (Berkeley: University of California Press).

Moore, Wilbur E.
1960 "A Reconsideration of Theories of Social Change." In *American Sociological Review*, 25.

Nicholas, Ralph W.
1973 "Social and Political Movements." In *Annual Review of Anthropology*, Vol. 2, Bernard J. Siegel, ed. (Palo Alto, California: George Banta Inc.).

Piaget, Jean
1970 *Structuralism*. (New York: Basic Books).

Pocock, David
1962 "Notes on Jajmaani Relationships." In *Contributions to Indian Sociology*, No. VI.

Turner, Victor
1967 *The Forest of Symbols: Aspects of Ndembu Ritual*. (Ithaca: Cornell University Press).

Wadley, Susan S.
1973 *Power in the Conceptual Structure of Karimpur Religion*. Unpublished dissertation submitted to the Department of Anthropology, University of Chicago.

Wagner, Roy
1972 *Habu: The Innovation of Meaning in Daribi Religion*. (Chicago: University of Chicago Press).

Wiser, William H.
1936 *The Hindu Jajmani System*. (Lucknow: Lucknow Publishing House).

FOUR

M. Shanmugam Pillai

Code Switching in a Tamil Novel

THIS STUDY ANALYZES the phenomenon of code-switching found in the conversations of the characters in the novel *Cila Nēraṅkaḷil Cila Manitarkaḷ* written by Jayagandan.[1] The novel received the Sahitya Akademi Award for the year 1972.

Indian Bilingualism

A prerequisite for code-switching is bilingualism or multilingualism, and hence an analysis of the bilingual situation in Tamil Nadu, which is similar to the situation elsewhere in India, with languages and people as varying factors, is appropriate. The bilingual situation is described here with particular reference to the City of Madurai, with which the author is very familiar and which he has been observing for the last few years in informal conversations. The Saurashtras, who consitute one third of the population of this city, speak Saurashtram and Tamil as their mother tongues.[2] The Malayalis

Professor Franklin Southworth, University of Pennsylvania, was kind enough to read a preliminary draft of this paper and to give critical comments which have been incorporated in the paper. The author thanks him for the same.

[1]Jayagandan, *Cila Nēraṅkaḷil Cila Manitarkaḷ* ("Some People at Some Time"), (Madurai; Meenakshi Puttaka Nilaiyam, 1970.)

[2]*Mother tongue* is defined here as a language or languages children learn to speak as infants from their homes and playmates before going to school.

speak Tamil and Malayalam; the Muslims, Tamil and Urdu; the Anglo-Indians, Tamil and English; the Naidus, the Cobblers, the Telugu Chetties and the Rajus, Tamil and Telugu; the Raos, either Tamil and Kannada or Tamil and Telugu; and the Narikkuravars, Tamil and Vagrivel.

A further classification of the above groups into *communal and caste bilingualism* is attempted here. The Malayali population consists of various castes, and bilingualism among them cuts across these caste variations. This is called *communal bilingualism,* an example of which is the bilingualism of the Malayali community in Madurai. Similarly, the Tamil community in Trivandrum speak Malayalam and Tamil as their mother tongues; in Bangalore, Kannada and Tamil; in Hyderabad, Telugu and Tamil; in Bombay, Maratha/Hindi and Tamil; in Delhi, Hindi and Tamil; and in Calcutta, Bengali and Tamil. A great percentage of the population living in the border areas between linguistic regions are communal bilinguals. As a community they identify themselves with either one of the linguistic regions and languages, depending upon the place of their residence. The northern and western districts of Tamil Nadu–Chingelput, North Arcot, Salem, Coimbatore, Nilgiris and Madurai–have a greater percentage of bilinguals than the eastern districts.[3]

The other is *caste bilingualism.* The Naidus are a specific caste which throughout Tamil Nadu speak Tamil and Telugu as their mother tongues. But all the Telugu-speaking castes in Madurai–the Naidus, the Rajus, and the Cobblers–do not feel united through the basis of their common language, Telugu, the way the Tamils in Bombay or Calcutta feel united on the basis of their common language, Tamil, irrespective of the variations in caste. There are Tamil Sangams in these cities where Tamil-speakers gather and schools where Tamil is taught to the children, but no such organizations are to be found for the Telugus in Madurai.[4] The Malayalis in Madurai have established

---

[3]P. K. Nambiar, ed. *Census of India 1961, Vol. IX, Madras, Part 1 (ii),* 1968.

[4]The Telugu migration to Tamil Nadu started perhaps during the

a Malayala Sangam. The Muslims and the Saurashtras in Madurai also come under the category of communal bilingualism because of their organization and unification on the basis of language and, for the Muslims, religion.

Both communal and caste bilingualism are the forms of *illiterate bilingualism.* One need not be educated or involved with an educational institution to be an illiterate bilingual. Such bilinguals acquire the capacity to speak these languages as native speakers, even as infants from their homes and from their playmates. One of the two languages is used in private, the code for communication within families or with people known to belong to the same caste or community, but not with others. The other is for public use, with every one, sometimes even with one's own family members.[5]

In *literate bilingualism* a person learns to speak and write in a second language in an educational institution. In the Indian situation, the second language is usually English. Proficiency in this language depends upon the number of years spent in schools and in colleges and the opportunities to use the language. Simultaneously with the acquisition of this second language, in many cases even earlier, one may learn to read and write one's regional mother tongue. Such a person can even be trilingual or multilingual. But in school one is not expected to learn to read and write one's non-regional mother tongue unless there is a provision to learn it as a minority language, which is a very rare situation. In the colleges one may have the opportunity to learn to read and write still another language,

---

Vijayanagar and Nayak rule over Madurai in the sixteenth century, and the Telugu people might have come from the different classes of Telugu society with different educational backgrounds. The Cobblers belong to the lower caste and the Naidus to the upper castes. Even now, education has not spread evenly among the Telugu-speaking population. But Tamils who migrated to cities are from the educated middle class, and the migration is recent. They are in the minority and a unification on the basis of language, irrespective of caste, contributes to their consolidation as a powerful force.

[5] J. John Gumperz, "Hindi-Punjabi code-switching in Delhi," in *Proceedings of the Ninth International Congress of Linguists,* (The Hague: Mouton and Company, 1962).

say, Hindi or Sanskrit or French. But still one may not be able to read or write one's non-regional mother tongue. A Naidu may not be able to read or write Telugu, even after finishing his college studies, though he can speak it fluently.

There is still another type of person who acquires knowledge of a second language (mostly speaking) as the result of contact, in adult life, with persons who speak that language. The cooks for British officers in pre-independence days and for western missionaries even now come under this category. They learned to speak English as a result of their professional association. English is not their mother tongue – because they did not acquire it as infants. They did not go to a school or have any systematic language training to acquire that language. In most cases they cannot read or write. There are many businessmen in Tamil Nadu who have business contacts in North India, where they visit occasionally. They acquire the capacity to speak Hindi because of their business contacts. This is called *professional bilingualism.* If they can read and write those languages, then they would be classified as educated bilinguals.

This classification is demonstrated below.

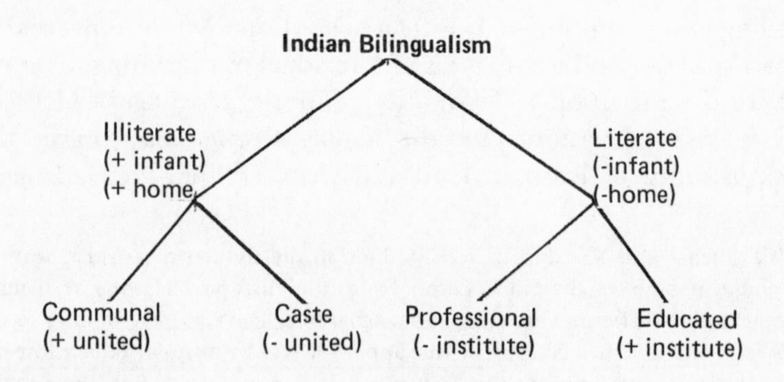

Code-Switching

A. Richard Diebold, Jr, writes, "By code-switching is usually meant the successive alternate use of two different language codes within the same discourse. It implies that the speaker is conscious of the switch."[6] With this definition for code-switching, let us look at code-switching in the Indian context.

Code-switching presupposes that the participants are at least bilinguals, if not multilinguals and/or bidialectals. There can be code-switching between language and/or between dialects, and hence language codes in the definition refer to all of these different codes. Sometimes there is a distinction made between code-switching, which involves alternate use of dialects, and language-mixing, when two or more languages are involved.

The language codes must alternate within the same discourse. Here it is *conversational discourse.* A conversational discourse consists of two or more *conversational slices.* A conversational slice is spoken by a single individual and is bound by a pause and another conversational slice or by conversational slices but never by pauses on both sides. It can be bound by breaks – the silences between two conversational slices. For a conversational discourse there must be at least two conversational slices bounded by pauses.

A Saurashtra in my university at Madurai will speak in Saurashtram to his Saurashtra friend and then turn and converse with me in Tamil, as may the other Saurashtra. Again, the two Saurashtras may converse in Saurashtram. It may be a continuation of the conversation or it may be something private. If I ask, they may explain their Saurashtran conversation to me in Tamil. My presence, as a non-Saurashtra, does not matter. But they will not talk to me in Saurashtram. Here in the United States of America my Hindi-speaking friends will switch to Hindi among themselves, even though they know I cannot follow the conversation and then explain in English what was said if I ask what they talked about. They switch to English when they talk to me. This kind of switching is *personal code-switching*, conditioned by the person one is talking to. The participants in personal code-switching have to be non-identical multilinguals, with at least one language in common.

---

[6] A. Richard Diebold, Jr., "Code-switching in Greek-English bilingual speech," *Georgetown University Round Table Selected Papers on Linguistics, 1961-1965.* (Washington, D.C.: Georgetown University Press, 1968).

While speaking to me in Tamil or to his friend in Saurashtram, a Saurashtra may speak in Tamil or in Saurashtram with no mixing of any other language code. This is *complete code-switching*. Or he may sprinkle other language codes within that conversational slice. This is *sprinkled code-switching*. If the sprinkled language is, say, English and if the person is educated, it is *educated sprinkled code-switching*. In the novel under study we have two kinds code-switching, *educated complete* and *educated sprinkled*, and both of them are non-personal.

Sprinkled code-switching occurs within a conversational slice, and personal code-switching within a conversational discourse. In a *non-personal code-switching* the participants are identical multilinguals, that is, all of them know the same languages.

Sprinkled code-switching is further divided into *reflected* and *non-reflected*. In a reflected sprinkled code-switching the *alternate code* will have a rendering, either a translation or the same idea, in the *base code*, either preceding or succeeding the alternate code. There is no such reflection in the non-reflected sprinkled code-switching. This will be illustrated later with the help of conversational slices from the novel.

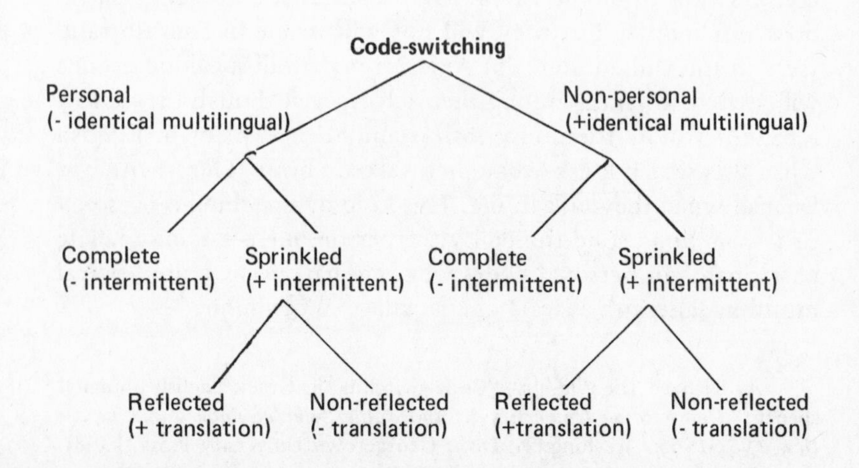

The last criteria in the definition is that the speaker is conscious of the switch. If he is not conscious, then the alternate code becomes a borrowing. In Tamil *bus stand* is a borrowing. An illiterate monolingual Tamil will use this expression. He is not conscious that it is English. But *change of dress*[7] is a code-switching. The same monolingual will not use this. Even the bilingual will not say "change of dress" if he talks to a monolingual, whereas he will say "bus stand." If he uses "change of dress," then he will quickly correct himself.

The Novel's Story

With this theoretical background about Indian bilingualism, we will now consider Jayagandan's novel. The novel is written in the stream of consciousness technique. The story progresses mainly through interior monologues and conversations.

The heroine Ganga and all her relatives in the novel belong to an educated middle-class Brahmin family. The hero, Brahbu, is a non-Brahmin millionaire. When Ganga was seventeen, during her first year of college in Madras, she was raped by Brahbu, whom she never knew and did not care to know till after a lapse of twelve years. Ganga was thrown out of the house by her brother Ganesan. Her mother Kanaga went along with her. They were supported by a distant uncle of Ganga, Venku Mama, a leading criminal lawyer and a great Sanskrit scholar at Tanjore. He gave Ganga a very good education. She received her M.A. in economics from Annamalai University and is now an important officer, a Section Officer, in the service of the government of Tamil Nadu. She is now at Madras.

Venku Mama is a sadist and hopes to have Ganga as his concubine. Under the protection of his old age, he is seventy now, he moves freely with her, embracing her and asking her to massage his body. He uses his Sanskrit scholarship to prove that Ganga can never be a wife again, that she was already a wife on the day when she was raped, and that she can only be a concubine to someone, implying himself. Ganga very carefully protects herself against this lecherous man.

---

[7] *Bus stand* and *change of dress* are expressions found in the novel.

Once Ganga overhears her uncle telling her mother that if Ganga wants she should search for the man who raped her and become his wife, thinking that she would never be able to find him, and that if she could succeed in finding him, he would not accept her. But after hard searching for six months, Ganga finds him, although by accident, and they become good friends.

Ganga enjoys the pleasure of being known as the concubine of Brahbu and thus protects herself from the advances of her old uncle, but she is Brahbu's concubine in name only. Brahbu is married and his daughter Manchu is now studying in the same college where Ganga once studied. Ganga and Manchu become good friends.

Brahbu feels very guilty about his earlier misbehavior with Ganga and wants her to get married and start a new life. But Ganga refuses. When a marriage proposal comes through, every one, including Brahbu, wants Ganga to accept the proposal. Brahbu refuses to see her till she gives her consent to the marriage. Ganga begs him to come and give his companionship. She is willing to live with him and marry him rather than anyone else. He refuses. Ganga loses herself in drinking and becomes an alcoholic.

Bilingualism in the Novel

All the above characters, except Ganga's mother, are educated bilinguals. Their communicative interaction is demonstrated below (*BL* = bilingual; *ML* = monolingual).

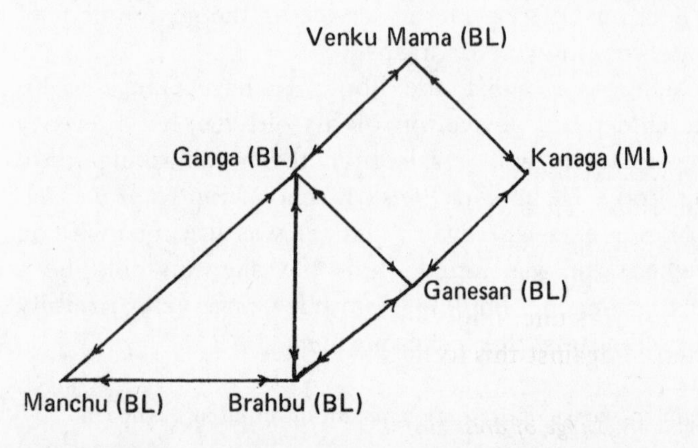

The square is the Brahmin family. Ganga is the link connecting that family with the family of Brahbu whose members are the lower corners of the triangle. The arrows indicate the directions of conversational interaction.

For our analysis the interior monologues are considered part of the conversational discourse; Ganga has these monologues throughout the story. She reflects how the several people would have conversed among themselves.

The figure demonstrates that Ganga is the central figure in the communicative chain of interaction in the novel. Venku Mama and Kanaga do not have any such interaction with either Brahbu or with Manchu. Ganga rarely speaks to her mother, though she appears frequently in Ganga's interior monologues. There is no interaction between Venku Mama and Ganesan either.

Kanaga is the only monolingual in the story. In the conversational discourses between Kanaga and Venku Mama there is no code-switching.

As has already been mentioned, we have in the novel educated code-switching, both complete and sprinkled. In a sprinkled code-switching there are three possibilities. The base code may be Tamil, into which English codes may be sprinkled. This is the only type which occurs in the novel. The other possibilities are where Tamil codes are sprinkled into an English base and where it may not be possible to decide which is the base, Tamil or English.

In the novel there are switchings to English words, phrases, and sentences. They are written in the Tamil script. There are two instances where they are given in the Roman script. One is a quotation, quoting a proverb (p. 345), and the other is a reading from a text (p. 351).

In an earlier paper[8] I theorized that whatever the part of speech of the English words (even verbs) in English, when borrowed into Tamil, they behave like nouns in Tamil. That

---

[8] M. Shanmugam Pillai, "English Borrowings in educated Tamil," *Studies in Indian Linguistics* (Volume presented to Prof. M. B. Emeneau on his Sixtieth Birthday). (Poona: Deccan College, 1968).

theory is found true in the code-switching involving words here.

At the level of phrase the same theory is supported, with the modification that only noun phrases are used in the code-switching. These phrases may fall into two classes. For one class of phrases, their corresponding translations or renderings into Tamil are possible and are used in formal style. But in the informal conversations their Tamil renderings would appear pedantic and presumptuous. "Ice-cream," "matinee show," "ladies' seat," "hand-bag," "bus stand," "Section Officer," and several others come under this category. There are sixty-three such phrases whose Tamil renderings are quite normal in informal situations. For "normal life" in the novel the Tamil expression will be *cātāraṇa vāḻkkai.* Similarly "change of dress" is *cāriyaikkaṭṭikkiṭṭatum* in the context, "straight line" is *nērā*, and so on. There are forty-five such phrases in the novel. There may be idividual variations in the distribution of the phrases in these two classes. But the second category seems to be definitely less frequently used than the first.

Complete Code-Switching

In the novel there are one hundred and sixteen conversational slices of one sentence in English, three conversational slices of two sentences, two conversational slices of three sentences, and only one of four sentences which the author writes with the Tamil script. There are seven instances where all of the conversational slices of an entire paragraph – more than four sentences – are supposed to be said in English. They are written with sprinklings of English into the Tamil base. But either in the beginning or at the end, the author or the participant who reflects says, "So he/she says this in English." The author perhaps adopts this technique because the secondary school students and the housewives who constitute the major component of his reading public[9] may not be able to follow if a whole paragraph is in English. We can make a generalization

[9]The novel was originally serialized in the weekly *Tiṉamaṇi Katir* under the name *Kālaṅkal Māṟum.* This weekly is widely read by students and housewives.

that the frequency of complete code-switching is greater if the conversational slices are smaller.

Of the one hundred and sixteen conversational slices of one sentence each, thirty-one are expressions like "Oh yes," "Yes," "O.K.," "Please," "No thanks," and so on. Thirty of them are used to express things of taboo and feelings of sorrow, dejection, and repentance. The rest are ordinary statements. It is taboo to discuss sex, particularly with ladies or by ladies. Here is an instance of a taboo where the switching takes place. Ganga is now talked about by every one as the concubine of Brahbu. Venku Mama advises her to be careful about becoming pregnant.

> *Rompa rakaciyamā inkilīsḷē kēkkar̲ār. "Precautions ellām eṭuttukkar̲yōn̲n̲ō?"* (He asks in English very softly "I hope you take precautions").
>
> *Precaution against what?*
>
> *Conception n̲u mar̲upaṭiyum kaṇṇaic cimiṭṭaṛār* (p. 211). (He says conception and winks his eyes again).

There are seven instances in the novel where the speaker switches to English when there is taboo (pp. 66, 148, 211, 227, 257, 300-302, 410). Here is a statement from one of the interior monologues of Ganga:

> *Avar aṭikkaṭi rompa paccaiyāvē colṛār. "Nī yārukkāvatu vaippāṭṭiyā irukkalām, ān̲āl evan̲ukkum pen̲ṭāṭṭiyā irukka muṭiyātu" ān̲āl atai rompa nācūkkā iṅkilīslē colṛār* (p. 66).

(He very often speaks obscenely, "You can be a concubine to someone, but not a wife to any one." But he says that in English in a civilized manner.) Ganga feels that it is civilized to speak of such taboos in English.

As for the other conversational slices which have two or more sentences, most of them are spoken by Brahbu, and all except two of them are spoken when he is under the grip of an intense feeling such as disgust with his life, humiliation by his father, misunderstanding with his wife, or repentance for having cheated at a game of cards.

In another interior monologue Ganga says *"Kōpam vantā ivarukku iṅkilīs vantuṭar̲atu. . . . Poriñcu taḷṛār"* (p. 321). (When he is angry he switches to English. He slashes on.) Ganga feels (or perhaps through her, the author of the novel feels) that there is a switching to English when a person is angry.

Sprinkled Code-Switching

There can be sprinklings at the beginning, middle, or at the end of conversational slices. There are sixty-four conversational slices which begin with English expressions. Of these, sixteen are expressions like "No," "No no," "Well said," "Never," "Oh yes," "Thanks," Lunch hour," and so on. Six of them are telephone conversations. Generally there are more sprinklings in telephone conversations than in personal conversations.[10] In the rest, except in four cases, the speaker is experiencing a strong emotion – grief, anger, disgust, worry, or repentance. A few such expressions are given here which will speak for themselves: "Oh, this is awful" (p. 111). "What are you talking?" (p. 145). "Why should I? This is my house" (p. 189). "One should have some purpose in life" (p. 339). The other four are normal unemotional expressions: "Just like this" (p. 152). "Sixth standard" (p. 275). "It is a good idea" (p. 277). "To put the whole story in a nut shell" (p. 302).

There are eighty-five conversational slices which end with switchings to English. Of these, fourteen are questions, usually questioning the statements in the conversation. Here is an illustration. Venku Mama speaks to Ganga. "*anta R.K.V. eḻutiṉa kataiyai nāṉum paticcēṉ. Uṅku ammā ataip paṭiccuṭṭu aḻutālām. . . . Uṅka ammāvai anta kataiyaip paṭikkaççoṉṉāyāmē. . . .* What do you mean?" (p. 69) (I too read the story written by R.K.V. Your mother, it seems, cried after reading that story. It seems you asked your mother to read that story. What do you mean?) All the other occurrences indicate decisions, conclusions, challenge, scolding, and repentance.

In the middle of the conversational slices there are fifty-six instances of code-switching to English sentences. Most of the

[10]In India, only people of the upper middle class and above can afford to have private telephones. Code-switching is a common style of speech among these people because of their education and profession. This may be the reason for more sprinklings in telephone conversations.

switchings at the level of words and phrases occur only in the middle and they are very frequent. Here again most of the sentences indicate feelings of anger, dejection, worry, and repentance, and also taboo. But this is not true of the words and phrases code-switched.

Reflected Code-Switching

There are thirty-five instances of reflected code-switching in the novel. Here is an illustration: Brahbu speaks to Ganga about her marriage.

> "No, no. That is right – *atu rompa tappu* – even though – *iruntālum*, there are many – *evvaḷavōpēr irukkāna.* I want your consent – *ni cari̲ṉṉu collu*" (p. 202).

This is an extreme case where a whole conversational slice is reflected for every word, phrase, and sentence. Usually it is a phrase or sentence within a conversational slice, which is reflected.

There are only five instances in which the Tamil expression precedes the English expression. In all the other, the Tamil rendering succeeds the English expression. One may think that the author adopts this technique so that his reading public may understand him. Though that may be partly true, reflected code-switching is quite common in actual informal conversation.

In twelve of the switchings here, the speaker speaks in disgust, dejection, or repentance. There are two instances of taboo.

We thus see that most of the code-switching at the level of sentences takes place when the speaker is disgusted, sorrowful, repentant, or angry – all involving some sort of emotional or intense feeling. Taboo is the one situation when there is code-switching all the time. There is a popular theory that one speaks only in his mother tongue when he is under such emotional situations. We have a saying in Tamil: If you want to know the mother tongue of a person, hit him hard unexpectedly. He will scream, shouting only in his mother tongue. I don't know whether there has been any empirical test conducted to find the truth of this popular theory. But our evidence here suggests just the opposite.

Now the question arises how far the style of code-switching in the novel reflects the actual situation. As a native speaker of Tamil, and as one who uses this type of code-switching often in informal conversations, I think the style faithfully represents the actual situation. Nonetheless, it will be an interesting study to compare Jayagandan's style with real conversations recorded in natural settings.

Among the modern short story writers it was Pudumaipitan (1906-1948) who used the dialects for the first time in conversational discourses. He used the Brahmin, the Vellala, and the Harijan dialects of Tirunelveli district,[11] according to the characters in his stories. Pudumaipitan himself belonged to the Vellala caste of that area. However, he did not use the dialects in his narratives or descriptions; the use of the dialects was confined to conversational discourses. At that time he was very much attacked for this. But now this has come to be an accepted pattern of writing short stories and novels, although there are still a few writers who will not use the dialects in any place in their writings. Novels using a particular dialect are now classified as *vaṭṭāra nāval* – regional novels. Usually the authors speak those dialects and each uses one or two dialects in his works.[12]

Jayagandan is the only one who is exploiting the use of many different dialects, according to the characters in his writings. In the novel under discussion, Brahbu uses a dialect which, according to Ganga, is not pure Madras dialect, for he speaks like an Anglo-Indian (p. 148). But I would identify his dialect as the standard spoken form, except for a few variants. Ganga speaks the Brahmin dialect. In the fifties when Jayagandan started writing, he was mainly using the slum dialect of Madras city. Most of his writing then was about the Madras slum-dwellers. Since then he has been exploiting the use of Harijan Tamil, standard spoken Tamil, Vellala Tamil, Brahmin

[11] Putumaippittan̠, Putumaippittan̠ Kataikaḷ. (Madras: Star Piracuvam, 1966).

[12] M. Shanmugam Pillai, "Merger of literary and colloquial Tamil," *Anthropological Linguistics* (Bloomington, 1965).

Tamil, and baby talk in his short stories and novels. In the later half of the sixties he started writing about middle-class people, and in these recent works he has successfully incorporated code-switching into his style.[13] He is the first Tamil writer to have done this.

---

[13]In the novelette *Vāḻkkai Aḻaikkiṟatu* he uses Vellala Tamil; in *Piraḷayam* he uses Harijan Tamil; in stories like *Pommai* he uses baby talk; in stories like *Yukacanti* and *Cuya Taricaṉam* he uses Brahmin Tamil; and in stories like *Orupaṭi Cōṟu* he uses the Madras slum dialect. I have given just one or two references for each dialect, though one can pick out quite a number of stories for each dialect. See also M. Shanmugam Pillai, "Tamil today," *Madurai University Journal*, 1971.

FIVE

Susan S. Bean

An Exploration into the Semantics Of Social Space in Kannada

AN ANALYSIS OF A NUMBER of Kannada words which exhibit some semantic and formal similarity is presented in this paper. Semantically the words appear to fall into three groups, each of which contains pairs of opposed meanings: words for male and female human beings, demonstratives indicating remote and proximate distance in time and space, and first and second person pronouns. In each of the three semantically distinguished groups, one of the opposed meanings in each pair is expressed formally by the morphs /i/ or /ii/, while the other is expressed formally by the morphs /a/ or /aa/.

The analysis presented attempts to show that the three apparently distinct groups of words are semantically related. Three solutions are offered. The solutions differ in the level of abstraction involved. The first is the most abstract; the third the least abstract. The solutions are related to each other by inclusion. The first encompasses the second; the second encompasses the third. Thus, the first solution can be accepted without the second and third, or the first and second solutions can be accepted without the third. The first solution involves the principle of opposition. The second solution incorporates the notion of markedness, thus specifying the structure of the postulated oppositions. The third solution contributes substance by assigning meanings to the marked and unmarked terms in the oppositions. After the three solutions are presented, the possibility will be discussed that a non-arbitrary association between sound and meaning accounts for the regular correspondence between form and meaning in this group of words. Finally, it will be suggested that this particular pattern of associated formal and semantic oppositions is not peculiar to Kannada but occurs commonly in the Dravidian languages.

The Data

The data on which the analysis is based are set out in the accompanying diagram (Figure 1). The diagram shows pairs of Kannada words in horizontal rows. In each case, the pair differs formally by one morph and semantically by one feature. In all cases the formal contrast involves the vowel /i/ in one of the paired words and the vowel /a/ in the other. The forms with /i/ are given in Column 1 in the diagram; the forms with /a/ are given in Column 2. The morphs with /i/ and /a/ are segmented by hyphens. Section 1 in the diagram contains the demonstratives.[1] In Column 1 of Section 1 are the forms with /i/, the proximate demonstratives: /illi/ "here," /iice/ "this side," /hiige/ "like this," /iiga/ "now," /iivattu/ "today," /iivaaga/ "now," /ii/ "this," /ivanu/ "he, proximate," /ivaLu/ "she, proximate," /iike/ "she, proximate," /idu/ "it, proximate," /ivaru/ "they, proximate." In Column 2 of Section 1 are the forms with /a/, the remote demonstratives: /alli/ "there," /aace/ "that side," /haage/ "like that," /aaga/ "then," /aavattu/ "that day," /aavaaga/ "then," /aa/ "that," /avanu/ "he, remote," /avaLu/ "she, remote," /aake/ "she, remote," /adu/ "it, remote," /avaru/ "they, remote."

Section 2 of the diagram contains words with masculine and femine suffixes. Column 1 of Section 2 contains forms with the femine suffix /-i/: /huDagi/ "girl," /muduki/ "old woman," /ajji/ "grandmother," and /raami/ a girl's name. Column 2 contains forms with the masculine suffix /-a/: /huDaga/ "boy," /muduka/ "old man," /ajja/ "grandfather," /raama/ a boy's name.

Section 3 of the diagram contains the personal pronouns. In Column 1 are the forms with /i/, the second person pronouns:

---

[1]The third person pronouns are included here since they consist morphologically of a demonstrative with a gender suffix.

THE DATA

Figure 1

Section 1.	Column 1		Column 2	
a) Demonstratives of place:	i-lli	"here"	a-lli	1. "there" 2. /allalli/ "here and there" 3. /maradalli/ "at the tree"
	ii-ce	"this side"	aa-ce	"that side"
	h-ii-ge	"like this"	h-aa-ge	"like that"
b) Demonstratives of time:	ii-ga	"now"	aa-ga	1. "then" 2. /aagaaga/ "from time to time 3. /bandaaga/ "at the time (he) came"
	ii-vattu	"today"	aa-vattu	"that day"
	ii-vaaga	"now"	aa-vaaga	"then"
c) Demonstrative adjective:	ii	"this"	aa	1. "that" 2. "which"

	Column 1		Column 2	
d) Demonstrative pronouns:	i-vanu	"he, prox."	a-vanu	1. "he, rem." 2. /bandavnu/ "he came"
	i-vaLu	"she, prox."	a-vaLu	1. "she, rem." 2. /bandavLu/ "she came"
	ii-ke	"she, prox."	aa-ke	"she, rem."
	i-du	"it, prox."	a-du	1. "it, rem." 2. /bandadu/ "it came"
	i-varu	"they, prox."	a-varu	1. "they, rem." 2. /bandavru/ "they came"
Section 2:				
Sex Suffixes	huDag-i	"girl"	huDag-a	1. "boy" 2. /heNNu huDaga/ "girl child"
	muduk-i	"old woman"	muduk-a	"old man"
	ajj-i	"grandmother"	ajj-a	"grandfather"
	raam-i	a girl's name	raam-a	a boy's name
Section 3:				
Personal pronouns	n-ii-nu	"you sing, nom."	n-aa-nu	"I nom."
	n-ii-vu	"you plural nom."	n-aa-vu	"we nom."
	n-i-n-	"you sing. obl."	n-a-n-	"I obl."
	n-i-m-	"you plural obl."	n-a-m-	"we obl."

/niinu/ "you singular, nominative case," /nin-/ "you singular, oblique stem," /niivu/ "you plural, nominative case," /nim-/ "you plural, oblique stem." Column 2 contains the forms with /a/, the first person pronouns: /naanu/ "I, nominative case," /nan-/ "I, oblique stem," /naavu/ "we, nominative case," /nam-/ "we, oblique stem."

Solution One

The first of the three solutions is immediately suggested by the arrangement of the data in the diagram. The horizontal rows contain paired words that contrast formally: morphs with /i/ in Column 1 and morphs with /a/ in Column 2. Semantically, the paired terms are in opposition. In Section 1 the opposed meanings are proximate and remote distance; in Section 2, female and male sex; in Section 3, hearer and speaker (i.e., second and first person). The most abstract solution states that there is a structural principle common to all of the paired words – semantic opposition. Thus, morphs with /i/ and morphs with /a/ occur in at least three unconnected semantic domains to express semantic oppositions: proximate and remote distance, female and male sex, second and first person.

Solution Two

Having observed that in every case forms in Column 1 with morphs represented by the vowel /i/ are in semantic opposition to forms in Column 2 with morphs represented by the vowel /a/, the second solution specifies the structure of these semantic oppositions. In each case the forms with /i/ are shown to be the marked terms in the opposition, while the forms with /a/ are the unmarked terms in the opposition.

Terms in opposition are not necessarily equal and opposite. Another kind of relationship is possible, that of marked to unmarked. The marked term in an opposition is characterized by the presence of something; the unmarked term in an opposition is characterized by the absence of that something. What is marked is positive; what is unmarked is negative. The interesting aspect of this relationship is that the unmarked, or negative, term takes on a meaning opposite to the marked term when the two are in contrast. In non-contrastive contexts, however, the unmarked member can occur with the opposition neutralized. For example, in English, feminine terms are semantically marked while masculine terms are semantically unmarked. The word *man* is semantically unmarked: *man* means "male person" in contrast with *woman* which is semantically marked, but *man* in the context of other animal species such as *dog* or *horse* is neutralized with regard to the opposition masculine-feminine and refers to both men and women. Thus the marked form is the specific presence of something, while the unmarked form is more general in meaning, taking on the sense of opposition in contrastive contexts and covering the whole class when the opposition is neutralized in non-contrastive contexts. Evidence of markedness consists in the discovery of environments in which an opposition is neutralized. The term occurring in that environment is unmarked. Secondary but supporting evidence exists in the more general meaning, and therefore wider distribution and more frequent occurrence of the unmarked term in the opposition.[2]

In Section 1 of the data (the demonstratives), there is clear evidence of neutralization for some of the terms in Column 2. Of the demonstratives of place, /alli/ "there" is neutralized in some contexts for the opposition of remote and proximate distance. Example 2 given with /alli/ "there" is a reduplicated form /allalli/ meaning "here and there." In the third example /alli/ occurs suffixed to a noun forming the locative case: /mara/ "tree" + /alli/ "there" = /maradalli/ "at the tree." In both examples, the opposition of remote and proximate distance is neutralized so that /alli/ means simply "location, place."

Among the demonstratives of time /aaga/ "then" occurs with the opposition between proximate and remote time neutralized. The second example shows the reduplicated form /aagaaga/ meaning "from time to time, occasionally." The third example

[2]For discussions of the concept of markedness see Greenberg 1964, Jacobson 1957, Lounsbury 1964.

shows /aaga/ suffixed to a verb form /bandu/ "having come" giving the expression /bandaaga/ "when (he) came," "at the time (he) came." In both examples the opposition between remote and proximate time is neutralized so that /aaga/ means simply "time."

The demonstrative adjective /aa/ "that" occurs with the opposition between remote and proximate distance neutralized when it functions as an interrogative adjective "which."

The demonstrative pronouns, /avanu/ "he, remote," /avaLu/ "she, remote," /adu/ "that one," and /avaru/ "they, remote" occur with the opposition between remote and proximate distance neutralized when they are suffixed to verb forms as person markers:

/bandu/ "having come" + demonstrative pronoun
/bandavanu/ "he came"
/bandavaLu/ "she came"
/bandadu/ "it came"
/bandavaru/ "they came."

Thus the demonstrative morph /a/ "remote" occurs with the opposition between remote and proximate neutralized. While there are not examples for each of the demonstratives with /a/ occurring with the remote-proximate opposition neutralized, the existence of the examples cited above and the lack of any examples of /i/ proximate with neutralization provide sufficient evidence to establish that in the case of the demonstratives, /a/ remote is the unmaried term and /i/ "proximate" the marked term in the opposition.

Further indirect evidence is available from the meanings of the /a/ and /i/ demonstratives. In each case it can be argued that the form with /a/ remote covers a wider, more general area in time or space, while the form with /i/ proximate is restricted in time and space. For example, /iivattu/ "today" means "this day that is happening now," while /aavattu/ "that day" refers to any day in the past or future, from the day after tomorrow to a day last month; /illi/ "here" said with reference to the speaker covers a much smaller area than /alli/ "there" referring to the area at a distance from the speaker. In general what is close to the speaker in time and space is a more restricted category than what is far from the speaker in time and space. Therefore the forms with /a/ "remote" are the unmarked, while the forms with /i/ "proximate" are the marked terms in the oppositions.

Section 2 of the data contains some terms for men with the masculine suffix /-a/. Of these terms only one occurs with the masculine-feminine opposition neutralized: /huDaga/ "boy" occurs in the expression /heNNu huDaga/ "female child." Thus, of the opposed terms /huDaga/ "boy" and /huDagi/ "girl," the masculine form /huDaga/ "boy" is the unmarked term in the opposition. Other examples make it clear that in Kannada masculine terms are unmarked:

/maga/ "son" . . . . /heNNu maga/ "female child, daughter"
/manushya/ "a man" . . . . /manushya dharma/ "the law of man (including women)"
/aaDu/ "he-goat" . . . . /heNN aaDu/ "female goat."

In general then, Kannada masculine terms are unmarked. In this section of the data the masculine suffix /-a/ is semantically unmarked, while the feminine suffix /-i/ is semantically marked.

Section 3 of the data includes the first and second person pronouns. The pronouns for addressee or second person, the forms with /ii/, occur in Column 1. The pronouns for speaker or first person, the forms with /aa/, occur in Column 2. In the opposition between second and first person, the first person pronoun is the unmarked term and the second person pronoun the marked term. This is demonstrated in Figure 2 which gives componential definitions of the first and second person pronouns.

Figure 2
Semantic Components of 1st and 2nd Person Pronouns

/niinu/ "thou"	-plural	-speaker	+hearer
/niivu/ "you"	+plural	-speaker	+hearer
/naanu/ "I"	-plural	+speaker	-hearer
/naavu/ "we"	+plural	+speaker	+hearer

The componential definitions show that only the first person plural can include both the speaker and the hearer: /naavu/ "we" can denote "speaker plus other" or "speaker plus hearer" or "speaker plus hearer plus other." The first gloss given with

/naavu/, "speaker plus other," like the gloss given for /naanu/ "I" opposes the speaker to the hearer. But in the second two glosses given with /naavu/ "speaker plus hearer" and "speaker plus hearer plus other." The opposition between speaker and hearer is neutralized. Thus /naavu/ "we" is the unmarked term in the opposition since in some contexts it excludes the hearer while in other contexts it includes the hearer. The opposed term /niivu/ "you plural" never includes the speaker, the only possible glosses being "hearer plus hearer" and "hearer plus other(s)" and "hearer plus hearer plus other(s)." Thus the term for first person is the unmarked member of the opposition between speaker and hearer.[3]

Building on the first solution, which showed that the forms with /i/ are in semantic opposition to the forms with /a/, the second solution demonstrates in all three sections of the data (the demonstratives, the sex suffixed nouns, and the personal pronouns), the forms in Column 1 with /i/ are semantically marked, while the forms in Column 2 with /a/ are semantically unmarked. That is, terms denoting proximate distance, female sex, and hearer are marked, while terms denoting remote distance, male sex, and addressee are unmarked.

Solution Three

The third solution contributes substance to the formal structures of opposition and markedness by revealing common semantic features underlying all of the morphs represented by /i/ and all of the morphs represented by /a/. The semantic feature underlying the forms in Column 1 with /i/ is proximate distance. The semantic feature underlying the forms in Column 2 with /a/ is remote distance.

In Section 1 of the data (the demonstratives), these features are obvious. In each case the forms with /i/ express either spatial or temporal proximity to the speaker, and in each case the forms with /a/ express either spatial or temporal remoteness from the speaker.

[3]It is interesting to note that many of the other Dravidian languages have two first person plural pronouns, one that excludes the hearer and one that includes the hearer. Kannada, however, does not.

The data in Section 2 (nouns with gender suffixes), is less transparent. The forms in Column 1 contain the suffix /-i/ "female," and the forms in Column 2 contain the suffix /-a/ "male." It is argued that underlying the meanings male and female are the meanings remote and proximate distance. In this case /a/ "remote" and /i/ "proximate" stand for social rather than spatial or temporal distance.

In the Kannada-speaking villages of Mysore, and in India as a whole, the social status of men is significantly superior to that of women. Formal political and economic authority resides with men. Women are always in positions of dependence on men, first on their fathers and then on their husbands. Their inferior social position is exhibited daily in the rules of etiquette which govern their interactions with men: women must eat after men, women must remain inconspicuously in the background when men are conversing, women must not speak the name of their husbands. Their inferior position is symbolized by two events in their lives involving pollution that are in no way matched in the life cycle of men. These are menstruation and widowhood. Both of these states involve the exclusion of women from certain aspects of social life in order to protect others from pollution.

The superior status of men is expressed linguistically in terms of social distance. Social distance can be used to express deference – the amount of social distance allowed or accorded another is roughly proportional to his social status.[4] Where alter is of high status, social distance will be greater; where alter is of low status, social distance will be less. Men, in contrast to women, in Indian society are of higher status. Symbolically allotting greater social distance to men is a way of expressing their comparatively higher status. Following this argument, the suffix /-a/ which has been glossed simply "masculine" can more accurately be glossed "those who are accorded more social distance (deference)." Similarly, the suffix /-i/ which was

---

[4] For an explanation of the concept of social distance and its relation to deferential behavior, see Goffman 1956 "The Nature of Deference and Demeanor."

glossed "feminine" can more accurately be glossed "those who are accorded less social distance." Thus the forms in Section 2, Column 1, like the forms in Section 1, Column 1, contain the underlying semantic feature "proximate" (here, socially proximate, female), while the forms in Section 2, Column 2, like the forms in Section 1, Column 2, contain the underlying semantic feature "remote" (here, socially remote, masculine).

In Section 3 of the data (the personal pronouns), a strange reversal is immediately apparent. If speaker and addressee are to be associated with the notion of distance at all, our expectation is that the addressee, the other, will be associated with the notion "remote" while the speaker, the self, will be associated with the notion "proximate." In this case we would expect to find the addressee in Column 2 with the /a/ forms and the speaker in Column 1 with the /i/ forms. In fact we find the exact opposite to be the case. That is, the data in Section 3 is not merely different from what was anticipated, but the exact opposite of what was anticipated. How can this be?

The speech situation involves a minimum of two actors, one in the role of speaker and the other in the role of addressee. These two actors are involved in an interaction in which something is exchanged. That is, utterances are produced by the speaker and received by the addressee. In India such an exchange is fraught with danger.

Speech is a bodily emission. From ancient times in India things excreted from the body were believed to be polluting. In the Laws of Manu there are twelve bodily emissions listed as polluting. While speech is not among them, spittle or saliva is (Bühler 1969). In discussing pollution beliefs, Hutton records the following customs for South India:

> in Travancore the breath of a courtier may pollute the king, while a low-caste man at a temple must wear a bandage over his mouth and nose lest his breath pollute the idol, and a Kudumi woman in her menstrual period must keep seven feet away from anyone, cover her mouth and nostrils with her hand, and take care that her shadow falls on no one. So too a potter making a household deity for the Kurubas must cover his mouth with a bandage . . .
>
> (Hutton 1946: 83)

Stephen Barnett reports that if, while eating, a member of the Kontaikkatti Velalar caste in Tamil Nadu hears an untouchable shouting in the street it is enough to stop the meal for a ritual bath (S. Barnett, personal communication). Thus spittle, breath, and speech itself can be polluting. It is not that speech is always and to the same degree polluting. It can be purifying as in the recitation of *mantras* by a priest. Speech is a vehicle for the transmission of purity and pollution. Like other transmitters, such as water, its danger in a particular instance depends on the relative purity of the source. Since a much wider range of people in the ritual hierarchy commonly talk to each other than take water or food from each other, the speech situation involves the exchange of a substance that is ambiguous and can often be dangerous.

In the first and second person pronouns the formal elements expressing proximity and remoteness are inverted. The inversion avoids, symbolically, the identification of ego with his role as speaker, and alter with his role as addressee. After all, speaker and addressee are roles that are played by individuals and not the individuals themselves. In this way distance, symbolic role distance, is created between the actors' individuality and the actors' roles.[5] In this analysis the first person forms with /a/ "remote" may be glossed "the role of speaker is remote from the speaker's self." The second person forms with /i/ "proximate" may be glossed "the role of hearer is proximate (to the speaker) in relation to the hearer's self." This symbolic distance between selves and roles reduces the potential danger of pollution inherent in the speech situation.[6] Thus, the association of speaker with remote and addressee with proximate does not violate the pattern of semantic relations between forms with /i/ and the meaning "proximate", and

---

[5] For an explanation of the concept of role distance, see Goffman 1961 "Fun in Games."

[6] That the third person pronouns are in fact demonstratives with gender suffixes, can also be seen as a way of avoiding the identification of an individual with his occurrence as referent in an utterance.

forms with /a/ and the meaning "remote." Rather the inversion that occurs in the personal pronouns is a result of the ambiguous and dangerous nature of the speech interaction, which serves to resolve that ambiguity by dissociating the individual selves from their roles as actors.

Three possible solutions have been offered to demonstrate the semantic relatedness of words from these separate lexical domains. In Figure 1 the words were arranged in two columns: words in Column 1 differed from corresponding words in Column 2 by only one morph expressed as /i/ in the former and /a/ in the latter. The words in Column 1 were shown to be in semantic opposition to the corresponding words in Column 2. Further, it was shown that in each semantic opposition, the morphs with /a/ were the unmarked terms, and the morphs with /i/ the marked terms in the opposition. Finally it was shown that these oppositions could be understood semantically as the opposition between remote and proximate distance: in Section 1, spatial or temporal distance; in Section 2, social distance; and in Section 3, role distance.

Sound Symbolism

A connection can be suggested between the formal representation of these morphs and their meanings, that is, a connection between the sound itself and the meanings associated with that sound.

In the basically five vowel system of Kannada /i, e, u, o, a/, /i/ and /a/ can be considered to be opposed phonemically, that is, high vowel vs. low vowel. Further, evidence on frequency of occurrence is consistent with an interpretation of the relationship between the vowels /i/ and /a/ as marked to unmarked. Nayak (1967: 64, 65) computed the frequency of occurrence of the phonemes of Kannada on the basis of a sample of the literary and colloquial styles, each containing about four and one-half thousand phonemes. In both styles /a/ was the most frequent phoneme, and /i/ the second most frequent in literary style and fourth in colloquial style. The gap however was great, /a/ having a frequency of occurrence in both styles about double that of /i/. Although such statistics are by no means conclusive, they do suggest that with regard to frequency of occurrence /i/ is marked in relation to /a/.

In addition, the formal association of /i/ with the underlying semantic feature proximate and /a/ with the underlying semantic feature remote may not be fortuitous. Rather, it may be the expression of a nearly universal tendency in sound symbolism for the notion of proximate to be associated with high and/or front vowels and the notion of remote to be associated with low and/or back vowels. A recent study on sound symbolism (Ultan 1970) showed that in a sample of 136 languages, one-third exhibited some kind of sound symbolism for the notion of proximate spatial distance. Of that third, the overwhelming majority (36 out of 46) showed an association between high and/or front vowels and proximate spatial distance. There were only three counter examples where high and/or front vowels were associated with remote spatial distance. I know of no statistical study for the association of low and/or back vowels with remote spatial distance, but the association has been noticed by many linguists. Of the following examples, the first four are from Jespersen (1964: 402) and the last three from Swadesh (1971: 141):

Figure 3

Examples of sound symbolism

Language	Proximate	Remote
English	this	that
French	ci	là
Malay	iki	ika
Hamitic	i	u
Chinook	i	u
Miwok	ne	no
Binga	ti	ta

On the basis of these observations, it is suggested that the association in all sections of the data (see Figure 1) between proximate distance and the vowel /i/, and remote distance and the vowel /a/, is a case of the non-arbitrary association of sound and meaning.

Proto-Dravidian

The pattern of oppositions between terms meaning proximate distance and terms meaning remote distance is not unique to Kannada. It may be common to the Dravidian language family as a whole. Remote and proximate demonstratives (see Section 1 of Figure 1) have been reconstructed for proto-Dravidian. The sources (Caldwell 1875, Bloch 1946) agree that proto-Dravidian contained three demonstrative bases: two of frequent occurrence, *a "remote" and *i "proximate," and one of limited occurrence *u "intermediate." The Kannada demonstratives therefore correspond to those postulated for proto-Dravidian, that is, /i/ "proximate" and /a/ "remote."

The masculine and feminine suffixes, /-a/ and /-i/ respectively, in Section 2 of the data are likely to be the result of borrowings and do not therefore reflect the existence of such an opposition in proto-Dravidian. It appears likely that the /-i/ suffix was borrowed from Sanskrit, and that the /i/-/-a/ opposition in sex suffixes developed in Kannada to fit with a pattern already well established in the language.

Several attempts have been made to reconstruct the personal pronouns (see Section 3 of Figure 1) of proto-Dravidian. Although there is some disagreement, the association of the vowel /i/ with the second person, and the vowel /a/ with the first person is prominent in all the attempts at reconstruction (Caldwell[7] 1875, Bloch 1946, Krishnamurthi 1968).

For proto-Dravidian then, like Kannada, the proximate demonstrative base is *i; the remote demonstrative base *a; and the distinctive contrast between the first and second person pronouns is based on the opposition of the vowel *a in the first

---

[7] In fact, Caldwell noticed the similarity between the form of the demonstratives and the form of the first and second person pronouns. He considered the possibility of understanding this in terms of distance but rejected this solution since he attempted to work it out in terms of spatial distance alone, the concepts of social distance and role distance not having been invented. He also suggested a formal relationship which resembles the twentieth-century concept of markedness (Caldwell 1875: 372).

person,[8] and the vowel *i in the second person. On the basis of the similarity between the demonstrative bases and personal pronouns in Kannada and proto-Dravidian, it is suggested that the relations of opposition and markedness, and the underlying semantic features remote and proximate distance, discussed here for Kannada demonstratives and pronouns might have existed in proto-Dravidian.

The argument for semantic features of distance underlying the personal pronouns was built on beliefs in pollution, particularly pollution caused by bodily excretions. The extension of this interpretation to proto-Dravidian implies the existence of similar pollution beliefs in Dravidian India perhaps five thousand years ago (see Andronov 1964). This is particularly intriguing in relation to archaeologists' reports on India's first cities, Mohenjodaro and Harappa, which flourished in the third millenium B.C. It has been hypothesized that the existence of elaborate baths, latrines, and sewer systems attests to the concern of the inhabitants of these cities with personal and ritual purity (see Allchin and Allchin 1928:246, Wheeler 1966). It is also considered to be quite possible that the inhabitants of these cities were speakers of a Dravidian language (see e.g., Parpola et al. 1969, Burrow 1969, Clauson and Chadwick 1969).

Summary

Following is a summary of the conclusions of this analysis. Data consisting of demonstratives, gender suffixed nouns, and personal pronouns have been presented. In each of these groups of data semantic oppositions are expressed formally on the one hand by morphs with the vowel /i/ and on the other hand by the morphs with the vowel /a/. The semantic oppositions so expressed are remote and proximate distance, male and female sex, and first and second person.

Three solutions were presented revealing the semantic relatedness of all the words in the corpus. First, it was pointed

---

[8]There is room for some disagreement here, because Bloch 1946 and Krishnamurthi 1968 reconstruct some first person forms, especially the oblique case, with */e/ instead of */a/.

out that in all three sections of the data the vowels /i/ and /a/ express semantic oppositions. The second solution showed that in each case the semantic features expressed by /a/ morphs were the unmarked terms in the semantic oppositions (remote, male, and first person) and that the semantic features expressed by morphs with /i/ were the marked terms in the oppositions (proximate, female, and second person). The third solution revealed that underlying all of the morphs with /a/ is the meaning remote distance, and underlying all the morphs with /i/, the meaning proximate distance. The kind of distance was different for each of the three sections of data. In Section 1 the underlying meaning was spatial or temporal distance; in Section 2 the underlying meaning was social distance, and in Section 3 the underlying meaning role distance. After the three solutions were presented it was suggested that the association between the vowel /i/, marked, and proximate, and the association between the vowel /a/, unmarked, and remote, was a case of the non-arbitrary association of sound and meaning. Finally, evidence from Dravidian historical linguistics was presented to suggest that the semantic structure disclosed for Kannada may have existed in proto-Dravidian.

REFERENCES

Allchin, B. and Allchin, R.
1968 *The Birth of Indian Civilization*. (Baltimore: Penguin Books).

Andronov, M.
1964 "Lexicostatistic analysis of the chronology of disintegration of proto-Dravidian," *Indo-Iranian Journal* 7: 170-186.

Bloch, Jules
1954 (1946) *The Grammatical Structure of Dravidian Languages*. (Poona: Deccan College and Post Graduate Research Institute).

Burrow, T.
1969 "Dravidian and the decipherment of the Indus script," *Antiquity* 43: 274-278.

Bühler, Georg (trans.)
1969 *The Laws of Manu*. (New York: Dover Publications Inc.). First published in 1886 as Vol. XXV of *The Sacred Books of The East*, Max Müeller, ed.

Caldwell, R.
1956 (1875) *Comparative Grammer of Dravidian Languages*. (Madres: University of Madras).

Clauson, G. and Chadwick, J.
1969 "The Indus script deciphered?" *Antiquity* 43: 200-207.

Greenberg, J.
1966 "Language universals." *Current Trends in Linguistics*. Volume III. T. Sebeok, ed. (The Hague: Mouton).

Goffman, E.
1956 "The nature of deference and demeanor." *American Anthropologist* 58: 473-502.

1961 *Encounters*. (New York: Bobbs-Merrill Company, Inc.).

Hutton, J. H.
1946 *Caste in India*. (Cambridge: Cambridge University Press).

Jakobson, R.
1957 *Shifters, Verbal Categories and the Russian Verb*. Harvard University.

Jespersen, Otto
1964 (1921) *Language*. (New York: W. W. Norton and Company, Inc.).

Krishnamurthi, Bh., ed.

1968 *Studies in Indian Linguistics: Professor M. B. Emeneau Sastipurti volume.* (Poona and Annamalainagar: Centers of Advanced Study in Linguistics, Deccan College and Annamalai University).

Lounsbury, F.

1964 "The Structural Analysis of Kinship Semantics," *Proceedings of the Ninth International Congress of Linguists.* (Horace Lunt, ed. pp. 1073-1093. (The Hague: Mouton and Company).

Nayak, H. M.

1967 *Kannada: Literary and Colloquial.* (Mysore: Rao and Raghavan).

Parpalo, A., et al.

1969 *Decipherment of the Proto-Dravidian Inscriptions of the Indus Civilization.* (Copenhagen: The Scandinavian Institute of Asian Studies, Special Publication).

Swadesh, Morris

1971 *The Origin and Diversification of Language.* (Chicago: Aldine Atherton).

Ultan, Russell

Size-Sound Symbolism. Vol. 3. (Stanford: Language Universals Project).

Wheeler, Sir Mortimer

1966 *Civilizations of the Indus Valley and Beyond.* (London: Thames and Hudson Ltd.).

SIX

Martha Bush Ashton

A Structural Analysis of Costume and Makeup in Yakṣagāna Baḍagatiṭṭu Bayalāṭa

IN THIS PAPER I will describe the costumes and make-up of Yakṣagāna Baḍagatiṭṭu Bayalāṭa and discuss how the actor-dancers put them together to create one of this art form's conventional concepts of various legendary characters.

Yakṣagāna Baḍagatiṭṭu Bayalāṭa is one of several forms of all-male religious dance and dance-drama in the tropical coastal region of Karnataka State. The performance, which includes music, dance, and impromptu dialogue, takes place in an open area such as a harvested paddy field, a temple compound, or a vacant plot close to a patron's house. Here the performers present their stories on a flat earthen surface demarcated for the occasion by decorated bamboo poles. The audience sits on three sides of this area. The performance is a long one, beginning around six-thirty in the evening when the drummers' rhythmical beat announces that the drama is about to commence and ending around six o'clock the following morning when the dance-drama is over. Villagers anticipate several performances of the touring troupes in their villages during the six months after the harvest (end of November) and before the monsoon begins (end of May).

As with many other Indian dance-dramas, the purpose is to teach the populace the ideals of Hinduism through the entertaining adventures of the gods, heroes, saints, and demons described in the *Mahābhārata, Jaimini Bhārata, Rāmāyaṇa,* and the *Purānas,* especially the *Bhāgavata, Padma,* and *Skanda.*

The author would like to acknowledge the editorial assistance of Mrs. Dorothy Doane.

To enter this world of fantasy the actor must almost completely disguise himself through make-up and costume – garments, headdress, ornaments, and weapons. Traditionally the colors include red, golden yellow, green, black, white, and metallic gold and silver. Unfortunately, no written works have been found that trace the development of the costumes and make-up or define the symbolism of their colors and designs. Nor do the sculpture and painting of this coastal region provide the key. *Sabhālakṣaṇa* (c. A.D. 1621), the only known ritual book relating to Yakṣagāna, does not even mention the existence of costumes and make-up.

It has been suggested by some Yakṣagāna enthusiasts that red may signify quick temper or a mischievous nature, that black denotes wickedness, and that the combination of red and black, extreme evil. Green might suggest that the character is righteous, serene, or is a forest dweller, and yellow may identify royalty; but there are no theories for the meaning of white. The metallic colors, of course, represent their respective precious metals. These logical guesses seem valid in many cases, but not in all, as the descriptions which follow will show. There seems to be no single color that symbolizes the same quality when used for different characters. For this reason, some Yakṣagāna scholars speculate that each combination of costume and make-up was created from locally available colors as a work of art to be appreciated for its design and color combination rather than for any implied significance.

Using the traditional colors, the creators have developed a variety of designs. They have used almost every shape and pattern imaginable. There are even two- and three-dimensionsl patterns, which are difficult to describe without visual aids. Thus far, there has been no written commentary or speculation on the symbolism of the shapes; this would be a project in itself.

While many characters wear similar costumes and make-up, others are very distinctively guised. In this paper I will limit the descriptions to those of the basic male characters (young princes, mature princes and kings, and elderly kings), the *gandharvas* (in Yakṣagāna stories the protectors of Lord Indra's pleasure gardens), hunters, demons and demonesses, two of the monkeys, the gods, and the basic female characters (young and mature princesses and queens, and elderly queens).

The visual representation of each character can be divided into four parts: the make-up, the costume, the headdress, and the weapon.

The make-up materials consist of pigment powders, coconut oil, water, rice paste, and lime, and they are mixed by each actor for each performance. The basic male make-up includes a pink-yellow base over which the actor draws the designs in red, white, and black as shown in Figure 1. This make-up pattern henceforth will be referred to as the "basic male make-up."

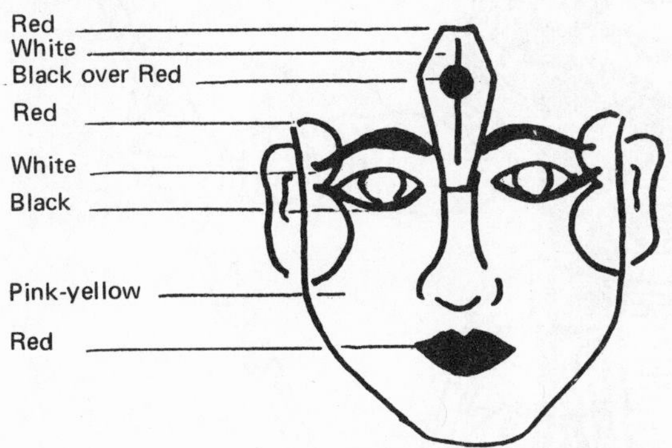

Fig. 1. The basic male make-up

The basic male character's costume consists of loose-fitting black cotton pajamas with a long string of tiny bells wound around the ankles. Just above the bells he fastens anklets made of aluminum (or carved of wood and painted silver or covered with silver paper). Over the pajamas he securely wraps and binds (in a way special to Yakṣagāna) a red and golden yellow checked, ten-yard cotton sari. Then, depending on the character he plays, he adds to his costume a red, green, or black jacket. The decorations include a belt, a breast plate, a girdle, and shoulder, upper arm, and wrist ornaments. These are carved of wood and either painted red or covered with gold or silver paper

Fig. 2. The basic male costume

and mirror pieces. Both the breast plate and girdle ornaments are sewn on red cloth backed with a coarse burlap-type fabric and decorated with black woolen puffballs. This costume will henceforth be referred to as the "basic male costume" (Figure 2).

A description of the headdresses is complicated by the number of items used in constructing the headgear and the intricate system of wrapping the head in preparation for wearing it. Most dancers have long hair which, when wrapped into a bun, serves as an anchor for the headdress. This hair bun is made at different places on the head, depending on the headdress; then the entire top part of the head is wrapped in either a red or black cloth, depending on the character.

At this point it is imperative that the actor place the ornament called *boṭṭu mundale* across the center of his forehead and tie it at the back of the head. The free-hanging strings are used to secure additional parts of the headdress at a later stage (Figure 3).

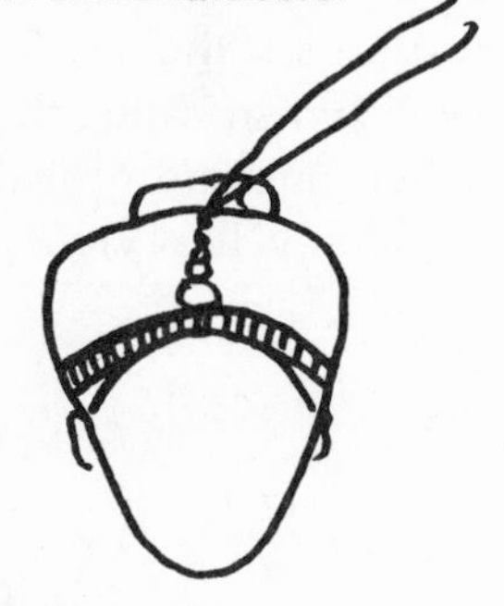

Fig. 3.
Wearing the *boṭṭu mundale*

The dancer is now prepared to wear one of the basic male headdresses—the *kēdage mundale*, the *muṇḍāsu*, or the king's crown. The *kēdage mundale* and the different styles of the *muṇḍāsu* are the most spectacular. They are constructed of bundles of dried rice grass in ever increasing sizes wrapped with cotton cloth (*aṭṭe*) (Figure 4) and plaited layers of dried rice grass, all bound together with cord to form a tear drop-shaped brim (Figure 5). The whole structure is made to curve slightly (Figure 6). Excess cloth from the head wrapping is then used to cover the structure, after which the actor entwines it in a radial pattern with brightly colored, and metallic gold and silver ribbons. He continues to decorate by adding the ear ornaments (*karṇa patra*); a fan-like adornment (the *kēdage*); a lotus-design ornament (*tāvare*); a red, white, and

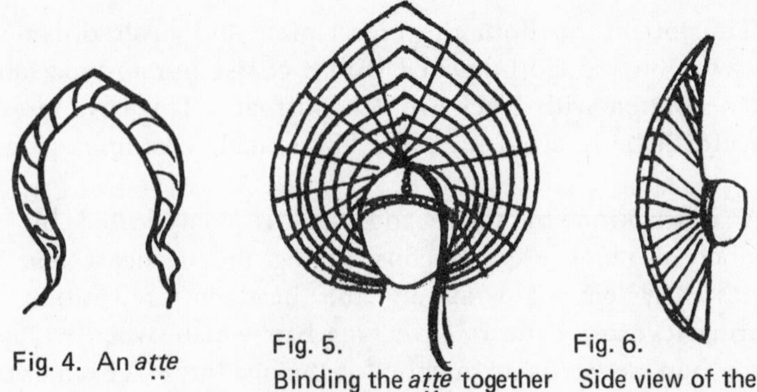

Fig. 4. An *aṭṭe*

Fig. 5. Binding the *aṭṭe* together and to the hair bun

Fig. 6. Side view of the *kēdage mundale*

green paper decoration (*suttu*); white paper flowers (*keñcu*), and an ornamented stick pin (*turāyi*) (Figure 7). On the upper curvature of the cloth-wrapped hair bun the actor places an embellishment called the *muḍi kēdage*. In addition he ties to the hair bun one end of a thin piece of white cloth with red border (or golden yellow cloth) called the *śelle* and tucks the remaining

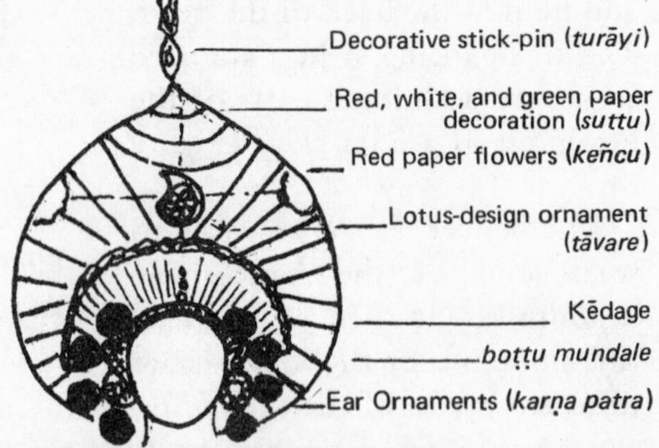

Fig. 7. Front view of the *kēdage mundale*

corners under the front sides of the girdle. This cloth both covers the strings used for securing the ornaments at the back and accentuates the whirling movements of the dance (Figure 8).

The *kēdage mundale* consists of five to seven *aṭṭe*, depending on the size of the actor's head, and is always wrapped in black cloth. The *munḍāsu* is a larger version of the *kēdage mundale* consisting of eight to ten *aṭṭe*, usually wrapped in red and worn

Fig. 8. The attachment of the *śelle*

with a *śelle*. The other varieties of this style will be discussed in relation to specific characters.

The king's crown is made of ornately carved wood covered with gold paper and mirror pieces; it is urn-shaped and flanked on either side by a swan. Attached to the swans are three black woolen puffballs. Peacock feathers extend from the top (Figure 9). Long false hair pieces, either black or white depending on the age of the character, are attached to the hair knot at the

Fig. 9. Complete king's headdress

back of the head. Like the *śelle* these hair pieces help to hide the untidy fastening of the ornaments and add to the movement of the dance.

The basic weapon is the bow and arrow; one basic male character, however, carries a mace. Other weapons will be discussed in relation to specific characters.

Energetic and ambitious young princes like Nakula and Sahadēva, the twin Pāṇḍavas; Abhimanyu and Babhruvāhana, Arjuna's sons; Vṛṣasēna, Karṇa's son; and Duhśāsana, Dhṛtarāṣṭra's son, wear the basic male make-up, the basic male costume with short-sleeved red jacket (short sleeves, made by tucking under the hemmed edge, symbolize youth), and the *kēdage mundale*. Each carries a bow and arrow.

The mature princes and kings wear these basic pieces with some additions. Arjuna, one of the Pāṇḍava princes, wears the basic male make-up to which he adds a black woolen mustache and a beard to suggest his maturity. This beard is drawn on the chin area with a mixture of soot and coconut oil and is smoothed down the neck to blend with the base make-up (Figure 10). This flattened beard resembles the lacquered and rolled beards worn by Sikhs.

Fig. 10. The black woolen mustache and the drawn-on beard

Arjuna wears the basic male costume with a short-sleeved red jacket, the short sleeve suggesting some remnants of youthfulness and the red color a quick temper. He wears the *kēdage mundale* and carries a bow and arrow.

Pradhyumna (Kṛṣṇa's son, also called Manmatha), a gentle prince, and Rukma (Rukmiṇi's brother), an obstinate, aggressive prince, both wear the basic male make-up with black woolen mustache and drawn-on beard, the basic male costume with long-sleeved green jacket, and the red *muṇḍāsu*. They each carry a bow and arrow. These two characters are so different in personality that it is puzzling why they wear the same costume – especially if colors do have a significance.

Bhīma, one of the Pāṇḍavas noted for his brute strength and highly explosive temper, wears the basic male make-up with black woolen mustache and drawn-on beard, the basic male costume with long-sleeved red jacket and, in addition, a red and white shawl. This shawl consists of two long pieces of cloth, one red and one white, and is worn in one of three ways: (1) draped around the neck and left to hang in equal lengths down the front (Figure 11a); (2) twisted together, wrapped around the waist and tied at one side (Figure 11b); and (3) draped around the neck, criss-crossed over the chest and tied in back at the waist (Figure 11c and d). The way it is worn depends on the character. (Sometimes it is even worn as a turban by the clown.) Although not a king, Bhima wears the king's crown and carries a mace.

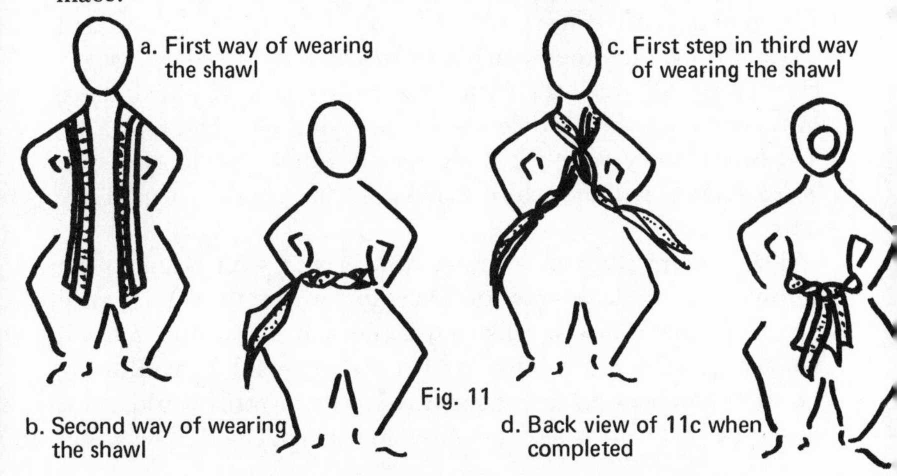

Fig. 11

The gentle mature kings like Dharmarāya, Rāma and Śatrughna, his half-brother, Nīladhvaja, and Haṁsadhvaja (kings mentioned in *Jaimini Bhārata*) wear the basic male make-up with added black mustache and drawn-on beard, the basic male costume with long-sleeved green jacket, and the red and white shawl. They each wear a king's crown and carry a bow and arrow.

The more spirited Bharata and Lakṣmaṇa (half-brothers of Rāma), Duryōdhana (king of the Kauravas), and Saindhava (King of the Sindhus) wear the basic male make-up plus black woolen mustache and drawn-on beard and the basic male costume with long-sleeved red jacket and red and white shawl. They each wear a king's crown and carry a bow and arrow.

Badrasēna, the determined king who abducts the princess; King Śalya, Karṇa's reluctant charioteer; and the heroic Vīramaṇi wear the basic male make-up plus black woolen mustache and drawn-on beard and the basic male costume with long-sleeved green shirt. They each wear a red *muṇḍāsu* and carry a bow and arrow. For this costume and headdress it is difficult to speculate on the significance of the colors. Perhaps the red in the headdress emphasizes the characters' passionate personalities, and possibly a green jacket is worn because a red jacket and a red *muṇḍāsu* would over-balance the color scheme.

The elderly kings, such as Daśaratha (Rāma's father), Dhṛtarāṣṭra, and Pāṇḍu, who have become more mellow and wise throughout the years, are usually depicted as gentle characters. All wear the basic male make-up with added white mustache and white woolen beard or blond false-hair mustache and beard. They wear the basic male costume with long-sleeved green jacket, red and white shawl, and the king's crown. They have no weapons.

The mature Bhīṣma, a prince who gave up his claim to the throne and took a vow of chastity, wears the basic male make-up with black woolen mustache and substitutes a black woolen beard for the drawn-on beard. Perhaps this free-flowing beard symbolizes his detachment from the material world, since this type of beard is also worn by the saints, elderly kings, and some of the gods. Bhisma wears the basic male costume with red jacket and red and white shawl. Although not a king, he wears the king's crown and carries a bow and arrow.

The characters Karṇa and his oldest son, Vṛṣakētu, wear a variation of the *muṇḍāsu* called the *pakku ellavastra*. This is a black *muṇḍāsu* without the *kēdage* ornament (Figure 12). The front edge of the *muṇḍāsu* is trimmed by a red fabric wrapped so that it completely covers the back of the headdress as well (Figure 13). Both wear the basic male make-up, black woolen

Fig. 12. Front view of the *pakku ellavastra*

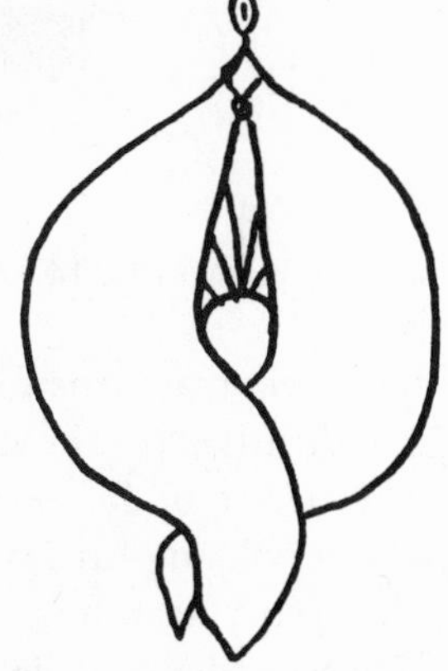

Fig. 13. Back view of the *pakku ellavastra*

mustache, drawn-on beard, and the basic male costume with red jacket. Each carries a bow and arrow. Again it is difficult to speculate on the symbolism of the colors. The suggestion that large areas of red and black indicate extreme evil certainly does not hold true in this case. Both characters are more gentle than fierce and, according to the suggested symbolism for this nature, should wear green jackets. However, perhaps because black and green in these proportions are not as aesthetically pleasing as black and red, a red jacket has been chosen to complement the black and red headdress.

A *gandharva* (in Yakṣagāna stories, one who protects Indra's pleasure gardens and frolics with the *apsarās*) has a special make-up. It includes red oval patterns around each eye and under these patterns a broken white line (Figure 14). Possibly the red signifies his mischievous personality and the accompanying broken white line indicates he is not malicious. He wears a black woolen mustache and drawn-on beard and

Fig. 14. A *gandharva's* make-up

dons the basic male costume with long-sleeved green jacket, perhaps indicative of the fact that he lives in the forest. He adorns the front of his red *muṇḍāsu* with wild fowl feathers possibly symbolizing his rather free and frivolous existence. To the back of his headdress above the hair bun and under the *muḍi kēdage* ornament, he inserts a red-squirrel's tail which jiggles as he dances, adding humor to his movements. He carries a bow and arrow.

The hunter, also a scatter-brained, mischievous character, wears make-up similar to that of the *gandharva*. He adds a tear-drop design on the bottom part of the nose, but unlike the *gandharva* he does not wear a black *tilaka* or the drawn-on beard (Figure 15). Hunters are often considered to be tribals, and in this region the tribals have their own gods and do not necessarily worship the Hindu gods. This may account for the hunter's not wearing a *tilaka*. Perhaps no beard is worn because it would get caught in twigs and branches when the hunter is camouflaging himself. He wears the basic male costume with long-sleeved green jacket over which he ties a string of mango leaves. Exposed at the front, they show him to be a forest dweller, and covered in the back, they suggest that he has bagged some game.

The hunter can choose one of two headdresses, the single-slanted *muṇḍāsu* or the double *muṇḍāsu*. For the single-slanted *muṇḍāsu*, the actor parts his hair to the left side,

Fig. 15. A hunter's make-up

makes a bun on the right side, and allows the remaining hair to hang freely. He wraps the *aṭṭe* (the cloth-covered, dried rice-grass pieces) from the right forehead to the left back of the head rather than from ear to ear as in the *kēdage mundale* and the *muṇḍāsu*. He decorates his headdress the same as the *kēdage mundale* and *muṇḍāsu*, but instead of the *kēdage* ornament, he sometimes adds a string of beads (Figure 16). For the double *muṇḍāsu*, the actor parts his hair in the middle and wraps a *muṇḍāsu* on each side of the head (Figure 17). He carries a bow and arrow.

Fig. 16. The single-slanted *muṇḍāsu* Fig. 17. The double-slanted *muṇḍāsu*

The mighty demon is usually a braggart, a very strong character who from the moment he begins his entrance toward the performance area commands the respect of the audience. The most popular demonic roles are Rāvaṇa, Śambarāsura, Narakāsura and Murāsura, Hiḍimba, and Bakāsura.

Most of the demon's costume and make-up is totally different from the basic pieces. The make-up is very complicated and takes approximately four hours to complete (Figure 18). The small round circles in Figure 18 represent one-half- to three-quarter-inch thorn-like protrusions made in layers from rice paste and lime (*ciṭṭe*). The beard is made of white cardboard with small areas painted red. Here the theory that large areas of red and black symbolize extreme evil seems to be confirmed.

The demon has his own breast plate, shoulder ornaments, girdle, and black jacket. However, he does wear the checkered

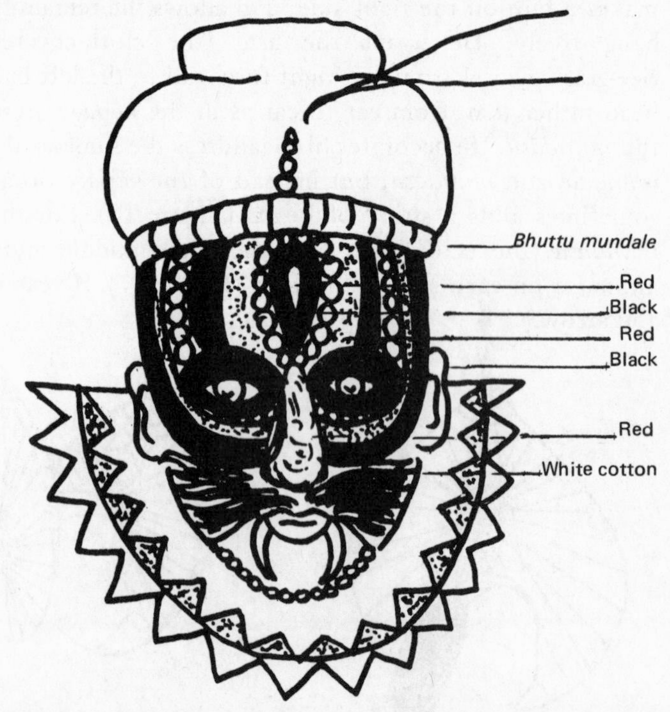

Fig. 18. The demon's make-up

Fig. 19. The demon in full disguise

ten-yard sari, the red and white shawl, the upper arm and wrist ornaments, and the belt of the basic male costume. He has his own crown and carries a sword (Figure 19).

The demoness does not command the same respect from the audience as the demon. She is usually a humorous character who, after the initial entrance as her terrible self, often resorts to disguise to accomplish her purpose. The most popular demonesses are Śūrpaṇakhi and Hiḍimbi (who married Bhīma and produced Ghaṭotkaca).

Like the demon, her make-up and costume are special to her character. The make-up is complicated and its application time comsuming; it includes the thorn-like protrusions, a cardboard beard, and a nose ring (Figure 20). Since the character is played

Fig. 20. The demoness's make-up

by a male, the actor wears a red jacket into which he stuffs large balls made of quilted cotton tape to give the appearance of a woman's breasts. Over his black pajamas, he ties bunches of mango leaves around the waist to enlarge the hips. A black

Fig. 21. The demoness's crown

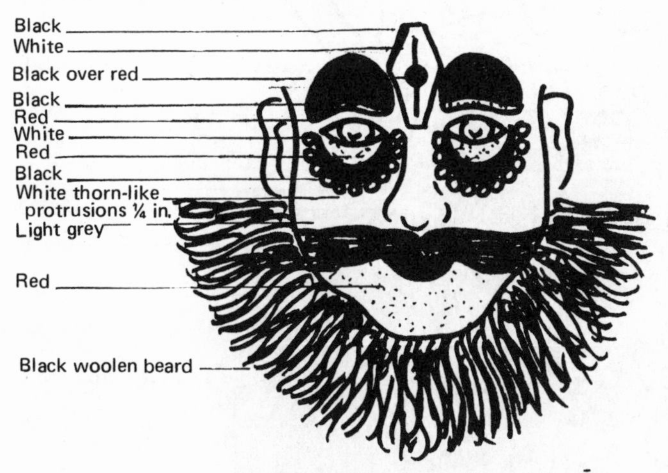

Fig. 23. Make-up of Vāli and Sugrīva

cotton sari with a red border design is gathered like a skirt on a length of quilted tape and tied around the waist. The demoness wears the demon's breast plate, shoulder, upper arm and wrist ornaments, and the red and white shawl, but has her own special crown (Figure 21). She also carries a sword.

Animal characters, so common in the stories of many cultures, also appear in Yakṣagāna. One such character is Vāli, a demon monkey-king, portrayed as an aggressive, strong, and valiant warrior. Another is his brother Sugrīva, who is constantly defeated by Vāli until he receives the help of Rāma. According to the story, Vāli and Sugrīva look so much alike that it is difficult for Rāma to distinguish them from one another. Likewise, it is difficult for the analyzer to speculate on color significance, in this case.

Vāli and Sugrīva wear make-up special to their character (Figure 23). They wear the demon's costume with long-sleeved black jacket and the demon's headdress. They carry mango leaves in place of a sword.

The gods, although having special places of residence in the heavens, are most frequently depicted in stories when they have descended to earth to live as men. Perhaps it is for this reason that most of the deities' costumes consist of basic pieces. The differences most often occur in the make-up and choice of

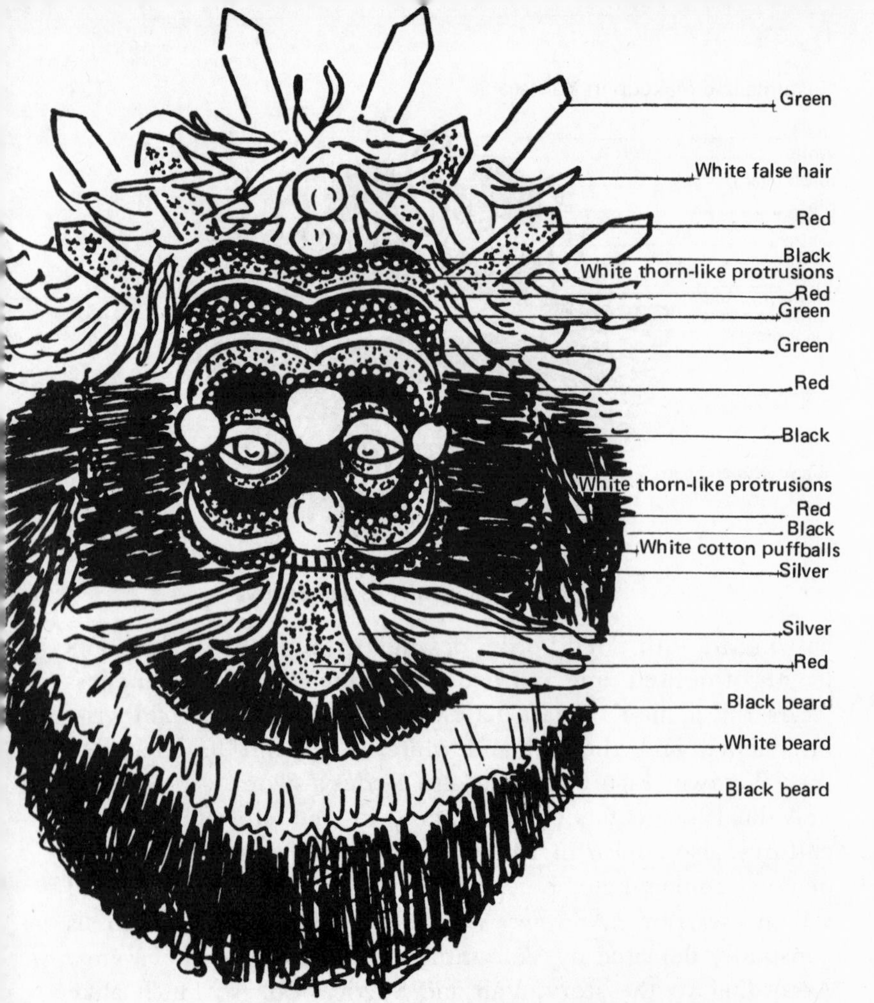

Fig. 24. Make-up and headdress for Nārasiṃha

weapons. Both the Vedic god Indra and Kṛṣṇa's brother Balarāma wear the same make-up, costume, and headdress as Bhīma, one of the Pāṇḍavas, and like him, they also carry a mace.

Lord Viṣṇu, a member of the Hindu trinity, appears in the stories about his incarnations as Nārasiṃha, Paraśurāma, Rāma, and Kṛṣṇa. Nārasiṃha the man-lion has his own special make-up (Figure 24). From the waist down he wears the basic male costume and above the waist he covers his body with white make-up; the only decorations are a few long garlands of fresh flowers and a few long strings of colorful beads that hang around his neck. His headdress is also peculiar to his character (Figure 24). It consists of long pointed pieces of cardboard each covered with either red or green paper. In between these cardboard pieces the actor adds white false hair to complete the lion's mane.

Paraśurāma's make-up varies slightly from the basic male make-up (Figure 25). He wears the same costume except for a red jacket and a headdress like that of the elderly kings. He also carries an ax.

Rāma is described in the mature king's section.

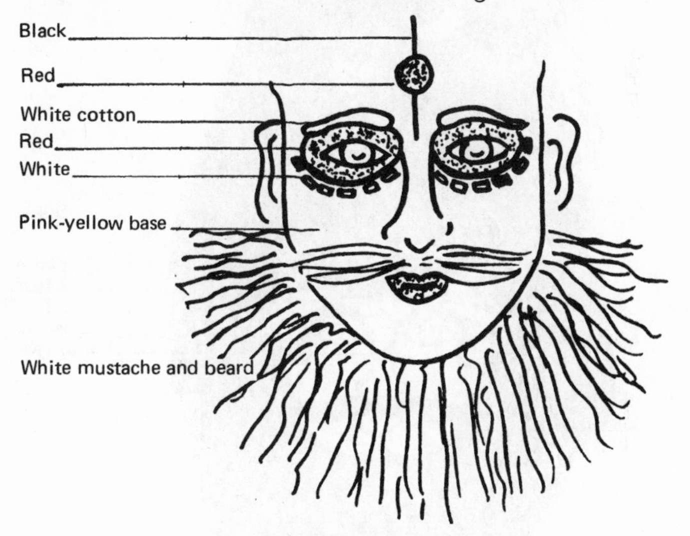

Fig. 25. Paraśurāma's make-up

In many dance-dramas, literary works, and paintings, Kṛṣṇa is represented as being black or a shade of blue, but in this style of Yakṣagāna he wears the basic male make-up which has a pink-yellow base. He is a combination of the gentle and the fierce. His lack of beard and mustache denote youth. From the waist up he wears the costume of a young prince to signify his virility and prowess. From the waist down, however, he wears the checked sari wrapped as a skirt rather than the special male wrap worn by princes and kings. Supposedly this attire represents Kṛṣṇa's strength as a warrior while at the same time suggesting his eternal youth and feminine gentility. He wears the *kēdage mundale* and carries a discus.

Lord Śiva has his own special make-up which includes "the

Fig. 26. The make-up and headdress of Śiva

third eye" (Figure 26). He wears the basic male costume with long-sleeved green jacket and red and white shawl. Here the green jacket does not seem appropriate for the usual fiery behaviour of this god. Those symbols with which he is so often associated in Hindu literature – the serpent, crescent moon, and Gaṅgā (the river Ganges) descending from the top of his matted locks – are seen in his headdress (Figure 26). His special weapon is the trident.

Lord Śiva's manifestation as Vīrabhadra also has a special

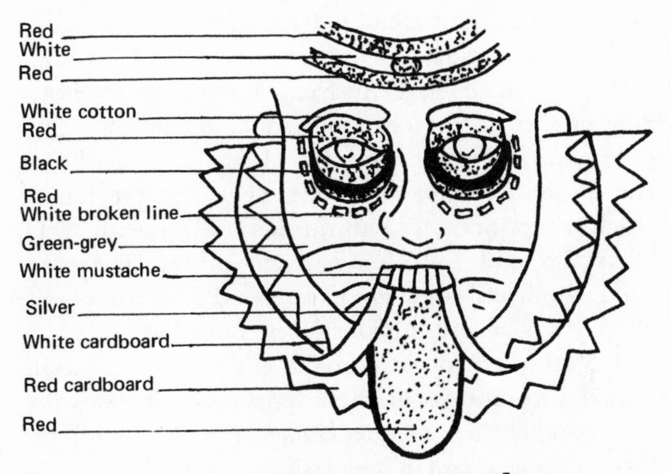

Fig. 27. Make-up for Vīrabhadra

make-up (Figure 27). He wears the demon's costume and the king's crown with a special back piece (Figure 28) and carries a sword.

While the demoness, who was discussed earlier, has a rather complex costume, the basic female characters have far less intriguing costumes and make-up. The base of the basic female make-up is the same pink-yellow paste used by male characters, over which the male actor playing the female role applies rouge, outlines his eyes and eyebrows with black, dabs his lips with red, and makes a design (usually a large dot) on his forehead. A few lines represent wrinkles on elderly female characters. The basic female costume is a six-yard sari of no particular color or design wrapped in modern fashion. The ornaments include nondescript bangles, necklaces, and

Fig. 28. The back piece for *Vīrabhadra's headdress*

earrings. The hairstyles for young and mature queens and princesses include both the single hanging braid and the bun at the back of the head. They are often augmented with flowers. The elderly queens' hair buns are powdered white.

The first recorded attempt to improve the female costume occurred in 1962 when Dr. Kota Sivarama Karanth created new designs adding vitality to the costumes while at the same time adhering to traditional concepts. He designed a girdle, a necklace, and upper arm and wrist ornaments for the female characters such as princesses and queens – Draupadi, Sīta, Subhadrā, Rukmiṇi and Satyabhāma, and others. These are made of carved wood, and some are painted red while others are covered with gold paper and mirror pieces. Both red and black woolen balls are attached to parts of the girdle for decoration. He also designed a headdress for these female characters which consists of a small replica of the *kēdage mundale* with red covering, silver ribbons, and a small silver tassel. These were designed for ballets which he choreographed using Yakṣagāna techniques. Dancers who performed in these shows often wear these ornaments when performing the dance-drama.

The female costume may still get another remodeling. At the time of this writing, Karanth is redesigning ornaments and sari patterns for an experimental production of Yakṣagāna under his direction at the National School of Drama in New Delhi.

The descriptions given above give some idea of the variety, complexity, and colorfulness of the traditional Yakṣagāna costumes and make-up. Although the individual parts seem particularly vivid and intricate, the end result, as with most art forms, is aesthetically pleasing. Unfortunately far too few have an opportunity to see and appreciate this spectacular form of South Indian artistry.

SEVEN

Charlotte Vaudeville

Paṇḍharpūr, The City of Saints

IN SEVERAL RESPECTS, the *bhakti* of Mahārāṣṭra is unique. Although Vaiṣṇava, it is clearly distinguishable from the southern Vaiṣṇava *bhakti* which was inspired by the Ālvārs poet-saints and codified in the scriptures of the "Four Sects" (catuḥ-saṁpradāya), beginning with the Srī-saṁpradāya of Rāmānuja. It is also distinct in many ways from the more modern Kṛṣṇaite sects of northern India, the most representative of the latter being the Vallabhite (or Puṣṭi-mārga) and Caitanya (or Gauḍīva) sects – both of them purely Kṛṣṇaite.

The main characteristics of Mahārāṣṭrian *bhakti* may be summarized under three headings: (a) The all-embracing importance of the Paṇḍharpūr image (Viṭhobā), the Paṇḍharpūr *kṣetra*, and the Paṇḍharpūr pilgrimage in this form of Vaiṣṇava *bhakti*; (b) The peculiar features of the central deity, the god Viṭṭhal or Viṭhobā of Paṇḍharpūr, worshipped as *svarūpa* (i.e., an original form) of Viṣṇu rather than as an *avatāra* of the same god, and partially identified with Kṛṣṇa-Gopāl, the Cowherd god of Mathurā and Dvārakā; (c) The absence of codified scriptures and the all-embracing importance of the popular religious lyrics known as *abhaṅgas*, composed in middle Marathi by the poet-saints of Mahārāṣṭra between the fourteenth[1] and

[1] If one admits what seems most probable, that the "Jñāndev" who composed a number of *abhaṅgas* was a different character from the Jñandev or Jñāneśvar who was the author of the famous versified commentary in archaic Marathi on the Bhagavad-gītā known as *Jñāneśvari*

the seventeenth centuries A.D. As great devotees of Viṭhobā and main exponents of Vaiṣṇava *bhakti*, these saints are themselves objects of a cult in Mahārāṣṭra. Their personal history appears closely connected with the Paṇḍharpūr pilgrimage.

The Paṇḍharpūr Kṣetra

The holy city of Paṇḍharpūr is situated on the left bank of the river Bhīmā, which is the main tributary of the upper Kṛṣṇa. The open plain in which Paṇḍharpūr is situated forms the south-eastern part of Mahārāṣṭra. The population is Marathi-speaking, though the linguistic boundary between Marathi in the North and Kannada in the south passes not far east from the town of Paṇḍharpūr.

The Bhīmā flows in a general northwest-southeast direction, but at Paṇḍharpūr it makes a curve in the shape of a crescent moon, facing the east, a situation similar to that of the Ganges at holy Kāśi (Benares). At Paṇḍharpūr, the Bhīmā takes on the name of Candrabhāgā, especially in the *abhaṅga* literature.

Since a number of problems are connected with the place itself, a brief historical sketch would be appropriate. The city is first mentioned in a copperplate inscription dated A.D. 516 carved under the Rāṣṭrakūṭa king Āvideya. In this inscription the place is called Pāṇḍarangapaḷḷī, i.e., "the village of Pāṇḍaranga."[2] There is no mention of Pāṇḍharpūr under the Cālukyas, who succeeded the Rāṣṭrakūtas in the Deccan. In A.D. 1187 the Yādava king Bhillama became independent from the Hoysalas and the Cālukyas, and he founded a dynasty with Devagiri, in the upper Godāvarī area, as his capital city and Marathi as its language: (There was at that time a general reaction against the prominence of Kannaḍa in most of the lands now included in Mahārāṣṭra.) In 1192 the Yādavas clashed again with the Hoysalas and retreated North into Gujarāt and Mālwā, while the Hoysalas retreated south towards Tamilnād. It

---

that was composed at the end of the thirteenth century. The Jñāndev of the *abhaṅgas* is more probably a contemporary of Nāmdev and other early Mahārāṣṭrian saints, who flourished in the fourteenth century.

[2] *Mysore Archaeological Department Annual Report.* (1929), pp. 198 ff. ff.).

appears that although Kannaḍa was still spoken – at least in southern Mahārāṣṭra during the thirteenth century – (i.e., in the poet Jñāneśvar's time), Marathi became prominent in that area in the period between the tenth and the twelfth century.

According to an inscription at Paṇḍharpūr deciphered by Dr. S. G. Tulpule a Viṭhobā temple might have been erected there as a small structure in A.D. 1189. We know, however, that the city of Paṇḍharpūr was still under Hoysala rule in 1237, as shown by the inscription in Sanskrit and Kannada found in the present Viṭhobā temple. This inscription mentions the presence of the god Viṭṭhal at Paṇḍharpūr, which is here called Pāṇḍarange and Pāṇḍarage. The same inscription mentions the Muni "Puṇḍarīka" (alias Puṇḍalīka).[3]

In a Sanskrit copperplate inscription dated Śaka 1171 (A.D. 1249), the city is mentioned as *Pauṇḍarīka kṣetra*, the *kṣetra* (or sacred land) of Puṇḍarīka," which confirms the impression that in the thirteenth century, Paṇḍharpūr was known as the place where the "Muni" Puṇḍalīk was honored. This *kṣetra* was situated on the Bhīmā river, "in the vicinity of god Viṣṇu," and we may surmise that Viṣṇu was none other than the popular Viṭṭhala or Viṭhobā, since *viṭho* appears as a Kannada form of the Sanskrit *viṣṇu* with the respectful and affectionate suffix-*bā*. This Viṭṭhal or Viṭhobā is otherwise known as a Kannada deity.[4] Evidence from inscriptions tends to show that the holy Paṇḍharpūr *kṣetra* was first known as the place of Puṇḍalīk, the

[3]Another gift inscription is found in the great temple, dated Śaka 1195-1199 (1273-1277 A. D.), published with an English translation by Dr. S. G. Tulpule in *An Old Marathi Reader.* (Poona, 1960), Extract 5, pp. 90-91; in the latter, the Yādava king Rāmacandradeva is called "The leader of the company of devotees at Paṇḍharī."

[4]Both A. G. Karmarkar and N. B. Kalamdani, *Mystic Teachings of the Haridāsas of Karṇatak.* (Dharwar, 1939), p. 25, and R. D. Ranade, *Mysticism in Maharashtra, History of Indian Philosophy,* vol. 7. (Poona, n.d.), p. 125 consider Puṇḍalīk as a Canarese saint. At any rate, Viṭṭhal is known to have been a favorite of the Hoysalas of Karṇātak, where a number of temples dedicated to him are found. But in the last quarter of the thirteenth century the cult of Viṭṭhal had already been adopted by the Yādavas, as shown by the inscription mentioned in Note 3.

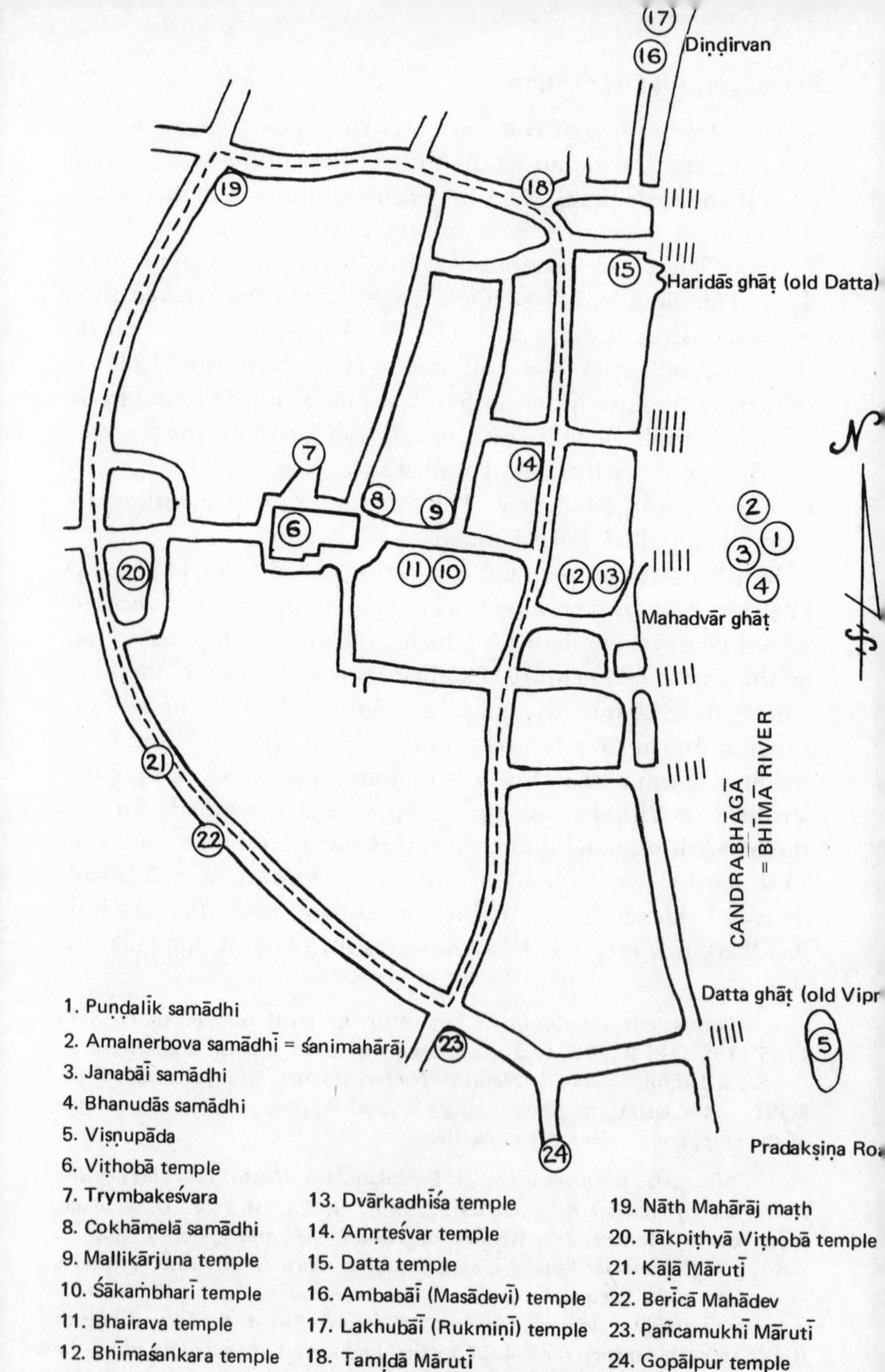

The Paṇḍharpūr Kṣetra

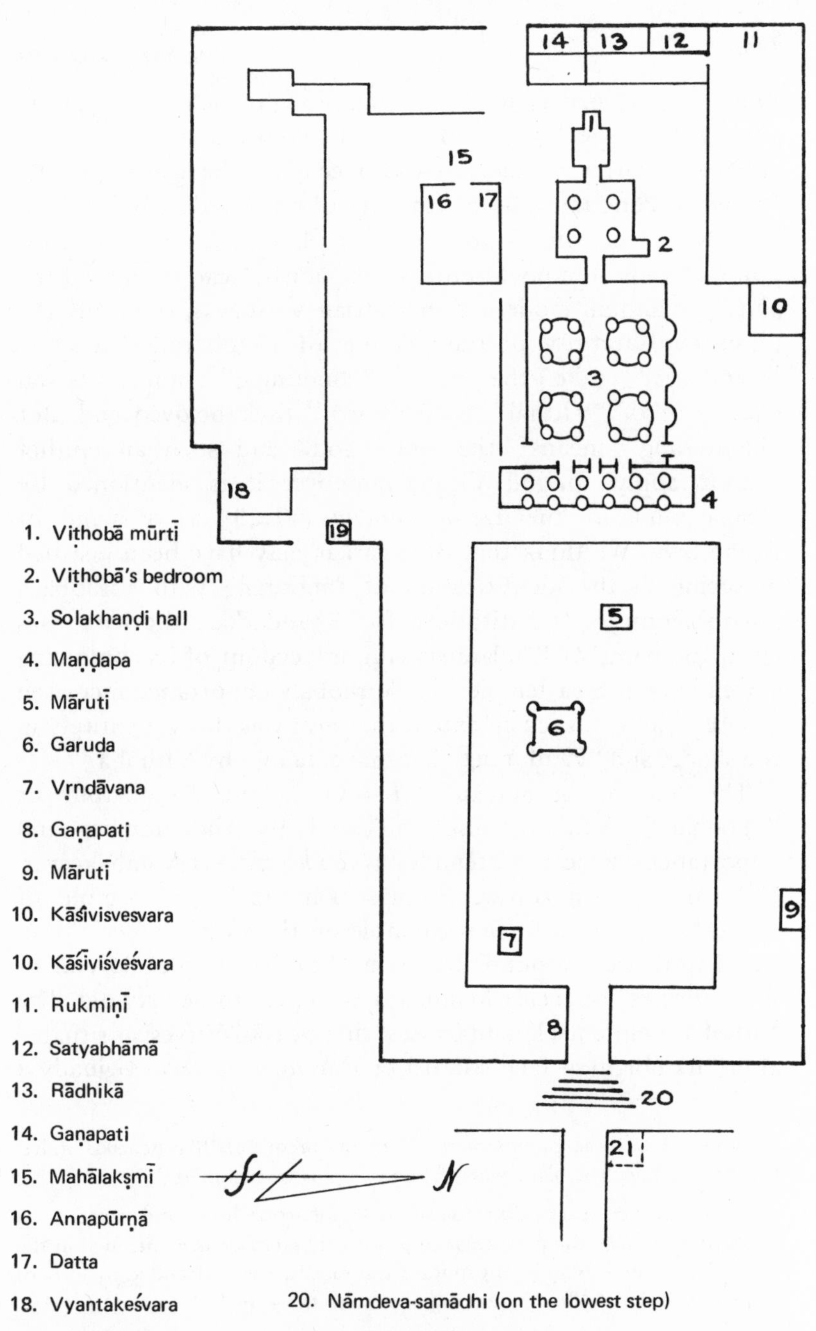

The Viṭhobā Temple

saint who, according to the legend, brought the god Viṭhobā to the bank of the Bhīmā.[5] But we also know that at least from the last quarter of the thirteenth century the place was also known as Pāṇḍurangapura, "the city of god Pāṇḍurang."[6]

However improbable from either a philological or a historical point of view, the poet-saints of Mahārāṣṭra who composed the *abhaṅgas* and all modern Mahārāṣṭrian Vaiṣṇavas, especially the pious confraternity of the Pilgrims of Paṇḍharpūr known as "Vārakarīs," take the name "Pāṇḍurang" simply as an equivalent of "Viṭṭhal" or "Viṭhobā," their beloved god. But "Pāṇḍurang" means "the white god" and such an epithet cannot apply to god Viṣṇu; moreover it is mentioned by Hemacandra in the *Deśīnāmamālā* (VI.23) as a name of Rudra-Śiva. We think that Bhandarkar may have been justified in seeing in the identification of Pāṇḍurang with Viṭhobā a phenomenon of substitution: for Bhandarkar, the city was given the name of Pāṇḍarangapaḷḷi on account of its containing a well-known Śiva temple. But Viṭhobā's importance increased in later times to such an extent that Śiva was thrown entirely in the shade, and "Pāṇḍurang" became equal with "Viṭhobā."[7]

The ancient prominence of Śiva in the Paṇḍharpūr or "Paṇḍharī" *kṣetra* is also indicated by the number and importance of the Śaiva temples in the *kṣetra* – Tryambakeśvar, Mallikārjuna, Amṛteśvar, Bhīmāśankar, the Devī temple of Śakambharī with a Bhairava temple on the side – especially in its central area, around the main Viṭhobā temple. Several of these shrines, especially Mallikārjuna, appear to be very old. The Viṭhobā temple itself contains a shrine of Kāśī-Viśveśvar situated along its northern face. Mārutī or Hanumān is also originally a

---

[5]In his *Caturvarga-cintāmaṇi*, Hemādri mentions "Pauṇḍarīka" (alias Paṇḍharpūr) as "the place where Pāṇḍuranga is worshipped."

[6]In another inscription found in Paṇḍharpūr itself and dated Śaka 1192 (A.D. 1270), the performance of a Vedic sacrifice is mentioned in the very place called "Pāṇḍurangapura"; the sacrifice was attended by crowds of people and also "by Viṭṭhal together with the gods."

[7]R. G. Bhandarkar, *Vaiṣṇavism, Śaivism and Minor Religious Systems, Collected Works*, vol. IV. (Poona, 1929), p. 125.

Śaiva deity. He appears not only as the son of the Wind (a *Vāyuputra*, therefore a great magician) but also as the eleventh of the eleven "Rudras," also known as "Maruts," who are worshipped in a temple on the bank of the Bhīmā, above the ancient river-bed temple known as "Puṇḍalīk-samādhi," (also a Śaiva temple). Hanumān or Mārutī, a deified *langūr* monkey, is the main godling of the hilly area known as the Ghāṭs. He is particularly popular in Mahārāṣṭra, and in Paṇḍharpūr he appears as the protective godling of the *kṣetra*. Several well-known and well-worshipped "Mārutīs" are found on its borders: Pañcamukhī Mārutī," a five-headed giant Mārutī, stands at the southern end of the long *pradakṣiṇā* road which crosses Paṇḍharpūr parallel to the river; at the northern extremity stands "Taṃbḍā Mārutī," while "Kāḷā Mārutī" stands at the crossing of the *pradakṣiṇā* road and the path leading to the Viṭhobā temple.[8] One may say that god Viṭhobā in Paṇḍharpūr is entirely surrounded by Śiva and his kith and kin.

The Arrival of Viṭhobā in Paṇḍharpūr

Mahārāṣṭrian *bhakti*, as we have said, sees in the Viṭhobā idol preserved in the main temple in Paṇḍharpūr a "svarūpa," i.e., an original form of the divinity – Viṭhobā is Viṣṇu living there for the sake of his devotees. A number of mutually conflicting legends purport to explain how and why he, the supreme divinity, came down to the sandy beach of the Bhīmā and remained there. The most widely accepted legend credits

---

[8]Hanumān appears in the *Rāmāyaṇa* as an ally of Rāma, but even there he keeps his own character of Vāyuputra, wind-borne magician, knower of medicinal plants, and great healer. When Rāma becomes an *avatāra* of Viṣṇu and the object of *bhakti*, Hanumān appears as a Vaiṣṇava *bhakta* – even as a *mahābhakta*, and is associated with the cult of Rāma as a perfect devotee. Late iconography represents him kneeling before Rāma who is flanked by Sītā and Lakṣmaṇa. But there is no doubt that this is a late development in the career of the popular monkey-god. His mother is said to be Añjanā or Añjanī devī, a popular goddess in the Western Ghaṭs, usually represented as a mere stone (like the god Narsobā) under a pīpal tree. Such a primitive shrine of Añjanā is found on the bank of the Bhīmā above the Viṣṇupāda rocks in the vicinity of the famous "Pañcamukhī Mārutī."

the "Muni" Puṇḍalīk with having attracted the god by his very holiness. This Puṇḍalīk is a rather mysterious figure. Karmarkar assumes that he may have been a Jaina ascetic from Karṇāṭak.[9] In that case he too would not have been an original resident of the *kṣetra* and he would not have been a Vaiṣṇava either. The saint Puṇḍalīk of Paṇḍharpūr might also be connected with the "Puṇḍarīka" mentioned in the southern recension of the *Mahābhārata* (Anuśana Parvan 124) as a devotee of the god Nārāyaṇa. The latter appeared in person visibly (*pratyakṣa*) before him and so Puṇḍarīka obtained Viṣṇu's own abode.

According to the tradition, Viṭṭhal was so pleased by Puṇḍalik's devotion towards his aged parents that he personally came and stood by him on the sandy bank of the Candrabhāgā. At that time Puṇḍalīk was so engrossed in the performance of his duties toward his father and mother that, unable to attend to his divine visitor, he simply threw a brick to him, bidding him to stand on it while he was busy. Viṭṭhal did not take offense: rather, out of love for Puṇḍalīk, he stood erect on the brick – and so he remained forever! That curious story brings out some interesting points: "Muni" Puṇḍalīk's behavior was the opposite of what would have been expected of a pious Vaiṣṇava. If he showed any *bhakti* at all, it was only towards his parents – and he actually went so far as to treat his divine visitor with contempt. Yet Viṭṭhal could not resist the attraction of his holiness, and he instantly placed himself entirely at his beck and call – just standing on the brick and waiting there. What the story actually exemplifies is the extraordinary power of devotion – no matter what the object – on the heart of the god Viṭṭhal. He is really the Lover of bhaktas, the true *bhakta-vacchala* who loves the saints as a mother loves her children, and, for the love of them, will accept any rebuke.[10]

[9]See Karmarkar, *Mystic Teachings*, p. 25; no evidence is brought to bear on this point. The remarkable devotion of "Muni" Puṇḍalīk towards his aged parents certainly does not point in this direction, since Jainism, like Buddhism, favors total renunciation and the breaking of family ties.

[10]This character of Viṣṇu-Kṛṣṇa is already strongly brought out in the literature of the oldest Kṛṣṇaite sect of Mahārāṣṭra, the Mahānubhava sect, in which Kṛṣṇa is the supreme deity and Dattātreya the perfect guru. The

In spite of his insolent behavior towards Viṭhobā (which may be interpreted as a kind of "trial" of the god's loving patience by his devotee), Puṇḍalīk is hailed by the whole Mahārāṣṭrian tradition, especially by the poet-saints of Mahārāṣṭra, as their great benefactor since it is he who brought Viṭṭhal to the spot. The place where the famous meeting took place is a river-bed shrine on the Bhīmā which is surrounded by water during the rains and known as "Puṇḍalīk-samādhi," the place where saint Puṇḍalīk attained *samādhi*. This Puṇḍalīk-samādhi, however, is nothing but a Śaiva shrine. It contains only a *Śiva-liṅga* covered with a brass mask in the Mahārāṣṭrian fashion. It is said to have originally been built by Cāṅgadeva or Vaṭeśvara, a well-known great Yogī or "Siddha," a Śaiva by faith said to have been converted to Vaiṣṇavism by Jñāneśvar, who himself was a disciple of the Śaiva Guru Gorakhnāth. The Śaiva shrine known as Puṇḍalīk-samādhi on the river bed is the first place to be visited by pilgrims, as they come to perform the *yātrā* of the Paṇḍharī-kṣetra.

The Puṇḍalīk shrine did not pass into the hands of the Bāḍve Brahmins as did the great Viṭhobā temple and most of the other shrines in the Paṇḍharī-kṣetra. It has remained to this day in the hands of the low-caste fishermen known as "Mahādev Koḷīs" who, like all the low caste people of Mahārāṣṭra, are Śaiva, and it is they who perform the *pūjā* to the *Śiva-liṅga* at Puṇḍalīk. The same Mahādev Koḷīs take charge of the pilgrims to ferry them from Puṇḍalīk to another famous shrine down the river,

---

Mahānubhava sect, which shows strong Yogic connection, particularly with the Nāth Yogī tradition (itself a Śaiva tradition), developed in the Deccan in the thirteenth century and possesses an interesting literature in old Marathi. In the *Śri Kṛṣṇa-caritra* (published with an introduction, critical notes and a lexicon in Marathi by Dr. S. G. Tulpule, [Poona, 1973]) of Cakradhara, the founder of the sect, the supreme love of Kṛṣṇa for his *bhaktas* and Kṛṣṇa's *bhakta-vacchala* character are strongly emphasized. The idea of *vātsalya-bhakti* as a form of *bhakti* in which it is the devotee who looks upon the god with motherly tenderness, rather than the opposite, seems to be a late development found in the Vallabhite or *Puṣṭi-mārga* sect. In this form of *bhakti*, the devotees imitate Yaśodā, the child Kṛṣṇa's foster-mother, in showing motherly tenderness towards the child Kṛṣṇa.

Viṣṇupāda. The responsibility, recognized to this day, of the Mahādev Koḷīs for the hallowed spot where Viṭhobā manifested himself to saint Puṇḍalīk, far from being a novelty, certainly marks the importance of the latter caste in former times and their close association with the holy *kṣetra.*

The Puṇḍalīk story does not say where Viṭṭhal came from. We may surmise that, as Viṣṇu, he came to the bank of the Bhīmā from Vaikuṇṭha to manifest himself to Puṇḍalīk. On the other hand, since we know Viṭṭhal to be a Canarese deity, we might suspect that the idol came from the South. But since the Viṭṭhal of Paṇḍharpūr is looked upon as a *svarūpa,* this origin is not mentioned in the Puṇḍalīk legend or in any other legend connected with the arrival of the god in Paṇḍharpūr.

In Vārakarī tradition however, the Puṇḍalīk legend is intermixed with another legend according to which Viṭṭhal, said to be identical with Kṛṣṇa-Gopāl, actually came from Dvārakā to Paṇḍharpūr as a wandering cowherd, followed by his companions, the Gopās, and his cows. After leaving Mathurā, Kṛṣṇa is said to have settled in Dvārakā and married Rukmiṇī, the Princess of Vidarbha. In Dvārakā, Kṛṣṇa-Gopāl is worshipped as Dvārakādhīśa, in a four-armed (*catuḥbhuja*) form. The Vārakarī legend says that Rādhā came to visit her beloved Kṛṣṇa in Dvārakā and sat in his lap, which irritated Rukmiṇī, his chief queen. Taking offense, she left him in anger and wandered about by herself. She finally arrived at Diṇḍīrvan, a densely forested area on the bank of the Bhīmā, just outside the northern limit of the present *kṣetra.* There, with the connivance of a local goddess, Masādevī, she remained in hiding in a stone, while Kṛṣṇa himself was wandering in search of her. If this story is to agree somehow with the previous one, the reunion of the two could not have taken place before Viṭṭhal – alias Kṛṣṇa – had revealed himself to Puṇḍalīk and taken his stand on the "brick." By itself, the Rukmiṇī story would be sufficient to explain how Viṭṭhal-Kṛṣṇa came to Paṇḍharpūr. Yet the tradition is unanimous in asserting that it was Puṇḍalīk's holiness and not Rukmiṇī's waywardness that actually brought Viṭhobā to that place. The Rukmiṇī episode may well be taken as an attempt to explain why Viṭṭhal stands alone in the great temple, without his consort by his side, and why the goddess is relegated to a different niche behind the main shrine.[11] Yet, from a mythological point of view, and from the point of view of the structure of the Paṇḍharpūr *kṣetra*, it is important to note that in Paṇḍharpūr, as in Dvārakā itself, the goddess Rukmiṇī shows her independence by arriving first, without her divine consort Kṛṣṇa, and by establishing herself independently by the river shore (as she established herself by the sea in Dvārakā) while her divine spouse, depicted as a wandering cowherd, searches for her. The mythical significance of the Rukmiṇī story is supported by the existence of an ancient shrine of Rukmiṇī in Diṇḍīrvan by the side of a primitive Masādevī shrine. There, in front of the Rukmiṇī image carved in black stone, is found a rounded stone daubed with red paint. This is said to be the very stone in which Rukmiṇī hid when Kṛṣṇa arrived on the spot looking for her. The pair were eventually reunited at Viṣṇupāda, the place where Kṛṣṇa crossed the river with his retinue of cowherds and cows, at the other (southern) extremity of the *kṣetra.*

The Viṣṇupāda shrine, situated on a small rocky island in the river bed which is entirely covered with water during the rainy season, is the third important shrine connected with the arrival of Viṭhobā in Paṇḍharpūr. Whereas on the central "Mahādvār Ghāṭ" (down the lane leading to the main temple) Viṣṇu, presumably coming down from Vaikuṇṭha, took a visible human shape on the "brick" for the sake of Puṇḍalīk, in Viṣṇupāda (as in Diṇḍīrvan) the god arrived in the well-known form of Kṛṣṇa-Gopāl. In Diṇḍīrvan, Kṛṣṇa, as Rukmiṇī herself, is said to come from Dvārakā; in Viṣṇupāda, he comes as a real cowherd with his cattle presumably from Mathurā. The shrine is an open *maṇḍapa* built over the rocks, which show clear imprints of human feet and apparently also cowprints – even the imprint of Kṛṣṇa's flute is there! According to the legend, it was by way of

---

[11]By the side of the Rukmiṇī shrine, along the western wall, are also found the smaller shrines of her "rivals," Satyabhāmā and Rādhikā (the name the Mahārāṣṭrian tradition gives to Rādhā, who appears to be assimilated as inferior queen).

this rocky island that Kṛṣṇa, his Gopā companions and his cows, crossed the river and eventually reached the left bank of the Bhīmā. There they held a festive party, supposedly in honor of the peacemaking between Kṛṣṇa and Rukmiṇī (the whereabouts of the latter at that crucial moment however not being very clear); what is certain is that they held a feast in which they consumed *kāḷā*, a kind of porridge made with rice and curds pressed together.

Viṣṇupāda is considered to be an especially holy spot by the pilgrims of Paṇḍharpūr, who never fail to visit it from Puṇḍalīk, using the boats plied by the Kolīs (Mahādev Kolīs) fishermen. Though Viṭhobā is held to be identical with Lord Kṛṣṇa of Mathurā and Dvārakā, Viṭhobā himself leaves his great temple once a year during the month of Mārgaśīrśa (November-December), when the rocks are clear of water, to hold a feast there with the cowherds. His *pādukās* (but not his *svarūpa-mūrti*) are taken to and from Viṣṇupāda in a procession. In fact, by the side of the "walking" imprints of Kṛṣṇa and the Gopās on the rocks, the imprint of the joined feet of Viṭhobā are found.

To the east of the Viṣṇupāda shrines in a niche built on the rock, a rough, reddened image of Mārutī (Hanumān) is found; this shrine is considered to be very old. The association of the footprints of "Viṣṇu" (as a Cowherd) with the monkey god Hanumān is interesting, as it recalls one of the anomalies found in the great Viṭhobā temple: the fact that the idol of Mārutī occupies the place just in front of the main shrine traditionally occupied by the divinity's own *vāhana* or divine vehicle (which in the case of Viṣṇu or Viṭhobā should, of course, have been Garuda). But the very position of this old "Mārutī" at the extremity of the rocky island which marks the southern border of the Paṇḍharpūr *kṣetra* also suggests that Mārutī is the guardian divinity of the *kṣetra*.

On the high bank above Viṣṇupāda is found the "Gopālpur" temple dedicated to Kṛṣṇa-Gopāl as the Flute Player, "Veṇugopāl," flanked by two gopīs called "Gopikā" and "Rādhikā" (the latter evidently standing for Rādhā). But in the enclosure of the Gopālpur temple, two Śiva shrines are found, one of Mahādeva and one of "Bhīmakrāj", the purported father of Rukmiṇī. Bhīmakrāj is also worshipped under the shape of a *liṅga* with a brass mask, as in the case of Puṇḍalīk. The Gopālpur precincts also enclose an underground cell, similar to those in which the primitive "Pātala-devīs" are usually found. Here the cell is said to have been occupied by the saint-poetess Janabāī, Nāmdev's maidservant. The present temple is comparatively recent (A.D. 1744). It is specially visited at the time of the Kṛṣṇaite feast of Gokulāṣṭamī in the month of Bhadra, but the Paṇḍharpūr pilgrims regularly visit it on the Āṣāḍhī and Kārttikī *pūrṇimās*, at the time of the two great *meḷās*, just after performing the *kāḷā* ceremony at Viṣṇupāda. The saints associated with Gopālpur are two female devotees of Viṭhobā: Janabāī (mentioned above) and the courtesan Kānhopatrā. These two low-born saints seem to stand there as "Gopīs" for the service of Kṛṣṇa-Gopāl. The whole assemblage of deities in the Gopālpur temple appears particularly incoherent.

So far we have been able only to describe the three main river-bank or river-bed shrines – all of them closely connected with some account of the "arrival" of Viṭhobā at Paṇḍharpūr. The very fact that all the current legends agree on that unexpected "landing," though they present rather conflicting accounts of how and why he got there, clearly suggests that the god had *not* always been there and that his presence on the spot had to be accounted for somehow. This serves to corroborate the hypothesis that Viṭṭhal, as a form of Viṣṇu or Kṛṣṇa-Gopāl, was not the original deity worshipped there and that his cult had displaced older cults, most probably that of Pāṇḍurang (alias Śiva), which was associated with some primitive Devī cult and with the cult of the monkey god Mārutī.

Viṭhobā and His Temple

The Viṭhobā temple is built on a small hillock at the foot of which runs the long lane known as "Pradakṣiṇā Road." The temple exhibits no remarkable architecture and no

Śrī Pāṇḍurang (Viṭhobā) of Paṇḍharpūr

Viṭṭhal and Rakhumāī (Rukmiṇī) as Worshiped in Vaiṣṇava Homes

magnificence. The main entrance is on the eastern side, facing the river, as in most temples. It is not a coherent structure but a rather curious assemblage of shrines, halls, and lodgings. In its center, beyond the so-called Solākhaṇḍī hall, is the *garbhagṛha* of Viṭhobā with a small antechamber, on one side of which is the *sej-ghar*, the "sleeping chamber" of the god. As noted before, the Viṭhobā idol stands alone in the inner shrine, whereas the shrines of Rukmiṇī and the other consorts are relegated to the back wall of the temple.

The image itself is made of black stone, about four feet high and roughly carved. It represents a rather plumpish boy with a large head, surmounted by a *Śiva-liṅga* as its headgear; the image wears a thin dhotī on the loins, the *Kauṣṭubha mālā* around the neck, and the *Śrī vatsalañchan* jewel on the chest. Very large *makara-kuṇḍalas* fall from the ear-lobes down to the shoulders. The image has only two arms, the left one holding the coach (*śankha*) and the other holding a lotus stalk, two of Viṣṇu's attributes. The two arms rest akimbo on the hips and the god stands perfectly erect and rigid, his two feet joined on a square block said to be a "brick" – the very brick Puṇḍalīk once threw at him! One may note that the position of the feet is exactly that of a pair of "pādukās" on a stone block, as worshipped from Buddhist times. But the position of the arms is rather suggestive of playfulness or even dancing; it resembles, in fact, the initial position of the dancer as described in the *Bhārata-nāṭyam* Actually, the whole Mahārāṣṭrian tradition reflected in the *abhaṅgas* agrees in seeing Viṭhobā as a child or a young boy – even as a playful child similar to the northern Kṛṣṇa-Gopāl or the southern Murukaṉ. As they enter the great temple and arrive in view of the god, the Paṇḍharpūr pilgrims appear to emulate their divinity as they perform a few jumps, feet joined and hands on the waist, in his presence.

Inconographically the Viṭhobā of Paṇḍharpūr is something of an exception. The image is clearly distinct from the usual representations of god Viṣṇu with four arms (usually flanked by two *devīs*). Though identified with Kṛṣṇa-Gopāl, Viṭhobā bears no resemblance to the popular representations of this god as a flute player (Veṇugopāla, Muralīdhara), yet it may be noted that, in the squarish proportions of his figure and the rigidity of his body, he somehow comes near to the Śrī Veṅkaṭeśvara of Tirupati, the Dvārakādhīśa of Dvārakā (both four-armed representations of Viṣṇu) and to the Śrī Nāth Jī of Govardhan (the latter two-armed, one arm raised to lift the Govardhan hill), three famous *svarūpa* images of Viṣṇu-Kṛṣṇa.

The image in the main temple at Paṇḍharpūr has been ascribed to the sixth century A.D., as has another Viṭhobā image found in another shrine of the same *kṣetra* and known as Tākpiṭhya Viṭhobā. Other representations of Viṭhobā are found in a dilapidated state in the Elephanta and Kānherī caves (dated eighth century A.D.). A number of images of the same god (as we have seen, a Kannada god) are found in Karnāṭaka. The one in Kolhāpūr, in southern Mahārāṣṭra, would belong to the twelfth or thirteenth century, while those in Kāḍūr (Mysore state), Luḷbāgal, and Tirupati belong to the Vijayanagar period. It is noteworthy that at least two of the Viṭhobās found in Mysore (and belonging to the Hoysala period) are found in Śaiva temples: one is carved on the wall of the Mallikārjuna temple at Basrāl, another is found in the Pañcaliṅga temple at Govindahaḷḷi. But in all these cases, the god wears a conical *mukuṭa* and not a *liṅga* as headgear. Later, the *mukuṭa* may be bell shaped and surmounted by a knob.

Images with arms akimbo are comparatively rare in Vaiṣṇava iconography, yet some are found in the Udayagiri hills in Madhya Pradesh.[12] Though there is a general resemblance, the Udayagiri images have four arms, no "brick" pedestal and no

[12]Cf. D. R. Patil, *The Monuments of the Udayagiri Hill.* (Gwalior: Archaeological Department, 1948), pp. 36 ff. The caves are situated near Bhīlsa in Madhya Pradesh (the ancient Vidīṣa, known from early Buddhist times and still flourishing under the early Guptas). The image of the standing Viṣṇu in cave Number 10 appears to have only two arms, though Patil says that the standing figures of Viṣṇu in caves Number 9 and 10 resemble the Viṣṇu figure in cave Number 6, which is four armed. All these figures are dated by the same author at c. A. D. 402. The photograph of the standing Viṣṇu in cave Number 10 has been graciously lent to us by the American Academy of Benares with permission to reproduce it, for which we are thankful.

liṅga as headdress. The *liṅga* headgear therefore could be a Mahārāṣṭrian innovation. Deleury mentions two local images, one of them found in a small temple in the Thāṇā district near

Image of Viṣṇu

Bombay that has the appearance of a stone cylinder (a *liṅga*?) on which a head and two arms akimbo have been roughly carved. No legs are visible, as if the deity were simply growing out of the platform.[13] The other image is found in the Archaelogical Museum of St. Xavier's College, Bombay. It is a brass statuette whose *mukuṭa* bears a *liṅga* and *śāluṅkā*.

Hypotheses have been offered concerning the possibility that

[13]See G. Deleury, *The Cult of Viṭhobā*. (Poona: Deccan College, 1960), p. 157; the image reproduced here is a photocopy of the one found in this work, opposite p. 156. The author adds that a statue of a similar type is found in a temple at Waī in the Satārā district.

Viṭhobā may originally have been identical with the Jain Tīrthankara Nemināth – or even with the Buddha – but none appears very convincing. On the other hand, there is probably a close link between the cult of Viṭhobā and that of Harihara, a divinity whose earliest representation is found at Badāmī. Harihara images are generally standing ones with stiff and parallel legs, like those of Veṅkateśvara, Dvārakādhīsa, and Śrī Nāth Jī. The Catalog of the Prince of Wales Museum in Bombay lists an image of Viṭhobā from Purandhara. Here the deity has four arms, two of them more or less akimbo, the left part being Viṣṇu and the right one Śiva.[14]

The importance of the joined feet on the square platform is constantly stressed in the *abhaṅga* literature, where it is given as a sublime proof of Lord Viṭhobā's absolute submissiveness to his devotees. The fervent Vārakarī devotion to the feet of Viṭhobā "on the brick" seems to correspond to the pilgrims' strong attraction to divine "pādukās". The latter may represent either Yogic deities (such as Dattātreya) or perfect Saints and Yogīs, such as Jñāndev, Tukārām, or generally any of the other great poet-saints who composed the *abhaṅgas*. As far as god Viṣṇu is concerned, it is well known that his feet, or the imprints of his feet (eventually on the chest of his devotees) have long been an object of ardent devotion. The Harihara iconography expresses the belief in the essential unity of Śiva and Viṣṇu by simple juxtaposition. As to Viṭhobā we may well consider his image as a kind of iconographical synthesis giving a human shape to a combination of two symbols: the *Śiva-liṅga* and the imprints of the feet of Viṣṇu.[15] According to this hypothesis, the rough image found at Thāṇā may be regarded as an attempt in the same direction. The fact that Viṭhobā's human shape is that of a young boy with squarish proportions and stiff legs would suggest a connection with the Tirupati

[14]For the representations of Harihara, see H. K. Sastri, *South Indian Images.* (Madras, 1916), p. 128.

[15]See the photograph of the characteristic railing built at the top of the Bhīmā embankment at Paṇḍharpūr, in which *pādukās* alternate with *Śiva-liṅgas*.

and/or the Dvārakā images. The Kṛṣṇa-Rukmiṇī legend which purports to explain Viṭhobā in Paṇḍharpūr would suggest a link between the latter god and the divinity worshipped as "Lord of Dvārakā" (Dvārakādhīśa), who is supposed to be none other than Kṛṣṇa-Gopāl from Mathurā.

Part of the Railing Over the Bank of the Bhīma at Paṇḍharpūr

The Paṇḍharpūr Pilgrimage and the Paṇḍharpūr Saints

The saints, i.e., the long lineage of the poet-saints of Mahārāṣṭra, cannot be dissociated from the cult of Viṭhobā and the Paṇḍharpūr pilgrimage. The *abhaṅga* literature composed by them constitutes the real "scriptures" for all Mahārāṣṭrian Vaiṣṇavas. As to the saints themselves, they are venerated and worshipped as the exponents of the way of salvation, and as embodiments of the grace of the Lord. It may be said that this ardent devotion to the saints is a characteristic of medieval Vaiṣṇava *bhakti*. What is peculiar to Mahārāṣṭrian *bhakti* is the unique link which exists between the Saints and Viṭhobā of Paṇḍharpūr, as well as the kind of relationship which is established between them. The mysterious figure of Puṇḍalīk stands at the head of this lineage, since he is credited with having brought Viṭhobā to Paṇḍharpūr. Yet the *abhaṅga* literature clearly exemplifies the belief that it is not for the sake of Puṇḍalīk alone but for the sake of all the saints that Viṭhobā chose to stay forever waiting on the "brick." Among the "historical" saints, i.e., among the composers of the *abhangas*, Jñāndev, who is considered to be the same person as the author of the Jñāneśvarī, is reputed to be the first, and Tukārām, a humble Kunbī of Dehū who lived in the seventeenth century, the greatest. Their joined names, "Jñāndev-Tukārām", symbolize all that is held most sacred and sublime in the religious tradition of Mahārāṣṭra.

Paṇḍharpūr is the City of the Saints, the place where all the saints and all those who endeavor to follow them have always converged. The famous biennial pilgrimage to Paṇḍharpūr, at Āṣāḍhī and Kārttikī *ekādaśī*, performed by the confraternity of the "Vārakarīs" (those who perform the *vārī* or regular trip to the holy city) is for them a way of joining all the poet-saints of Mahārāṣṭra in Paṇḍharpūr. The strenuous effort of the pilgrims is motivated not only by the longing to contemplate the joined feet of their beloved Viṭhobā on the "brick" but also to congregate with all the saints in their holy city. The pilgrimage has a markedly social character. It may be said that it is a form of mass communion in the exaltation of Viṭhobā's presence and of the presence of his beloved saints. Actually, each procession of pilgrims follows a *pālkhī*, a decorated chariot carrying the *pādukās* of their particular saint, whom they joyfully escort to Paṇḍharpūr.

The twenty-eight main *pālkhīs* all come from the Marathi-speaking area limited in the north by the Tāpti and in the south by the Kṛṣṇa river. In this way, the great pilgrimage is a uniquely Mahārāṣṭrian phenomena, not only a religious but also a "national" performance, and it has thus probably played an important role in developing a national consciousness among the Marāṭhās, who form the immense majority of all "Vārakarīs." Although Paṇḍharpūr itself is situated near the Kannada linguistic boundary, the fact is that it attracts no procession of pilgrims from the Kannada area, and none from the Konkaṇī-speaking or Telugu-speaking areas. It is also a very remarkable fact that two extreme groups, the southwestern one, which starts from the vicinity of Kolhāpūr, and the northeastern one, from the Nāgpur and Amarāvati districts (in Berār, ancient Vidarbha), distinguish themselves in having as "leaders" some non-Vaiṣṇava saints or deities. From the vicinity of Nāgpur come the *pālkhīs* of Śrī Bhūteśvar (a name of Śiva), Rukmiṇī (worshipped as a goddess in Berār), Śankhar Mahādev (another name of Śiva) and Śeṣanārāyaṇa, the great Nāga which, in Mahārāṣṭra, is regularly associated with the *Śiva-linga.* From the vicinity of Kolhāpūr come the *pālkhīs* of Macchindranāth and Gorakhnāth, the two earliest Gurus of the Nāth Yogīs, a Tantric Śaiva sect.

The most famous *pālkhīs* are those of Jñāndev, from Ālaṇḍī, and Tukārām, the greatest *abhaṅga* poet of Mahārāṣṭra, from Dehū, near Poona. Two famous saints and composers of *abhaṅgas*, however, have no *pālkhīs*, since they are considered residents of Paṇḍharpūr: Nāmdev, a low-born tailor (*śimpī*) whose "*samādhi*" is found on the lowest step of the great Viṭhobā temple, where his presence is marked by a brass bust,[16] and Cokhāmeḷa, a Mahār, therefore an "untouchable," whose own "*samādhi*" is on the other side of the lane, facing the door of the temple. Being a Mahar, Cokhamela was excluded from the temple as a matter of course. The fact that

---

[16]Near by, in what is said to have been Nāmdev's house, is found a small shrine of Keśiraja (Keśava ?), apparently a slightly different form of Viṭhobā. The body is the same, but the head wears a *mukuṭa* instead of the *Śiva-liṅga*. It is said that Nāmdev's family was traditionally devoted to Viṭhobā, though an episode in Nāmdev's legendary biography shows that his devotion to Lord Śiva, at Aūḍhā Nāgnāth in Mahārāṣṭra, was rewarded by a miracle. Nāmdev remains a rather mysterious figure; he is believed to have been a contemporary and close companion – if not an actual disciple – of Jñāndev or Jñāneśvara. The question of the identity of the Marathi Nāmdev with the Hindi Nāmdev, author of the hymns recorded in the *Guru-Granth* of the Sīkhs, is also a matter for controversy. In spite of his Vaiṣṇava background, he is generally believed to have become the disciple of Visobā Khecar, a Śaiva and a Vedāntin. It is a fact that Nāmdev's Hindi hymns at least have a strong *nirguṇā* flavor which seems to contradict the saint's legendary devotion to the Viṭhobā image of Paṇḍharpūr. This is explained as reflecting the saint's spiritual evolution.

Nāmdev is "buried" under the lowest step of the temple, as well as some incidents narrated in his legendary biography seem to indicate that he too was not welcome within the sacred precincts. Yet both these saints are foremost among the *abhaṅga* composers – especially Nāmdev – and both may be considered as "founder saints," real pillars of the Paṇḍharpūr cult. Their devotion is said to have been all the more ardent since they were condemned to contemplate the feet of Viṭhobā from a distance, and Viṭhobā himself manifested his special tenderness for them. Like the other poet-saints, they themselves are objects of cults, their respective shrines being tended by members of their respective castes. But all the castes worship them, as they worship Jñāndev and Tukārām in Ālaṇḍī and Dehū. The worship of the saints is a sacred duty for all devotees of Viṭhobā, since Viṭhobā himself worships them!

The poet-saints of Mahārāṣṭra demonstrate a curious tendency to form families or clusters. According to the Mahārāṣṭrian tradition, Jñāndev or Jñāneśvar was the second of an orphaned family of three brothers and one sister: Nivṛttidev, Jñāndev, Sopān, and Muktabāī, respectively. The eldest, Nivṛtti, having been initiated in Tryambak by his guru, Gahīnīnāth (a spiritual descendant of Gorakhnāth), in his turn initiated his brother Jñāndev. Nothing historical is known about this remarkable family, but all the *abhaṅgas* attributed to them (and some attributed to Gahīnīnāth) are strongly Advaitic in flavor; this is particularly true of Muktabāī's *abhaṅgas*. Nivṛtti, a disciple of the Nāths, must have been a Śaiva. His *pālkhī* starts from Tryambak near Nāsik, a famous Śaiva pilgrimage center, which was the place of his own initiation. As to Muktabāī, there are three distinct *pālkhīs* carrying her *pādukās*, all situated on the southern bank of the Tāpti river in East Khandesh, i.e., in the extreme north of the area "drained" by the Paṇḍharpūr pilgrimage.

From the Satārā district in the southern part of the Western Ghāṭs comes the *pālkhī* of Rāmdās, a seventeenth century saint who was the guru of Śivajī and himself a staunch Śaiva and a devotee of Tuljā Devī of Tuljāpūr, Śivajī's family goddess.

Tuljāpūr is the starting point of another *pālkhī*. It may therefore be said of Paṇḍharpūr that it is a Vaiṣṇava pilgrimage which attracts a number of apparently Śaiva saints and devotees. Actually the great mass of the Marāṭhā population, including the lowest castes, are to this day predominantly Śaivas. Though the Vārakarīs consider themselves Vaiṣṇavas, and are strictly vegetarian and faithful keepers of the *ekādaśī vrata*, there is no doubt that the clientele of Viṭhobā of Paṇḍharpūr is drawn from social groups which are traditionally Śaiva and that Śaiva saints have been easily accepted as Vaiṣṇava *bhaktas* – since Śiva himself is considered to be a great devotee of Viṭhobā! Several of the saint-poets of *abhaṅgas* are said to have been converted to the cult of Viṭhobā, but ultimately this "conversion" matters little. Whoever walks the way to Paṇḍharpūr is walking along with the saints, placing his feet in their feet. The great Paṇḍharpūr *meḷā* is really the gathering of all the saints.

While the whole joyous army of the "Vaiṣṇavas," singing all the way, marches forward, Viṭhobā himself, standing on his brick, is depicted as waiting for them with ardent expectations and longings: he deeply loves the saints, he is their "Father and Mother"; but even more of a mother![17] One may say that,

---

[17]The expression *māybāp* "Mother and Father," in Marathi (just as the Hindī *mā̃-bāp*) addressed to one single person, indicates that this person is conceived as all-merciful, a very fountain of compassion, from whom all bounty may be expected. It is, therefore, often found on the lips of the supplicant praying to his god – or on the lips of beggars asking for alms. In Mahārāṣṭra *māybāp* is the traditional way for an outcaste, "untouchable" Mahār to address his social superiors, whose merciful gifts he craves (himself being entitled only to contempt). The most famous *abhaṅga* of the Mahār saint Cokhāmeḷa, still very popular and often sung all over Mahārāṣṭra, is the one which begins with these words addressed to Viṭhobā:

Johār, māybāp, johār
tumcyā mahārācā mī mahār. . . .

"Hail, O Father and Mother, hail!
I am the Mahār of your Mahār. . . . (i.e., of your devotee)

The conception of God as a "mother" filled with tenderness for the devotee, her child, is implied, as we have seen,[10] in his character of

without the saints there would be no Paṇḍharpūr and no Viṭhobā; for Viṭhobā is the form assumed by the supreme Lord, Bhagavān, to meet the saints and to enjoy their presence, from the time of Puṇḍalīk to this very day. It is this conception of Paṇḍharpūr as the meeting place of all saints, the very fountain of holiness, a place of superhuman joy and overflowing tenderness, which gives to that holy city and to the great pilgrimage its unique character. The mass of the Vārakarīs who trudge the long road to Paṇḍharpūr, following their *pālkhīs*, represent all the castes of Mahārāṣṭra, especially the low-castes. Even if they were Śaiva by birth or tradition, all have somehow become "Vaiṣṇavas" insofar as they have recognized Viṭhobā, the beloved of the saints, as their "Father and Mother" and Paṇḍharpūr itself as their *māher*, the longed-for maternal house of the bride, the one and only true home of all the saints. Leaving Paṇḍharpūr, the feet of Viṭhobā, and the company of the saints, therefore, is felt as a painful separation, not unlike the heart-rending departure of the young Hindu bride from her mother's house – in the often-quoted words of Saint Tukārām:

> *kanyā sāsuryāsī jāye*
> *māgẽ paratoni pāhe . . .*
> As the young girl leaving for the father-in-law's house,
> eagerly turns and looks behind . . .

---

bhakta-vatsala (bhakta-vacchala). In the case of Viṭhobā, his motherly love for the saints is so prominent a characteristic that the composers of the *abhaṅgas* frequently address him using the feminine "Viṭhe" ("O [Mother] Vitha"), rather than the expected masculine "Vitho" or "Viṭhobā."

EIGHT

David Buck

The Snake in the Song of a Sittar

SURROUNDING CIVAN̲ (ŚIVA)* in his heavenly abode, "like bees around their queen bee,"[1] are countless numbers of immortal beings called Cittars. They heal our souls – and our bodies, for many of them have also been physicians – and teach us to attain the immortality they themselves have attained. It was among us on earth that they began their own spiritual perfection: they pursued *tapas* and *yoga* in caves and in the forests; they performed miracles; and they taught the path to immortality, the *Citta-Mārk̲am*, to those who would learn. Born human, they left our society and renounced its values. They sing for the spiritual well-being and growth of all individual souls,[2] but acts to promote the well-being of society in general, such as demon slaying, are conspicuous only in their absence. Their relationship with the followers of orthodoxy has, in general, been antipathetic in the extreme, both because of their

[1] Thiru. Kanagaratnam of Colombo used this image during a personal interview in June, 1972.

[2] Cf. "The Song of Pāmpāṭṭi-Cittar," stanza 111, for example.

* Transliteration of Tamil words is done according to the Tamil Lexicon system, except in cases where a particular word is so well known in its Sanskrit form that transliteration of the Sanskrit cognate aids clarity. In most cases, however, the extent of morphological similarity is not indicative of the extent of the semantic similarity of these cognates. Hence, in several cases, the Tamil form has been used because it is the nuances of that word that this paper treats, and the Sanskrit cognate has been included in parentheses for reference only.

atraditional behavior and because of their vociferous rejection of conventional worship and book learning.[3]

The Cittar does not fit at all neatly into any of the traditional types commonly referred to in the academic study of Hinduism. True, we can see elements of the *yogin*, for the Cittar is committed to *yoga* practice, but also of the *bhakta*, for he adores his God; of the philosopher, for he ridicules certain philosophical beliefs and espouses others; and of the folk, the people of Tamil Nadu, for he comes much closer to their language in his folk-song style than most poets and singers. At times he even reminds us of the shaman: for example, he speaks of leaving his body and flying through the air.[4] But to the Cittar himself he is none of these. He is certainly not a shaman, for his meditation is purely enstatic and his goal the release of the spirit into the *mokṣa* of Immortal Bliss.[5] He is not of the folk, for he renounces worldly life altogether and lives as a celibate.[6] He is not a philosopher, for he denounces book learning.[7] Insofar as he is a *bhakta*, he is highly unusual in his preoccupation with *yoga* and rejection of temple worship; and insofar as he is a *yogin* he is unusual, for his *yoga* culminates in a *bhakti*-type attitude of love for God. It is to one of these Cittars, and the Song he sang, that we are turning.

He is known to us as "Pāmpāṭṭi-Cittar," the "Cittar who makes snakes dance," or the "Snake-Charmer Cittar." When he lived we do not know, for he himself went up in a poof of unrecorded history behind the smokescreen of this epithet. But from looking at his song, and at the other songs and writings

[3]Cf., e.g., K. Kailasapathy, *Oppiyal Ilakkiyam.* (Madras: Pāri Nilayam, 1969), pp. 189-90; W. D. O'Flaherty, "Asceticism and Sexuality in the Mythology of Śiva, Pt. I," *History of Religions.* (Chicago: University of Chicago Press), VIII:4, p. 323; Sāmi. Chidambaranār, *Cittarkaḷ Kanṭa Viññānam-Tattuvam.* (Madras: Ilakkiya Nilayam, 1969), pp. 43-50; et. al.

[4]Cf. "The Song of Pāmpāṭṭi-Cittar," stanzas 16-17.

[5]Cf. ibid., entire.

[6]Cf. ibid., sections on "Renunciation of the Desire for Wealth," "Renunciation of the Desire for Women," and "Avoidance of Self-Love."

[7]Cf. ibid., stanza 98 (quoted below).

subsumed under the general rubric of Cittar literature, we can guess that he sang his song some time after the opening of the fifteenth century, and probably before the beginning of the eighteenth century, A.D. It is probable that most of the literature of the Tamil Cittars comes from this period. This would place it at a time of political tension in Tamil Nadu: Vijayanagar rule was weakening from within and being attacked from without by the Muslims, and the British were establishing the roots of their long stay.[8] Aruṇakiṟinātar had recently sung his elegies on Murukaṉ, and elsewhere in the literary world, there were the writing of *stala purāṇams*, the beginnings of dramatic composition, commentaries on Tamil classics, Tamil translations from Sanskrit (including the Bhagavad-Gītā), continuations of court poetry and the other so-called minor literatures, and the eruption of folk-song motifs and folk-song meters into literature.[9] In terms of the history of Tamil literary forms, the Cittar songs fit well into this last category, for most Cittars, Pāmpaṭṭi included, used this form. The sparkling *bhakti* poetry of the Śaiva and Vaiṣṇava faiths and the formation of orthodox philosophies, rounded off by the Śaiva Siddhānta Śastrams in the fourteenth and fifteenth centuries, had passed, and there are those[10] who consider the Cittar movement a reaction to the ossification of those great traditions.

But that is not to say that the tradition began then. The oldest specific reference to Cittars that I have seen is in Arjuna's vision, in chapter eleven of the Bhagavad-Gītā, but the tradition is reputed to be even older than that. It is associated with an ancient tradition of medicine somewhat similar to, but clearly independent from, the Sanskrit Ayurvedic tradition. The man in the street reveres Cittars for their attainment of both

[8] A. Krishnaswami, *The Tamil Country Under Vijayanagars*, (Annamalainagar: Annamalai University, 1964), chapters 13-15.

[9] T. P. Meenakshisundaran, *A History of Tamil Literature*. (Annamalainagar: Annamalai University, 1965), chapters 8 and 9; and T. V. S. Pandarathar, *A History of Tamil Literature (13, 14, & 15th Centuries)*. (Annamalainagar: Annamalai University, 1963), entire.

[10] Cf., e.g., A. V. Subramania Iyer, *The Poetry and Philosophy of the Tamil Siddhars*. (Chidambaram: Manivasakar Noolakam, 1969), pp. 4-6.

miraculous powers and the immortal state of perfect release from the bondage of death and life.

In this presentation I hope to introduce philosophical Cittar literature through an examination of Pāmpaṭṭi-Cittar's symbolic use of the serpent. Secondly, I hope to illustrate how cultural, mythological, and psychological referents can be marshalled in the presentation of a symbol. I even hope to be able to throw some light on a type of religious man not heretofore often considered in our scholarship – and significant, at the very least, in his novel combination of better-known types.

Pāmpāṭṭi-Cittar's whole song revolves around the image of a snake dancing to the melody of a snake-charmer. Essentially, this snake is a poetic device, and the snake charmer motif functions, like the ordinary snake-charmer's show, to attract our attention. It does.

perceive,
perceive,
perceive,
and
dance,
snake!

see
Civaṉ's
Glorious Feet,
perceive,
and
dance,
snake!

dance,
snake!
perceive,
and
dance,
snake!

that we've seen
Civaṉ's
Twin Feet,
dance,
snake!
dance![11]

And right here lies hidden the basic function of Pāmpāṭṭi's snake symbol. He is speaking to us, but his words are addressed to a snake. Much of what the Cittar has to say is striking enough, and forcefully enough put, that we might be offended by it to the point of not listening to his message; but this indirect mode of address permits him to tell us clearly what he wants to say, without unduly offending us individually.[12]

[11] "The Song of Pāmpāṭṭi-Cittar," stanza 1 (all translations from this Song are my own).

[12] He calls people "dogs" (stanza 41); he calls our bodies "stinking pots, where pus and feces, oozy blood and fat are stuck together" (stanza

So we see the serpent as a symbol for us, the listeners. But Cittar symbolism is complex, sometimes to the point of real obscurity.[13] "Everything which can be thought is untrue," said a *ñāni (jñānin)* near the end of the last century.[14] It is only through paradox that we can reach that which cannot be thought, the ultimately true, and as often as not, it is through symbolism that the necessary paradoxical situation is established.[15] Symbolism in Cittar songs often relies on the age-old phenomenon of the mystical inner meaning. Discovery of an inner meaning is simply the explanation of the import of the symbol in philosophical or religious terms, lacking only the immediacy which the symbol affords. It gives a fullness to our understanding of the symbol, the natural obscurity of which may often simply leave us empty-handedly wondering what a stanza is about. The most common way to discover inner meanings is simply to postulate one, based on associations the symbol brings forth and to follow the implications of that meaning through in all important directions. After that has been tried several times, the postulate generating the fewest difficulties is presumed to be the correct one. Employing this principle, then, I postulate that the major snake in the Song of Pāmpāṭṭi-Cittar is the Soul, as an extension of its symbolic usage in addressing the most real and vital part of the individuals in his audience. The remainder of the paper shows how this postulate works out in its further implications.

So, with the serpent as the Soul, the next question is: why use a snake to symbolize the Soul? Why not some other object? Of course, any object could be chosen, and other Cittars have in fact chosen other symbols – and with remarkable effect – but

---

63); and he makes fun of the rich (cf. section on "Renunciation of the Desire for Wealth") and the orthodox (stanza 99).

[13] Iyer, *Tamil Siddhars*, pp. 1ff. has an interesting discussion of this point.

[14] Edward Carpenter, *A Visit to a Gñāni.* (Chicago: Stockham, n.d.), p. 97.

[15] I am indebted on this point to M. Eliade, *Yoga, Immortality and Freedom*. (Princeton: Princeton University Press, 1969), pp. 250-54.

Pāmpāṭṭi chose the snake, and his utilization of its symbolic potential makes it particularly appropriate.

Serpent symbolizes Soul, or our "life-essence," in many another song, myth and legend both in India and elsewhere. Patañjali is regarded as an incarnation of *Āticēṭaṉ (Ādiśeṣa)*,[16] and Evans-Wentz speaks of "the Wise Men, who have long been symbolized by the *Nagas*, or Serpent Demigods."[17] The souls of Greeks and Egyptians seem to have changed into serpents when their bodies died, to live with the mother of death as snakes in the underworld,[18] and the same association is common in Zulu, Malagasy, and many other cultures.[19] In Europe, "the form of the serpent, like that of the mouse, may be assumed by the soul of a sleeper."[20] The snake symbol is of deep importance in initiation rites in many cultures, where it often expresses the pattern of a return to the womb and rebirth as an initiate.[21] English romantic poets have also linked the Soul with the serpent.[22]

Examination of extra-Indian serpent imagery does more, however, than merely establish world-wide currency of a usage we are considering. It hints at something of the influence that serpent imagery can have on the very conception of the Soul it conveys. The Soul symbolized by a snake is almost always

---

[16] H. Zimmer, *Philosophies of India*. (New York: Pantheon Books, 1951), p. 283.

[17] W. Y. Evans-Wentz, *Tibetan Yoga and Secret Doctrines*. (New York: Oxford University Press, 1958), p. 344.

[18] C. G. Jung, *Psychology of the Unconscious*. (New York: Dodd, Mead, and Company, 1922), p. 408.

[19] N. W. Thomas, "Animals," in James Hastings, ed., *Encyclopedia of Religion and Ethics*. (New York: Charles Scribner's Sons, 1921), Vol. 1, pp. 525-26.

[20] Ibid., p. 526.

[21] Cf., e.g., M. Eliade, *Rites and Symbols of Initiation*. (New York: Harper & Row, 1958).

[22] L. N. and D. T. Pedrini, *Serpent Imagery and Symbolism: A Study in the Major English Romantic Poets*. (New Haven: College and University Press, 1966), p. 54 and chapter III.

explicitly bound up in earthly existence. And as its importance in initiation rites suggests, it simultaneously shows us how to slip out of that bondage into New Life. Heinrich Zimmer sums up this point in specific reference to India by stating that the serpent represents "life-force in the sphere of life-matter."[23] To illustrate the applicability of these insights to the Song of Pāmpāṭṭi-Cittar, consider stanza 74:

as oil and water
won't mix,
so must
we achieve
right in this world.

cut your bonds,
and
live!

see the Light,
the eye
of eyes,
stand,
and
dance,
snake!
dance!

Souls are bound to live on this earth, yet must strive to separate themselves from it as oil separates from water, to cut that bondage in order truly to live and to perceive the Light of God.

Consider for a moment the *nāgas* of Hindu art and literature. Though they are rarely taken explicitly as symbols of the Soul, much of the mythology surrounding them is based on the type of symbol structure that can be applied to the Soul, in India at least. We have within us the incalculably precious potential of attaining immortal bliss; the *nāgas* are also immortal, and the treasure of their immortality is concentrated in a precious gem of incalculable worth hidden *inside* them – the proverbial *nākarattiṉam (nāgaratna).* They are also considered the paragons of asceticism and *yoga*,[24] the embodiments, as it were, of those strenuous paths toward the final slipping out of earthly bondage into the Absolute State of Perfection. Thus they fit perfectly the requirements of a symbol for a Soul conceived of as an immortality surrounded by physical and

[23] H. Zimmer, *Myths and Symbols in Indian Art and Civilization*. (New York: Harper & Row, 1964), p. 75.

[24] J.-P. Vogel, *Indian Serpent-Lore*. (London: Arthur Probsthain, 1926), p. 13; this attribution was confirmed by His Holiness Brahmasri Swami Sankarananda of Five Falls, Courtallam.

mental encumbrances, but which has at the same time before it the promise of eternal release from that bondage. That is, though the explicit reference, "serpent symbolizes Soul," is lacking,[25] the mythico-symbolic framework of *nāga*-lore is seen not only to allow, but even to encourage, such a connection.

Like the inward ghosts and bejewelled ladies of other Cittars, then, Pāmpāṭṭi-Cittar's snake-symbol for the Soul serves as the focus of attention for an audience;[26] and it performs this function particularly well because of the incredible mass of cultural, mythological, and psychological materials on which it can draw, all well embedded in the lives of his hearers.

But *how* does he do it? Stanza 83 goes like this:

snake
that lived
in a hole
in the trunk
of the banyan tree!

you
went into
a hole in the trunk
of the pīpal tree.

watch,
watch

the tip
of the tail,
coil,
hang,
and
dance,
snake!
dance!

The outer meaning is clear enough. And so are the cultural references to the marriage of the trees and the fact that sacred snakes are associated with sacred trees. Snakes do coil up, maybe not exactly as though watching the tips of their tails, but even such a reference is at least not ridiculous. But all of this belongs to what is known as the "outer meaning." The inner meaning of this stanza relates the Soul to God's Feet.

---

[25]Though in one Gandhāra example, according to Zimmer, it *is* explicit: a *nāginī* symbolizes Psyche caught up by Spirit (Garuḍa). Cf. Zimmer, *Myths and Symbols . . .*, p. 76n.

[26]On this function of the serpent see the interesting information on the serpent in Hebrew culture in M. Bodkin, *Archetypal Patterns in Poetry*. (London: Oxford University Press, 1934), pp. 276-77.

Banyan trees have long been used in Tamil literature as metaphors for the womb;[27] those magnificent spreading trees that give and renew life, and protect us from the miseries of the hot sun. Thus, the snake who lived there in a hole can reasonably be said to symbolize the Soul, which lived in the womb while developing its physical body. Pīpal is known as *araca-maram* in Tamil, that is, "king-tree," and the word for trunk is *aṭi*, which also means "foot." Now, we know that "king" in Tamil religious poetry commonly means "God," and, indeed, Pāmpāṭṭi-Cittar himself has used it clearly in that meaning more than a few times.[28] Thus, "trunk of the pīpal- or king-tree" is a sort of metaphor hiding the Cittar's real meaning, to wit, "the Feet of God." There is a poetic convention in Tamil whereby a verb in the past tense can be used to indicate a present, or future, action that is certain to occur. Thus it also implies, of course, the potential to occur, and "went into God's Feet" implies "can most certainly go into God's Feet." Again, "go into," or "enter," here is simply a very appropriate poetic way of hinting at the total immersion in bliss that comes to the Soul with Release at the Feet of Civan. Thus, the Soul, or snake, which was born in a physical womb, or hole in the trunk of a banyan tree, has the sure potential of becoming absorbed in God's Feet, or entering a hole in the trunk of a pīpal tree.

But what of the tip of the tail? First of all, the circle thus formed symbolizes the wholeness and endlessness of the Soul in Bliss,[29] the immortality about which the Cittars sing in so many stanzas.[30] Having reached the Feet of Civan, the Soul can enjoy uninterrupted, everlasting bliss – spoken of sometimes as "sleep without sleeping."[31] That is what the snake's coiled

---

[27] Cf. *Kuṟṟālak-Kuṟavañci*, for one example.

[28] Stanzas 28, 29, 30, 33, 55, 104, et. al.

[29] Cf. Aniela Jaffé in C. G. Jung, et. al., *Man and His Symbols.* (Garden City, N. Y.: Doubleday & Co., 1964), pp. 240-41

[30] Cf. "The Song of Pāmpāṭṭi-Cittar," stanzas 18, 19, 77, 80, 113, 116, et. al.

[31] Cf. ibid., stanza 116; also Tirumūlar, *Tirumantiram*, stanza 129 and Tāyumāṇavar, "*Kāṇbēnō, Veṉ Kaṇṇi!*" stanza 10, and many others.

position indicates: eternal rest.[32] But that is not all: the snake is still to do something – watch, watch the tip of its tail. It must keep an eye on itself to make sure it does not give up its immortality, and it must come to know its own self perfectly. But there is still more: "tail," *vāl*, also means "pure,"[33] and the word for "tip" here again is *aṭi*, or "foot." So "the tip of the tail" means "the pure feet," and there is no question about whose feet – Civaṉ's. The Cittar doesn't want us to think that *we* will be the whole story when we attain final Release. We can only attain to God's Holy Feet, and our Bliss is, in essence, purely the experience of uninterrupted absorption in the thought – not ordinary thought, of course, for we will have transcended what we now think of as thought long before – but the pure thought, "Civan." The verb "hang"[34] implies a support, and just as the snake can only hang from something, so we must simply recognize Civaṉ as our only support. And, for the sheer joy of attainment, the snake must dance to the snake-charmer's tune, and we must attune ourselves to God's rhythms. Ultimately our souls, too, will be able to dance in God's presence.

Having finished an interpretation of this stanza, we find that we can write a word-for-word transcription of its inner meaning:

> O Soul, who was born into a mortal body, you have the certain potential of attaining Ultimate Release! Concentrate on it, and with Civaṉ's help,[35] you can rest blissfully absorbed in His Presence.

Examination of this stanza has accomplished several ends. It has shown how Pāmpāṭṭi, the snake-charmer, actually uses his

---

[32]Cf., e.g., J. Woodroffe, *The Serpent Power*, sixth ed. (Madras: Ganesh & Co., 1958), p. 35.

[33]Cf. Tiruvaḷḷuvar, *Tirukkuraḷ*. 1:2.

[34]Some editions (Aru. Rāmanātan's, for example) have "sleep" in the place of "hang." "Sleep" would imply meditation, rather than realization of Civaṉ's superiority. Such a reading would illustrate the *yoga* strain of the Song, whereas "hang" illustrates the *bhakti* strain.

[35]Or, when "sleep" is read for "hang," the hidden meaning would read "through meditation" instead of "with Civaṉ's help."

snake-symbol in a specific literary situation, and it has shown, through poetry, what kind of Soul, God, and Release he is concerned with.

His ability to insert religious and philosophical ideas into cultural, *purāṇic*, and psychological imagery is frankly ingenious. One of the best known stanzas in all of Cittar literature is Pāmpāṭṭi-Cittar's stanza twenty, in which he uses *purāṇic* as well as cultural material in this way:

o snake
on top
of the crown
of the Lord!

o cobra snake
with a bag
of venom!

o snake
that enters into
and dwells in
the underworld!

sing,
sing,
stand,
and
play,
snake!
play!

In terms of symbolism, it is the third half-line of this stanza that is the most intriguing:

o snake
that enters into
and dwells in
the underworld!

Here through a single mythico-cultural reference, the Cittar's Song exhibits not only a way of utilizing the snake as a soul symbol, but also the functioning of a symbol in two opposing ways, as well as expressing the two mutually contradictory attributes of the snake-symbol which were just developed while looking at world mythologies on a somewhat broader scale. All this is accomplished because this line can be interpreted to mean two opposing things. On the one hand, the underworld means the unevolved universe, because underneath the earth's crust is the home of the *nāgas*, descendants of Ādiśeṣa, himself a symbol of the unevolved cosmos,[36] and relatives of Vṛtra, the

[36]Cf. Zimmer, *Myths and Symbols . . .*, p. 61 and Jung, et. al., *Man and His Symbols*. p. 152.

"embodiment," as it were, of it. That is, it refers our thoughts to the subtle reality supporting this false world; it sings of the transcendence of our phenomenal existence, and of the transferral of our sphere of presence to that which is the Root Cause of Nature and ourselves, which is God. Thus, "to live in the underworld" is to be liberated from the bondage of mortal life.

But as the Cittar reminded us in the first line of this stanza, the snake lives by nature in the most exalted of all places, on top of Civaṉ's head. To enter into, and take up residence in the underworld would, in this case, mean descent from the Supreme State at the top of the evolutionary ladder, acquiring all the *tattuvams (tattvas)* of creation, and ending up with a physical body here on earth. That is, besides referring to the liberation of the innately bound Soul,[37] it also refers to the seemingly contradictory happening of the accrual to it of those very same earthly bonds. Thus this line symbolizes at once both the bondage of the immortal Soul and its potential for transcending that bondage to exist in the presence of God. Each of these interpretations can also be considered separately, however, enabling a listener whose individual needs are answerable by the exhilarating message of the reality of Release to be served, while at the same time it can serve another listener (or, perhaps, the same person at another time) with the sobering realization of the truth of his own very real bondage to the world and death. Mythological snakes, through this poetic usage, serve religious ends through the insights of Pāmpāṭṭi-Cittar.

But the Cittar nowhere implies that Release, certain though it is, will come to us without work on our part. *Bhakti* is the culmination of his religion, and his constant insistence on worshipful devotion and love brings to mind the many carvings of *nāgas* in poses of rapt devotion to God.

> meditate! meditate
> on the Fragrant Flower
> of God's Feet
> that permeate the Soul
> like the oil in the sesame seed!

[37] Cf. also, "The Song of Pāmpāṭṭi-Cittar," stanza 90.

control yourself,
submit,
and perceive
just so that
love and *bhakti*
truly stand
Supreme,
and
dance,
snake!
dance! [38]

worship
worship
worship
the Feet
of the Light that shines
everywhere
as a pure gem,
and
dance,
snake!
dance! [39]

Behind this devotional religion, though, and supporting it in all its aspects, lies *yoga*. The Cittar sang thus in his 118th stanza:

we let out the snake
that stood in the pot
of the body
and immersed it
in the ocean of compassion;

Here is a new snake. To get at its meaning, note first that the body is often called a pot in many traditions, especially the Cittar tradition. So that image is no problem. The "ocean of compassion" is to be taken as the grace of Civaṉ, *aruḷ*, since compassion, *karuṇai*, is often used as a synonym for *aruḷ*; ocean implies the vastness of the Cittar's feeling for this grace. In this stanza, then, the Cittar is singing of the conclusion first, the attainment of complete immersion in Civaṉ's *aruḷ*. The next line goes:

we made the friendly *cuḻumuṉai*
flow long,
and steadfastly searched
for the Eternal Being;

The reference to *cuḻumuṉai (suṣumṇā)* displays unequivocally the *yoga* nature of this stanza. *Cuḻumuṉai* is the central one of the 72,000 subtle veins in the body. It is located along the spinal cord of the physical body. When breath is controlled, and the mind united with it, they both flow up the *cuḻumuṉai* to

[38]Ibid., stanza 4.

[39]Ibid., stanza 70.

realization of the presence of Civaṉ. Strenuous breath control exercises – Pāmpāṭṭi-Cittar refers to them in stanza 30 also – are required to control these two and make them flow through the *cuḻumuṉai*. The process culminates, however, in presence at God's Feet, and can thus be beautifully described as a steadfast search for the Eternal Being.

All the things of the world are transcended in this *yoga* practice. Indeed, our consciousness becomes completely clear of thought of any kind whatsoever. It remains simply as an open, empty, endless space. This is pure *cit*– intelligence, or conscious existence. When our own consciousness shines as purely, as openly as that, we have rid it of all the *tattuvams* of earthly bondage and brought it to its own innate Immortal Bliss. This space is referred to in the next line:

we ascended into
the Magical Great Space
and
sought to attain
the Faultless Being

who is, being eternally perfect, of course, God Himself.

But what of the new snake we met with a few minutes ago? It is not the snake to whom the stanza is addressed, who is told to dance, as usual, at the end of the last line. This new snake is the breath, who is at first tamed and bottled up inside the body. Let us shift to stanza 125 to illustrate this usage:

we'll bottle up
the snake
in the
needle-hole pot;

Needle-hole pot means the body, because in *yogic* meditation there is only one way for the breath to escape: through the *Piramā-rantiram (Brahma-randra)*, an infinitesimally small hole in the top of the subtle body, at the end of the *cuḻumuṉai* vein. Also, it can be considered a purely poetic metaphor: the breath is tied to the body – that is, the pot – and goes where it goes, just as the thread is bound to follow the movements of a needle-hole. Thus, the snake is bottled up in the body. It cannot, therefore, be the Soul, as the Cittar wants to free the

Soul from the body, and would not suggest that we bottle ourselves up here. But it does admirably suggest the breath, which we must control and keep inside the body in *yoga* practice. The reference is particularly apt in view of the association of snakes with air: they eat it, according to some, when they flick out their tongues,[40] and by their very nature they practice *yoga* continuously, being able to show no signs of outward breathing.[41] The reference to bottling up a snake in a pot is another example of the Cittar's symbolic use of cultural material: snake-charmers have often kept their snakes in earthen pots.

The Cittar spins out the snake-means-breath metaphor more fully in these and other stanzas, but we have time to note only two more lines in this regard. To explain the usage at the beginning of stanza 118, that is,

> we let out the snake
> that stood in the pot
> of the body

etc., listen to a later line of the present stanza (stanza 125). After having controlled and refined the snake of breath, the Cittar sings

> we'll let it out
> in the
> space
> dear to the mind,
> and make
> it
> dance[42]

The purified breath, having united with the mind, dances its version of the sacred dance in the Empty Space of Pure Intelligence, that "space dear to the mind" because it is there that we enjoy the blissful Release of Immortality which is, of course, pleasant to think about, and which we attain by concentration.

---

[40] Vogel, *Indian Serpent-Lore*, p. 13.

[41] His Holiness Brahmasri Swami Sankarananda of Five Falls, Courtallam.

[42] "The Song of Pāmpāṭṭi-Cittar," stanza 125.

Later in the same stanza, the Cittar says that he himself will climb up to this space and dance, an equation of himself with the dancing snake which supports our view that the serpent in the "dance, snake! dance!" formula does in fact represent the Soul. The stanza ends with the half-line,

we've
cut off
birth
and death,
so
dance,
snake!
dance![43]

Practically speaking, the Cittar has raised himself by *yoga* practice to perfection, through raising mind and breath through the *cuḻumuṉai*. He has attained, however, not the *yogic* isolation of *kaivalya mukti*, but immortality in a *bhakti*-type union with the Lord.

Having considered the nature of the snake-symbol for Soul and breath, and Pāmpāṭṭi-Cittar's use of cultural, mythological, and psychological connections in the structure of his snake-symbol, consider now for a moment the nature of the Soul symbolized by this snake. It is a real individual entity, typologically much like the *puruṣa* of classic *yoga*, but the seeds of *bhakti* already discernible in Patañjali exert a much stronger influence in the philosophical understanding of the Cittar. The Soul's eternal freedom in isolation is not the focus of the Cittar song, as it is in the *yoga darśana*; superseding that, the Cittar seeks refuge at the Feet of his God,[44] and destroys the isolation of *yoga*.[45] The emptiness of isolation is but a step to the attainment of the true Immortality in the bliss of existence in the very presence of God.[46]

In terms of the philosophical atmosphere in which Cittar

---

[43]Ibid.

[44]Ibid., stanza 17 and many others.

[45]Ibid., stanza 8.

[46]Ibid., stanzas 71 and 76, for example.

literature is currently interpreted (and note here that such an approach is particularly valid in view of the fact that today's major philosophies were already well established in Tamil Nadu by the time the Song of Pāmpāṭṭi-Cittar was probably sung) it is interesting to note, for example, that nowhere in the Song is there a denial, such as an Advaitin would most certainly have made, of the individual reality of the Soul. And the few references that could be interpreted in that way – to the Guru as "our Soul,"[47] to God appearing as the Soul,[48] etc. – can all be better interpreted in accordance with a whole basketful of Śaiva Siddhāntic metaphors (such as the iron-filings-around-the-magnet metaphor for the Souls drawn to God at Final Release[49]) than in accordance with an Advaita Vedāntic type of denial of the plurality of souls. Moreover, the Cittar speaks clearly in stanzas three, four, and others, of the essential difference, yet enduring relationship, between Civaṉ and what he outright calls "the myriad eternal souls."[50] The style and diction – using the verb "to see" for Release, and carefully inserting phrases like "in the proper manner"[51] when he uses the verb "to join" – support the assertion that Pāmpāṭṭi-Cittar accepts the real existence of a plurality of souls.

Yet neither is there full accord with the Śaiva Siddhānta. Though both accept the eternality of the Soul, the Śaiva Siddhāntin would never be caught playing it up to the proportions Pāmpāṭṭi-Cittar sings of when declaring its immortality. And while Pāmpāṭṭi clearly accepts the eternal superiority of God, even in Release – a Release which is itself pictured as presence at God's Feet – Śaiva Siddhānta develops the theme of this eternal superiority more precisely and insistently. Pāmpāṭṭi-Cittar sings with less rigid philosophical precision, and hence his Song can be interpreted to show some

---

[47] Ibid., stanza 14.

[48] Ibid., stanza 7.

[49] Ibid., stanza 91.

[50] Ibid., stanza 3.

[51] Ibid., stanza 116.

degree of accord with various systems, as is indeed the case with the Śaiva Tēvāram. In any case, Pāmpāṭṭi-Cittar is clearly unconcerned with the question of his relation to any philosophical system:

the four *vedas*,
the six kinds
of *śāstras*,
the myriad
tantras
the *agamas*
which relate
purāṇic lore

and the other texts,
kind by kind,

are all just useless
books,
so
dance,
snake!
dance![52]

Pāmpāṭṭi-Cittar's snake-soul is an immortal, conscious entity, surrounded by physical and mental encumbrances, working to refine itself until it attains its innate state of pure, unclouded consciousness, the Empty Space of Intelligence mentioned above, also known as the "own-form of Consciousness," *ciṟ-corūpam (cit-svarupa)*.[53] Upon attainment of that state, the Soul will find itself the equal of Civaṉ, who is also *ciṟ-corūpam*. Pāmpāṭṭi-Cittar sings,

we'll even
live
as equals
of the Lord[54]

---

[52]Ibid., stanza 98 (Some editions, including Aru. Rāmanāthan's and Sadānandam's, would read

the *āgamas*
which relate
purāṇas
and the arts,

[53]Ibid., stanzas 71 and 76, for example.

[54]Ibid., stanza 32.

It is important to note here the non-Śaiva Siddhāntic flavor in the influence that the *yoga* strain seems to have exerted on the *bhakti* strain, as well as the inappropriateness of this statement to any kind of *Vedānta*.

The eternal Soul is indestructible; it is immortal, and it is from this immortality – the transcendence of both the life *and death* of this world – that the Cittars beckon to us, calling us to follow them, time and time again.

we were
purified;

truthfully,
our body
won't be
destroyed;

we'll even live
forever,
so

dance,
snake!
dance![55]

those who put
their hearts
in the Father
forever
will never be destroyed,
so
dance,
snake!
dance![56]

But what of us now? We are grinding out our lives on the plane of gross matter and physicality. Our Soul is trapped in our bodies. Like the incalculably precious *nāgaratna*, we have within us the gem of immortal life and bliss. But we must unencumber ourselves of the physical and mental bonds of our present lives, refine ourselves as the alchemists refine base metals, and then, and only then, can we transcend this, as Pāmpāṭṭi-Cittar calls it, "filthy body"[57] and attain the golden purity of Immortality.

[55]Ibid., stanza 77. [56]Ibid., stanza 44. [57]Ibid., stanza 128.

Serpent imagery is associated with the idea of immortality in India and all over the world as well.[58] There are those[59] who believe that the snake's sloughing off of its skin is its means of renewing its life without having to undergo the bothers connected with death and rebirth, and it is a well-established fact of Hindu tradition that the *nāgas* became immortal during the episode of the churning of the ocean by the *devas* and *asuras* to obtain the drink of immortality which had been hidden there. Again we see Pāmpāṭṭi-Cittar's ingenuity in applying religious meanings to the traditional figure of the snake.

This presentation has accomplished four ends: first, an introduction to Cittar literature; second, illustration of some of the actual ways in which a symbol laden with mythological, cultural, and psychological referents has been used to convey a religious meaning; third, the introduction of a somewhat new type of conception of the Soul; and fourth, a step toward the understanding of the Cittar way as a synthesis of many religious types (most notably of *yoga* and *bhakti* patterns), a synthesis achieved, in the Song of one Cittar, through the symbol of the dancing snake.

[58]Cf. *Tāṇḍya Mahābrāhmaṇa* xxv, 15, quoted in Vogel, *Indian Serpent-Lore*, p. 14.

[59]Vogel, *Indian Serpent-Lore*, p. 14.

REFERENCES

Balaramaiah, V., *Cittar Meypporuḷ*. (Madras: Aruṭperuncōti Patippakam, 1972).

Bodkin, Maud, *Archetypal Patterns in Poetry*. (London: Oxford University Press, 1934).

Carpenter, Edward, *A Visit to a Gñani*. (Chicago: Stockham, n.d.).

Chidambaranār, Sāmi, *Cittarkaḷ Kaṇṭa Viññānam-Tattuvam*. (Madras: Ilakkiya Nilayam, 1969).

Crooke, W., "Serpent-Worship (Indian)," in J. Hastings, ed. *Encyclopedia of Religion and Ethics*. (New York: Charles Scribner's Sons, 1921) 11:411-19.

Eliade, M., *Patterns in Comparative Religion*. (New York: World Publishing Company, 1958).

________. *Rites and Symbols of Initiation*. (New York: Harper & Row, 1958).

________. *Yoga, Immortality and Freedom*. (Princeton: Princeton University Press, 1969).

Evans-Wentz, W. Y., *Tibetan Yoga and Secret Doctrines*. (New York: Oxford University Press, 1958).

Iyer, A. V., Subramania. *The Poetry and Philosophy of the Tamil Siddhars*. (Chidambaram: Manivasakar Noolakam, 1969).

Jones, Rex L., "Shamanism in South Asia." *History of Religions*. VII: 4, pp. 330-47.

Jung, C. G. *Psychology of the Unconscious*. (New York: Dodd, Mead and Co., 1922).

________. et. al. *Man and His Symbols*. (Garden City, N. Y.: Doubleday & Co., 1964).

Kailasapathy, K., *Oppiyal Ilakkiyam*. Madras: Pāri Nilayam, 1969).

Krishnaswami, A., *The Tamil Country Under Vijayanagar*. (Annamalainagar: Annamalai University, 1964).

Māṇikkam, Irā, "Tamil Nāṭṭu-c-Cittarkaḷ," in V. I. Subramaniam, ed. *Proceedings of the II International Conference-Seminar of Tamil Studies*. Vol. III (Tamil) (Madras: International Association of Tamil Research, 1971), pp. 149-55.

Mascaro, J., trans., *The Bhagavad-Gita*. (Baltimore: Penguin Books, 1962).

Meenakshisundaran, T. P., *A History of Tamil Literature*. (Annamalainagar: Annamalai Unversity, 1965).

O'Flaherty, W. D., "Asceticism and Sexuality in the Mythology of Śiva," Part I in *History of Religions*. VIII:4, 300-37.

Pandarathar, T. V. S., *A History of Tamil Literature (13, 14 & 15th Centuries)*. (Annamalainager: Annamalai University, 1963).

Pedrini, L. N. and D. T., *Serpent Imagery and Symbolism, A Study of the Major English Romantic Poets*. (New Haven: College and University Press, 1966).

Pillai, K. Subramania, *The Metaphysics of the Saiva Siddhanta System*. (Madras: The South India Saiva Siddhanta Works Publishing Society, 1958).

Raghavan, A. Srinivasa, "Mystic Symbolism in the Work of the Alwars," in *Proceedings of the First Conference-Seminar of Tamil Studies*. Kuala Lumpur, 1969.

Raghavan, V., *The Great Integrators: The Saint-Singers of India*. (New Delhi: Publications Division, Ministry of Information and Broadcasting, 1966).

Sastri, K. A. Nilakantha, *Development of Religion in South India*. (Madras: Orient Longmans, 1963).

Sastri, Jyotirbhushan V. V. Ramani, "The Doctrinal Culture and Tradition of the Siddhas," in *The Cultural Heritage of India*. Vol. IV. (Calcutta: Ramakrishna Institute of Culture, 1956). pp. 303-18.

Sen, Sukumar, "The Nātha Cult," in *The Cultural Heritage of India*. (Calcutta: Ramakrishna Institute of Culture, 1956), IV:280-90.

Tangavēlu, M. P., "Tamiḻakamum Citta Vaittiyamum," in V. I. Subramaniam, ed., *Proceedings of the II International Conference-Seminar of Tamil Studies*. Vol. III (Tamil). (Madras: International Association of Tamil Research, 1971).

Tāyumānavar, *Tiruppāḍalkaḷ*. (Madras: Ārumuka Nāvalar Vittiyānubālana Accakan, 1963).

Tirumūlar, *Tirumantiram*. (Srivaikuntam: Sri Kumaragurubaran Sangam, 1938).

Tiruvaḷḷuvar, *Tirukkuṟaḷ*. (Madurai: Aruṇā Patippakam, 1970).

Venkatasāmi, Mayilai Sīni, *Samaṇamum Tamiḻum*. (Madras: South India Saiva Siddhanṭa Works Publishing Society, 1970).

Vogel, J.-P., *Indian Serpent-Lore*. (London: Arthur Probsthain, 1926).

Woodroffe, J., *The Serpent Power*. Sixth ed. (Madras: Ganesh & Co., 1958).

Zimmer, H., *Myths and Symbols in Indian Art and Civilization. (New* York: Harper & Row, 1964).

__________. *Philosophies of India*. (New York: Pantheon Books, 1951).

The following are four different editions of the text of "The Song of Pāmpāṭṭi-Cittar." The first three contain many other Cittar works as well:

Rāmanāthan, Aru, ed., *Cittar Pāḍalkaḷ*. (Madras: Prema Pirasuran, 1968).

Saravanamuttu Pillai, V., ed. *Periya Ñāna-k-Kōvai.* (Madras: B. Irattina Nayakar Sons, 1949).

Satānantam, ed., *Periya Ñāna-k-Kōrvai*. (Madras: R. G. Pati Company, 1968).i,

"Pāmpāṭṭi-Cittar Pāḍal." (Madras: R. G. Pati Company, n.d.).

NINE

Sign and Paradigm: Myth in Tamil Śaiva and Vaiṣṇava Bhakti Poetry

Glenn E. Yocum

ANY STUDENT OF THE HISTORY of South India is well aware of the great upsurge of popular devotional religion which swept through Tamilnad beginning about the year 700. This *bhakti* movement, which seems to have continued with unabated fervor for at least several centuries, not only decisively influenced the subsequent course of religious expression in South India but also triggered a series of similar devotional movements throughout the subcontinent. In fact, it would be only a slight exaggeration to say that Hinduism, as we know it today, received its final definitive impulse from the Āḻvārs and Nāyaṉārs, the great Tamil poet-saints of the *bhakti* movement. Indeed, the significance of Tamilnad for the later development of Hindu *bhakti* is seen in a passage from the *Bhāgavatamāhātmya* where personified *bhakti* says, "Born in Drāviḍa country, I grew up in Karnāṭaka. In Mahārāṣṭra and Gujarat I became old. There, owing to the terrible *kali* age, I had been mutilated by the heretics . . . Having arrived then at Vrindāvan, renewed and all beautiful, I have become young now with the most perfect and lovable charm."[1] In the context of this paper, all this is merely a way of stating that to compare the various functions of myth which appear in the devotional poetry of the Nāyaṉārs and Āḻvārs is to deal with an issue which

[1] *Bhāgavatamāhātmya* 1:45-50 as quoted in Mariasusai Dhavamony, *Love of God according to Śaiva Siddhānta: A Study in the Mysticism and Theology of Śaivism.* (Oxford: Clarendon Press, 1971), p. 102.

has ramifications extending far beyond South India. And it is also a manner of excusing in advance a few subsequent references to phenomena which fall outside of our more immediate South Indian focus.

In comparing Tamil Vaiṣṇava and Śaiva mythology we shall also hopefully be gaining insight into some of the more general differences between Vaiṣṇavism and Śaivism as expressed in a devotional, popular, non-systematic, and non-intellectualized context. Although difference and contrast will be our principal concern, this represents no attempt to deny or to devalue the all-important common soil of pan-Indian, Brahmanical concepts and indigenous Tamil traditions in which both Vaiṣṇava and Śaiva *bhakti* were nourished. Our way of proceeding will be to examine the place of mythology first in Śaiva *bhakti* poetry and then in the Vaiṣṇava literature, and finally to indicate the salient differences between the two.

While there is little doubt about how this essay relates to South India, I must confess that my understanding of "structure" is a rather broad one. For in undertaking a comparison of the myths cited by the Tamil Śaiva and Vaiṣṇava poets, I have not been concerned to discover Lévi-Straussian oppositions. Rather, I shall attempt to show how various mythological motifs influence the mode, or structure, if you will, of relationship between the devotee and the deity. My claim will be that the myths about the deity toward whom devotion is directed characterize to a large extent the type of relationship which the devotee experiences with God. Stated so baldly, that may well appear to be rather self-evident. But perhaps it will offer us an avenue leading to some less obvious and more interesting conclusions regarding the differences in structure between Vaiṣṇava and Śaiva *bhakti*.

Myth in Śaiva *Bhakti*

In view of the manifold richness of the myths about Śiva and also the vast body of Śaiva devotional literature in Tamil, we cannot hope to be even reasonably comprehensive in our discussion of Śaiva mythology. Rather, I shall selectively focus our attention on several of the most frequently mentioned myths while making only passing reference to other aspects of Śaiva mythology. Hopefully, this will provide a sample representative enough to permit some generalizations regarding the function of myth in Śaiva devotion.

What is almost undoubtedly the most popular myth among the Tamil Śaiva poets is that of Śiva's immeasurable, incomprehensible *liṅga* of fire. In both the *Tēvāram* and Māṇikkavācakar's *Tiruvācakam* there are innumerable references to the inability of Visnu and Brahmā to reach the ends of this immense *liṅga*, thus showing themselves to be inferior to Śiva, the supreme Lord of the universe. While the myth obviously proclaims Śiva's preeminence in the pantheon, it also functions for the *bhaktas* as a primary indicator of Śiva's inability to be known, to be comprehended, and consequently to be controlled by the thought or action of all other beings, be they the divine likes of Brahmā and Viṣṇu or humans who would seek power and understanding through the practice of austerities. As presented by the Tamil Śaiva poets, this myth makes a very definite and unmistakable epistemological-theological point about the primacy of revelation in the devotees' relationship with Śiva. The relationship is God-initiated and is sustained by God's willingness to continue his gracious manifestations toward his devotees. This idea is clearly intended, for mention of the illustration of Viṣṇu and Brahmā is commonly juxtaposed with descriptions of Śiva's willingness to reveal himself to his unpretentious, apparently undeserving devotees. For example, the following verse from Māṇikkavācakar's *Tiruvācakam*:

> Although great, red-eyed Māl [Viṣṇu] dug down,
> that expanding flowery foot he could not see.
> But the Lord of that same foot
> graciously came upon the earth,
> cut off our rebirth,
> and accepted as His servants even people like us.
>
> The Lord of the South,
> where abundant coconut groves grow,
> the Lord of Peruntuṟai,
> He with the beautiful eyes,

appeared as a kind and learned sage [*antaṇaṉ*],
called us,
and graciously granted us release.

Let us sing about
His beautiful, merciful, adorned foot.
O Ammāṉai.[2]

There are several striking features in this passage which are widely characteristic of Tamil Śaiva devotion. First, we have the reference to the myth in question. Viṣṇu assumes the form of a boar and delves down, seeking the foot of the *liṅga*, but to no avail. This myth in its Purāṇic forms is usually played out against a cosmic backdrop. Neither Viṣṇu nor Brahmā can claim to create the universe, for Śiva precedes, transcends, and contains them both.[3] Hence, Śiva is superior. He is the Lord of the universe. From this cosmic framework of the myth Māṇikkavācakar quickly shifts to the personal idiom of grace and salvation – and this in highly concrete terms. The cosmic Lord who hid himself from Viṣṇu and Brahmā is the same Lord who assumed the form of the sage whom Māṇikkavācakar met in Peruntuṟai. Thus, the myth of the *liṅga* with its cosmic focus is appropriated in a highly personalized context. That the one who has revealed himself in such concrete form at Peruntuṟai is

[2]*Tiruvācakam* 8:1. Ammāṉai refers to a village game engaged in by women, during the playing of which songs are sung. On the myth of the *liṅga* of fire also see *Tiruvācakam* 11:1, 3, 5, 7, 14; and 12:6. Translations from the *Tiruvācakam* are mine, based on the Tamil text found in G. U. Pope (ed. and trans.), *The Tiruvāçagam or 'Sacred Utterances' of the Tamil Poet, Saint, and Sage Māṇikka-vāçagar*. (Oxford: Clarendon Press, 1900). My references list the usual hymn and verse numbers, not hymn and line numbers, which is Pope's peculiar method of *Tiruvācakam* citation.

[3]See Heinrich Zimmer, *Myths and Symbols in Indian Art and Civilization*. Joseph Campbell, ed. (New York: Harper Torchbooks, 1962), pp. 128-130; and M. A. Dorai Rangaswamy, *The Religion and Philosophy of the Tēvāram: With Special Reference to Nampi Ārūrar (Sundarar)*. (Madras: University of Madras, 1958), Book I, pp. 196-199. The study by Dorai Rangaswamy is a mine of information on myth in the poetry of Cuntarar, and I am indebted to this book for most of my references to the *Cuntarar Tēvāram*.

also the Lord of the cosmos only serves to heighten the miracle of Māṇikkavācakar's conversion.

This concretization of religious symbols and concepts, which is usually explicitly associated with experiences at particular holy places and temples, is not restricted to Māṇikkavācakar. It is common to virtually all the medieval Śaiva poets in Tamilnad. There is a short verse by Tirunāvukkaracu (Appar) which is remarkably similar in structure to that of Māṇikkavācakar just quoted:

> Vishnu, spouse of Lakshmi, and four-ways-facing Brahm,
> Searched the heights and depths, but Thy feet could never see.
> Yet, O only Lord, who in Athihai doest dwell,
> Formless in Thy grace, grant the sight of them to me.[4]

One constantly discovers that the cosmic reference of the Purāṇic myths about Śiva is balanced by the intense personal experiences of the individual *bhaktas*, experiences as varied as the number of devotees. One only need read the legends about the sixty-three Nāyaṉārs in the *Periyapurāṇam*, the twelfth-century Tamil Śaiva hagiology, to appreciate the variety of ways in which Śiva manifests himself to his devotees.

Another myth which is very prominent in the Śaiva devotional literature is that of Śiva's destruction of the Tripura, the three fortresses of the *asuras* which were invulnerable to the attacks of the *devas* and from which the *asuras* terrorized the cosmos. Śiva is said to have demolished all three fortresses with a single arrow or, less frequently, is pictured as causing their destruction merely by smiling.[5] This myth too declares Śiva's supremacy among the gods. He alone is capable of vanquishing the forces of evil. His destruction of the Tripura is really an act of preservation, an act of grace. Indeed, in the eyes of the Śaiva devotees all of Śiva's apparently bizarre and destructive acts are

---

[4] F. Kingsbury and G. E. Phillips (trans.), *Hymns of the Tamil Śaivite Saints*. (Calcutta: Association Press, 1921), p. 39.

[5] See the synopses of the Tripura myth in Kingsbury and Phillips, ibid., pp. 7-8; and in Dorai Rangaswamy, *Religion and Philosophy of the Tēvāram*, pp. 304-306.

essentially acts of grace and salvation. In the case of the Tripura myth this gracious aspect is explicitly emphasized in its conclusion: the *asuras*, recognizing Śiva's greatness, take refuge in him and become part of his entourage.[6] In the Śaiva *bhakti* hymns this myth, like others, is frequently personalized and brought into association with particular holy places, as seen in the following verse by Cuntarar (Sundaramūrti):

> When the three fortresses were burned
> by the flames rising high,
> the three [*asuras*] thought of you
> and took refuge in you.
> You then made them rulers of the world of gold.
>
> Having understood this famous act of your granting grace,
> I worshipped your exalted foot,
> wept aloud,
> and took refuge in you,
> O Lord of the Vedas!
> O Supreme Being!
> O our Lord who wears on your waist a belt of bells
> and beads!
> O our supreme Lord of Āvaṭuturai![7]

Another example of Śiva's destructive power is found in the myth describing the havoc which Śiva, appearing as Vīrabhadra, wreaked at Dakṣa's sacrifice. Here it would appear to be more difficult to rationalize Śiva's seemingly wanton actions as a manifestation of his grace, although there is no dearth of references to this myth in the Tamil devotional hymns. If ever Śiva appeared as a *pittaṉ* (madman),[8] an epithet occasionally used by his devotees to characterize him, it is in his antics at Dakṣa's sacrifice. Within the compass of twelve short verses

[6]E.g., see *Tiruvacakam* 14:4; and *Cuntarar Tevaram* 55:8.

[7]*Cuntarar Tēvāram* 55:8. – my translation of the text as found in the edition of Catāciva Ceṭṭiyār, ed., *Tēvārappatikaṅkaḷ, Tirumuṟai 7.* (Tinnevelly and Madras: South India Saiva Siddhanta Works Publishing Society, 1929), p. 167.

[8]E.g., *Tiruvācakam* 11:15; 12:9; 30:2; 37:8; *Campantar Tēvāram* 295:10; *Tirunāvukkaracu Tēvāram* 116:5; 158:6; and *Cuntarar Tēvāram* 53:5.

Māṇikkavācakar enumerates the following results of his actions: Agni's hands were cut off; the priest's head was severed; Dakṣa was given a goat's head; Bhaga's eye was plucked out; Sarasvatī and Brahmā also had their heads removed; Soma's face was crushed; and Sūrya's teeth were broken and swept away.[9] Several times in his delineation of this riotous tableau Māṇikkavācakar makes what must be the understatement of the *Tiruvacākam*: "the sacrifice was confounded." In this particular account Viṣṇu is the only participant to escape unscathed.

How is this myth related to the *bhaktas'* devotional context? Specifically, it is cited several times as a type of antidote for spiritual arrogance, for such was the pride of Dakṣa and the *devas* in not inviting Śiva to the sacrifice.[10] Twice in the above-mentioned passage Māṇikkavācakar simply announces that Śiva acted in such a way so that rebirth might cease.[11] I would also suggest that this myth exemplifies the same sort of apparent arbitrariness in Śiva's character as is displayed in his relations with his devotees. His capricious behavior at Dakṣa's sacrifice and his periodic revelations to and abandonments of his *bhaktas* are all of a piece. The epithets "madman" and "deceiver" (*kaḷvaṉ*)[12] are based as much upon the personal experience of individual devotees as on Śiva's mythical actions. His is not a love which smothers one in sweetness. Rather it is an aggressive love, possessing and intoxicating, but also by fits leaving his devotees in moods of rejection and utter desolation, testing their faithfulness to him. Indeed, in a religious world of

---

[9] *Tiruvācakam* 14:5-16; also cf. 8:15.

[10] Dorai Rangaswamy, *Religion and Philosophy of the Tēvāram*, pp. 333-334. Also cf. *Tiruvācakam* 13:4.

[11] *Tiruvācakam* 14:10, 12.

[12] E.g., *Tiruvācakam* 5:6; also cf. 8:6 (*kiṟi ceyta āṟu oruvaṉ*), 34:3 (*paṉavaṉ eṉai ceyta paṭiṟu*), and 34:6 (*paraṉ tāṉ ceyta paṭiṟē*). *Kaḷvaṉ* is also a popular epithet of Śiva in the poetry of Campantar – see the selections in J. M. Somasundaram Pillai (ed. and trans.), *Two Thousand Years of Tamil Literature: An Anthology*. (Madras: South India Saiva Siddhanta Works Publishing Society, 1959), pp. 316-319.

such divine unpredictability there is little room for pride of spiritual achievement.

There are several myths recounting instances of Śiva's merciful action, which are understandably popular in the devotional literature. Particularly noteworthy here are the stories of Śiva's drinking the poison which surfaced during the churning of the ocean of milk[13] and of his catching the falling Ganges in his hair.[14] Both myths have a pronounced cosmic dimension, for in each case Śiva's action is deemed to have rescued the world from imminent ruin. And again one notes an emphasis on Śiva's greatness vis-à-vis the other gods. As before, however, the *bhakti* poets render the myth personal and concrete. Śiva's drinking the poison and bearing the Ganges are typically cited to show that the *bhaktas'* individual experiences of Śiva's grace are confirmed in his world-saving acts. There is little interest in the myths apart from their immediate, existential significance.

Finally, attention must be given to Śiva as Naṭarājan, the Lord of the dance, although we cannot begin to present a full account of this many-faceted form, as it covers a whole series of myths in which Śiva appears as the dancing Lord. One meets with frequent references to Śiva simply as the "dancer" (*kūttaṉ,*[15] *naṭamaṭi,*[16] *niruttaṉ*[17]). Māṇikkavācakar often mentions

[13]E.g., *Tiruvācakam* 4:173; 5:69; 6:7, 32; 11:20; 13:10; 16:4, 5; 23:7; 35:9; *Campantar Tēvāram* 145:9; 184:4; *Tirunāvukkaracu Tēvāram* 253:9; and *Cuntarar Tēvāram* 6:5; 16:8; 23:3; 51:3; 55:5; 67:9; 70:1; 81:6; 93:7; 99:1; and many others. Further, any mention of Śiva's blue throat, an extremely common motif, is based upon this myth. (Śiva's throat turned blue when he drank the poison.)

[14]E.g., *Tiruvācakam* 5:64; 6:26; 23:9; 24:6; *Tirunāvukkaracu Tēvāram* 34:10; 211:15; *Cuntarar Tēvāram* 1:8; 4:1; 5:2; 7:2; 38:4; 55:7; 77:2; 82:6; 92:10; 96:8.

[15]E.g., *Tiruvācakam* 1:90; 5:43; 7:12; 9:2, 15; 15:8; 21:7, 8; 51:2; and *Cuntarar Tēvāram* 61:11; 62:4; 92:6.

[16]E.g., *Tiruvācakam* 50:6; and *Cuntarar Tēvāram* 17:9; 41:6; 46:4; 63:3.

[17]E.g., *Tiruvācakam* 4:202; 5:61; 29:2; *Campantar Tēvāram* 287:2; 377:3; and *Tirunāvukkaracu Tēvāram* 71:3.

Chidambaram in connection with Śiva's dancing,[18] and in these instances Śiva's cosmic dance, symbolizing his infinite sovereignty and energy, is called to mind. But it must be emphasized that Chidambaram was a particularly significant place of personal experience for Māṇikkavācakar, quite apart from its being the location par excellence of Śiva's dance. By Cuntarar much is made of Śiva's dancing in the crematorium.[19] Coupled with Cuntarar's other references to Śiva's night dance[20] and his fiery dance of destruction,[21] the total image which emerges from these often overlapping features would seem to be a rather unlikely one for inspiring *bhakti*.

But might it be that these images of Śiva's terrific aspect provide at least a two-fold insight into the nature of Śaiva *bhakti*? First, we see here again something of the unpredictability and caprice which distinguished Śiva's behavior at Dakṣa's sacrifice, an aspect of his character reflected in his relationship with his devotees. Second and more significant, these examples graphically depict Śiva's transcendence of the physical limitations and social restrictions of human existence. If one were to do a "structural" analysis in terms of category oppositions, a plausible interpretation of these "negative" and "destructive" aspects of Śiva's nature would be to view them as indicative of salvation's transcendence of and opposition to the mundane, saṃsāric sphere not merely of birth, death, and rebirth but also of the accepted norms of personal and social behavior. Measured by the world's standards, Śiva is mad. As Māṇikkavācakar says,

> The One who did not appear [to Viṣṇu],
> our eternal Lord,
> is dancing right now in the burning ground
> with the demons,

---

[18]E.g., the entire twenty-first hymn of the *Tiruvācakam* and also 1:90; 2:140-141; 4:92; 5:61; 7:12; 11:20; 12:9, 17; 13:1, 7, 14; 15:1; 35:3, 7; 40:1; 42:4; 50:6.

[19]E.g., *Cuntarar Tēvāram* 9:8; 10:2; 42:6; 55:8; 72:7; 92:5; 98:4.

[20]E.g., *Cuntarar Tēvāram* 4:6; 15:2; 29:3; 47:2.

[21]E.g., *Cuntarar Tēvāram* 17:8; 40:8; 46:1; 72:7.

whirling and swaying,
mad,
clad with a tiger's skin,
homeless.[22]

Śaiva mythology provides the *bhaktas* with a vivid image of transcendence which they seek to internalize, but it must be noted that this does not entail myth's functioning as a pattern for human imitation. For myth in the Śaiva tradition emphasizes Śiva's otherness, his complete transcendence of the human condition, and consequently does not usually invite overt imitation. Only within certain ascetic traditions (e.g., among the Kāpālikas) do some of Śiva's bizarre acts become models for human devotional practice.[23] Although, as we have seen, there is no lack of reference in Tamil devotional poetry to Śiva's more eccentric features, there is a relative absence of interest in his role as master *yogin*, a form which could very well be viewed as paradigmatic for ascetic practice. This is not surprising, for the Tamil *bhakti* movement represents an attempt to reconcile a concern for the ultimate transformation of existence, on the one hand, with an acceptance of life in the world, on the other.

While myths about Śiva may often seem to deny the worth of the socio-economic order, in the case of the Tamil devotees this is not interpreted as a call to renunciation. Rather, these myths are appropriated at a symbolic level by the Tamil *bhakti* cult. Thus, we find a Cuntarar who had not one but two wives[24] and

---

[22]*Tiruvācakam* 5:7.

[23]On the aspects of Kāpālika practice which imitate various of Śiva's mythical actions, see David N. Lorenzen, *The Kāpālikas and Kālāmukhas: Two Lost Śaivite Sects*. (Berkeley and Los Angeles: University of California Press, 1972), pp. 73-95.

[24]Cuntarar, lamenting the difficulty of keeping two wives happy, pleads for sympathy and help by referring to Śiva's own situation of being the husband of both Gaṅgā and Pārvatī (*Cuntarar Tēvāram* 20:3, 54:8). Mention of Śiva's spouses is rather frequent in the *bhakta* literature, and Professor M. Shanmugam Pillai has suggested to me that the devotional poets' fondness for this image of divine marriage correlates with the *bhakti* movement's rejection of celibacy and asceticism.

a Māṇikkavācakar who, although giving up his high position in the Pāṇṭiyaṉ administrative hierarchy, wrote devotional poetry to be sung by villagers during their daily activities.[25] The *bhakti* movement is above all a popular movement. While in it we can discern the renouncer's concern for salvation, this concern is translated into activity which need not nullify the devotee's social and economic ties.[26]

To sum up, what does our sketch of Śaiva mythology in the Tamil devotional hymns tell us about the mode of relationship between Śiva and his *bhaktas*? The principal myths cited reveal Śiva's greatness, his transcendence, and his generally uncanny nature, all of which leave an imprint on the relationship with him experienced by individual devotees. Rather than providing a model of relationship, the myths furnish the devotee with signs, indicators which give insight into the divine nature, confirming each *bhakta's* own personal experience of Śiva's greatness, transcendence, and uncanniness.[27] In short, Śaiva mythology does not direct the *bhakta's* devotion along a predetermined course. While the myths may stress the discontinuity between Śiva's nature and the human condition, this does not preclude a dynamic relationship between man and God. In fact, I would maintain that the crucial elements in the Tamil Śaivas' relationship with the deity are those of individuality, of dynamism, and of openness. Both the myths and accounts of individual devotional experience leave no doubt

---

[25]See especially *Tiruvācakam* hymns 7, 9, and 13, and also those hymns for accompanying various village games – numbers 8, 11, 12, and 14.

[26]Cf. Louis Dumont, "World Renunciation in Indian Religions," *Religion/Politics and History in India: Collected Papers in Indian Sociology*. (Paris and The Hague: Mouton, 1970), pp. 56-57.

[27]In some instances one can discern human models for the relationship between the devotee and Śiva. For example, the *guru-śiṣya* relationship, later of great significance in the Śaiva Siddhānta, is important for Māṇikkavācakar, who also sometimes pictures deity and devotee as lover and beloved. But these are forms of relationship based mainly upon individual personal experience rather than derived from mythical precedent.

that Śiva is the sovereign Lord, but what impresses one is the individuality of the *bhaktas'* experience, the sense that each devotee is left to "work out his own salvation in fear and trembling." And although much of the mythology about Śiva is concerned with cosmic motifs, the Tamil poets are able to correlate these myths with their various personal situations. Individuality, development, and instability are the hallmarks of the Śaiva devotional relationship, features which, while not simply derived from the mythology of Śiva, are certainly consonant with its principal themes.

Myth in Vaisnava *Bhakti*

Whereas Śaiva mythology is rich in images of transcendence, Vaiṣṇavism with its doctrine of God's *avatāras* discloses the human face of the divine. This is not to deny, however, that in the literature of Tamil Vaiṣṇava *bhakti* there are instances where myth functions in a manner similar to that noted in Tamil Śaivism. In the Vaiṣṇava devotional poetry one also notices the same emphasis on specific sacred places, although without quite as extensive a proliferation of individual sites as among the Śaivas. (Tirupati and Śrīraṅgam enjoy special prominence in the Vaiṣṇava hymns.[28]) Myths signifying Viṣṇu's greatness and cosmic sovereignty are likewise not wanting, although their impact is tempered by the frequent references to the Kṛṣṇa and Rāma *avatāras*. Finally, there can be no doubt about the intensity of individual *bhaktas'* sense of personal relationship with the deity. Nonetheless, what does differentiate the Vaiṣṇavas from the Śaiva poets in this regard is that among the devotees of Viṣṇu devotional emotion flows along more clearly defined channels, and thus their relationship with God appears to be more structured than is the case among the Śaiva *bhaktas*. And this distinction between Tamil Vaiṣṇavas and

---

[28]See especially Toṇṭaraṭippoṭi Āḻvār's *Tirumālai* and *Tiruppaḷḷi Eḻucci*, both addressed to the Lord as enshrined at Śrīraṅgam. Both hymns are translated in K. C. Varadachari, *Āḻvārs of South India*. (Bombay: Bharatiya Vidya Bhavan, 1966), pp. 86-99 and 101-104. I have drawn many of my citations to the Āḻvār hymns from Varadachari's book.

Śaivas is not a little connected with the differing mythologies of the two great Hindu gods. But before we turn to the points at which the function of myth diverges, we should mention at least one prominent example of similarity.

One of the most popular myths in the hymns of the Āḻvārs is the story of Viṣṇu as Trivikrama, who in three steps encompassed the universe and conquered Bali, the *asura* who was threatening the cosmos with his evil designs.[29] Although the details of the myths may be quite different, the theme of the Trivikrama episode is strongly reminiscent of Śiva as the destroyer of the Tripura or as Nīlakaṇṭha, the drinker of the poison. These myths all declare both the supremacy of the deity, be it Śiva or Viṣṇu, and the gracious intention of his action. But it must also be noted that the myth of Trivikrama appears in the context of Viṣṇu's Vāmana (dwarf) *avatāra*. Hence, even here where there is a clear thematic analogy with some of the myths about Śiva, the uniquely Vaiṣṇava doctrine of the *avatāra* is evident, indicative of the major difference between Śaiva and Vaiṣṇava mythology.

Of Viṣṇu's ten *avatāras* by far the most important for the Āḻvār poets are those of Rāma and Kṛṣṇa. Prefiguring later Vaiṣṇava *bhakti*, several of the Āḻvārs were especially devoted to the figure of Kṛṣṇa as the mischievous child and youthful lover of Vṛndāvana. Rather than considering references to these two *avatāras* separately, I shall review the myths according to the type of devotion they inspired; for already among the Āḻvārs we find individual devotees tailoring their devotional attitude and expression along lines suggested by incidents related in the myths about Rāma and Kṛṣṇa.

In the mythologies of both Rāma and Kṛṣṇa the Āḻvārs found images of parental affection which they translated into their own personal expressions of devotion to God. Where Bālakṛṣṇa, the child Kṛṣṇa, is the object of devotional attention, his

---

[29] E.g., see Periyāḻvār's *Tirumoḻi* I:4:8; and Nammāḻvār's *Tiruviruttam* 42, 58, 61, 64 – all found translated in J. S. M. Hooper (trans.), *Hymns of the Āḻvārs*. (Calcutta: Association Press, 1929). Also cf. Pēyāḻvār's *Tiruvantāti* 4, 5, 9, 18, 47; Tirumaḻicai Āḻvār's *Nāṉmukaṉ Tiruvantāti* 9, and the same author's *Tiruccanta Viruttam* 105, 109.

foster-parents, Yaśodā and Nanda, typically serve as models with whom the devotee seeks to identify himself in his relationship with Kṛṣṇa. In his *Tirumoḻi* Periyāḻvār adopts this attitude with telling effect. Viewing Kṛṣṇa through Yaśodā's eyes, Periyāḻvār becomes the archetypal mother doting on her infant son, even indulgently taking pleasure in his pranks:

> Come see the flowerlike feet the silly babe
> Takes to his mouth and munches.[30]
>
> Come watch the lips, the eye, the mouth, the smile,
> The nose, of the little man whom Yasōdai
> With powdered turmeric cleans the tongue and bathes.[31]
>
> He'll tip over the jar of oil;
> He'll pinch and wake the babe,
> And roll his eye in mischief.[32]

And there is this charming incident, where Periyāḻvār-Yaśodā describes Kṛṣṇa calling the moon:

> He rolls round in the dust, so that the jewel on his brow keeps swinging, and his waist-bells tinkle! Oh, look at my son Govinda's play, big Moon, if thou hast eyes in thy face – and then, be gone! My little one, precious to me as nectar, my blessing, is calling thee, pointing, with his little hands! O big Moon, if thou wishest to play with this little black one, hide not thyself in the clouds, but come rejoicing![33]

Kulaśēkarāḻvār is another Vaiṣṇava devotee whose poetry shows him in the role of a parent vis-à-vis God. In his case, however, the scope of the mythical paradigms is widened to

---

[30]*Periyāḻvār Tirumoḻi* I:2:1 in C. and Hephzibah Jesudasan, *A History of Tamil Literature*. (Calcutta: Y.M.C.A. Publishing House, 1961), p. 102. On parallel examples from North India in the works of Vallabha and Sūrdās, see Charles S. J. White, "Kṛṣṇa as Divine Child," *History of Religions* 10, No. 2 (November 1970): 156-177; and S. M. Pandey and Norman Zide, "Sūrdās and His Krishna-*bhakti*," *Krishna: Myths, Rites, and Attitudes*, Milton Singer, ed. (Chicago: University of Chicago Press, 1968), pp. 173-199.

[31]*Periyāḻvār Tirumoḻi* I:2:15 in Jesudasan, ibid.

[32]*Periyāḻvār Tirumoḻi* II:4:6 in ibid., p. 103.

[33]*Periyāḻvār Tirumoḻi* I:4:1-2 in Hooper, *Hymns of the Āḻvārs*, p. 37.

include Devakī, Kṛṣṇa's actual mother, and Daśaratha and Kausalyā, Rāma's parents, thus considerably broadening and deepening the range of emotion in the parent-devotee/child-God relationship. In the sixth hymn of his *Perumāḷ Tirumoḻi* Kulaśēkara casts himself as Devakī, from whom Kṛṣṇa was taken away to protect him from Kaṃsa, the evil king of Mathurā.[34] Kulaśēkara as Devakī sings bitter-sweet cradle songs, imagining the pleasures of motherhood enjoyed by Yaśodā. Here the element of separation is introduced into the devotional relationship in a particularly poignant way, inspired by mythical precedent.

Kulaśēkara draws upon the myths about Rāma in a rather unusual manner. At one point he pictures himself as Kausalyā, Rāma's mother, recounting in a lullaby her son's great deeds. Hence, he transforms the usual account of Rāma's heroic feats by recalling them in an atmosphere tinged by a mother's pride and love.[35] The ten verses of *Perumāḷ Tirumoli* hymn 9 are from the perspective of Rāma's father Daśaratha, who was forced to exile his son. The prevailing mood of this hymn is sorrow due to the son's (i.e., God's) absence, for which the father-devotee must be held responsible. Or to translate the devotional emotion expressed here into more abstract theological terms, this is a poem about separation from God caused by error and guilt. For our purposes, it is significant that even this kind of attitude is mythically based.

Through their depictions of God as a child and themselves as parents, Periyāḻvār in particular, and to a lesser extent Kulaśēkara and Tirumaṅkai Āḻvār,[36] were responsible for the creation of a new genre of Tamil poetry – *piḷḷaittamiḻ*, which extols the various stages of childhood and other themes relating

---

[34]In this and the following paragraph I am relying on Varadachari, *Āḻvārs of South India*, pp. 75-80; and Jesudasan, *History of Tamil Literature*, pp. 99-100.

[35]*Perumāḷ Tirumoḻi* 8:1-10.

[36]E.g., Tirumaṅkai's *Periya Tirumoḻi* 4, 5.

to children.[37] Also contributing to the development of *piḷḷaittamiḻ* is a verse by Āṇṭāḷ, the only female Āḻvār. Imagining herself to be one of the *gopīs*, Āṇṭāḷ relates how the naughty Kṛṣṇa knocked down her dollhouse.[38] As is so often the case in the history of Tamil literature, literary form and religious expression are seen here in symbiotic relationship, mutually influencing each other.

Certainly the group of myths having the most pervasive effect on the expression of Vaiṣṇava *bhakti* deal with Kṛṣṇa's amorous "sports" with the *gopīs* of Vṛndāvana. Identification with the *gopīs* is central to the devotion of several of the most prominent Āḻvārs. We shall also have occasion to note how the mythical basis of this erotic relationship is reinforced by literary traditions indigenous to Tamilnad. But first a few examples of Āḻvār reference to the myth about Kṛṣṇa and the *gopīs*.

Āṇṭāḷ, who according to legend considered herself to be the spouse of Kṛṣṇa, is even reported to have undergone a full wedding ceremony formally uniting her to the deity in marriage. It is not surprising, then, that her devotional poems display an erotic type of mysticism. In the *Tiruppāvai*, Āṇṭāḷ pictures herself as one of a group of *gopīs* attempting to awaken Kṛṣṇa by singing outside of Nanda's and Yaśodā's house:

> Govinda! whose greatness and sweetness subdue even your enemies! The reward that we shall obtain by singing of you and obtaining the Parai [drum] from you shall be the following, all excellent ones which all the world will praise and extol as the highest. All the several ornaments such as wrist ornaments, shoulder ornaments, ornaments for the lower ear, ornaments for the upper ear, ornaments for the ankles; all these we shall wear. We shall wear dresses (hallowed by your contact). Then we shall take food cooked in milk and covered with ghee so lavishly that the ghee flows down the elbow of the receiver. And we shall always be united with you and thus we shall feel cool and happy.
>
> We are small and insignificant Gopis born of a race whose vocation is to go to the forest behind the milch cattle and eat there, a race

---

[37]T. P. Meenakshisundaran, *A History of Tamil Literature*. (Annamalainagar: Annamalai University, 1965), pp. 144-147.

[38]*Nāyacciyār Tirumoḻi* II, as related in Jesudasan, *History of Tamil Literature*, pp. 110-111.

> which has no claims whatsoever to knowledge. But it has been our great good fortune that You should have been born into the race we call our own. You Govinda! who have no wants and no imperfections whatsoever! The relationship between you and ourselves here cannot be done away with, try as you, or we, or all of us together may. (This much we beseech of you). We young girls in our ignorance have called you by small names in the abundance of our love towards you. Pray do not get offended at that.[39]

Āṇṭāḷ's other extant work, the *Nāycciyār Tirumoḻi*, is more overtly erotic. For example, she addresses these lines to Kāma, the god of love:

> I pray thee, Manmatha, let thy arrows of flower hasten me to my Beloved! Let it plunge me into the splendour of Krishna! Destine me, O god of love, for the sweet embrace of Ranga! I have consecrated my swelling breast unto Him alone! If any one mentions that my love-laden breast is meant for the human touch, I shall cease to live, O Manmatha! Is a fox of the forest to smell the sacred offering meant for gods? O let the lovely hands of Krishna alone possess me! I do penance for that, O god of love![40]

As related in the myths about the pranks Kṛṣṇa plays on the *gopīs*, Āṇṭāḷ imagines Kṛṣṇa to have hidden her sari while she and the other *gopīs* were bathing. The *Nāycciyār Tirumoḻi* also contains, among others, an account of a dream which Āṇṭāḷ had about her wedding to Kṛṣṇa and a section addressed to Kṛṣṇa's conch, where Āṇṭāḷ sensuously dwells on the beauty of Kṛṣṇa's lips and mouth.[41]

---

[39] *Tiruppāvai* 28-29 in D. Ramaswamy Iyengar, trans., *Thiruppavai*, 2d ed. (Madras: Sri Visishtadvaita Pracharini Sabha, 1967), pp. 25-26. Hooper suggests that the *paṟai* (drum) indicates "the triumph of acknowledged love; if he gives her a drum, it is so far a sign that he has commissioned her to proclaim his praises" (*Hymns of the Āḻvārs*, p. 49).

[40] Quoted without specific textual reference by Shuddhananda Bharati, *Alvar Saints and Acharyas*, 2d ed. (Madras: Shuddhananda Library, 1968), p. 20.

[41] See Jesudasan, *History of Tamil Literature*, pp. 107-108, 110-111. Another famous female devotee of Kṛṣṇa whose *bhakti* bears resemblance to Āṇṭāḷ's was the Hindi poet Mīrābāī. Cf. S. M. Pandey, "Mīrābāī and Her Contributions to the Bhakti Movement," *History of Religions* 5, No. 1. (Summer 1965): 54-73.

Judging from her poetry, Āṇṭāḷ's experience of Kṛṣṇa was limited to that of a *gopī* seeking her beloved. Other of the Āḻvārs, however, were not so exclusive in the mode of devotional relationship which they enjoyed. Kulaśēkara, whom we have already mentioned as an exponent of relating to God as a parent does to a son, also exemplifies a love for God which is modelled on that of a *gopī* attracted to Kṛṣṇa.[42] And Periyāḻvār, who commonly casts himself in the role of Yaśodā doting upon the child Kṛṣṇa, on occasion changes costumes, as it were, and becomes a *gopī*. Thus, we find Periyāḻvār saying, "Lo, that shepherd boy comes playing on his flute, laughing with his mates! Sisters, I have known nothing so charming like this pretty Gopal! My passion for Him breaks the bounds of my breast! See the sweet smile of His coral lips!"[43]

According to Tamil Vaiṣṇava tradition, the devotion of the Āḻvārs reached its apex in Nammāḻvār (Our Āḻvār). Throughout his *Tiruviruttam* and also at many points in his *Tiruvāymoḻi*, Nammāḻvār adopts the erotic mode as his way of relating to the deity, with the example of Kṛṣṇa and the *gopīs* serving as his source of inspiration.[44] The *Tiruviruttam* is modelled on Tamil Caṅkam poetry of the *akam* type. Nammāḻvār here imagines himself to be a woman waiting for the return of her lover, who is identified with Viṣṇu-Kṛṣṇa. Consequently, he is able to draw upon a whole system of imagery which subtly serves to intensify the spiritual-psychological desperation of the soul separated from God. Night is often referred to as a particularly painful time:

> Love's glow is paling, and instead, a dark
> And sickly yellow spreading;—and the night
> Becomes an age! This is the matchless wealth
> My good heart gave me when it yearned and sought
> Keen discus-wielding Kaṇṇan's tuḷasī cool![45]

---

[42] *Perumāḷ Tirumoḻi* 6:1-10.

[43] Quoted without reference by Bharati, *Alvar Saints and Acharyas*, p. 17.

[44] C. Vaudeville, "Evolution of Love-Symbolism in Bhagavatism," *Journal of the American Oriental Society* 82 (1962): 37.

[45] *Tiruviruttam* 12 in Hooper, *Hymns of the Āḻvārs*, p. 64. In *akam*

And at one point the heroine desperately pleads simply to gaze upon the Lord, her lover, even if in the company of other women:

> E'en among groups of beauteous girls, or in
> The festivals of the great—or anywhere—
> 'Tis thee that I would gaze upon, with disc
> Of gold and conch all white within thy hand,
> Thou dark-hued one, thou Sapphire, Pearl—my Gem![46]

Nammāḻvār's *Tiruvāymoḻi* is also based on the structure of love between man and woman, its vision of union with God unmistakably tied to a mystical viewpoint in which the soul is conceived of as female and God as male.[47]

The *Ciriya Tirumaṭal* and the *Periya Tirumaṭal* by Tirumaṅkai make use of an image from Tamil poetry to express Tirumaṅkai's sense of desperate, unrequited love for God. *Maṭal* refers to a practice whereby a man could publicly express his extreme love for a woman and thus hopefully force her to reciprocate his affection.[48] While this practice was a male prerogative in South India, Tirumaṅkai, nevertheless, imagines himself to be a woman and God to be male, rather unconvincingly attributing the female performance of the *maṭal* to North Indian custom.[49]

---

poetry the heroine's complexion takes on a yellow-green appearance (*pacalai*) when she is particularly love-sick for her absent lover.

[46]*Tiruviruttam* 84 in ibid., p. 84.

[47]Cf. the passages of *Tiruvāymoḻi* in Varadachari, *Āḻvārs of South India*, pp. 189-191.

[48]The *maṭal* is a palmyra stem which the frustrated lover fashions into a type of saw-horse and then rides through the streets while proclaiming his love. The *maṭal* custom is mentioned in *Kuṟuntokai* 17 and 32, both verses translated in A. K. Ramanujan (trans.), *The Interior Landscape: Love Poems from a Classical Tamil Anthology*. (Bloomington: Indiana University Press, 1967), pp. 27 and 34. Also see *Kuṟuntokai* 17, 173; and *Naṟṟiṇai*, 146, 152, 342, 377.

[49]*Ciriya Tirumaṭal* 64-77, as cited in Varadachari, *Āḻvārs of South India*, pp. 117-118. The references to "North Indian custom" are mainly to several mythical incidents in Sanskrit works which are not, strictly speaking, concerned with riding the *maṭal*. Rather, Tirumaṅkai interprets *maṭal* in terms of the female practice of *satī*, and this probably explains

Whereas some of our examples of the Vaiṣṇava devotional relationship based on love between the sexes, such as the *maṭal*, are not directly dependent upon mythical paradigms, it is certain that this devotional structure would not have been so conspicuously favored by the Āḻvārs were it not for the popularity among them of the stories about Kṛṣṇa's dalliance with the *gopīs* of Vṛndāvana. Clearly, in the case of the Tamil Vaiṣṇavas, myth functions significantly as a source of devotional attitudes, as a means for defining appropriate types of relationship with God and for guiding devotion along particular, rather well-defined paths. That this function of Vaiṣṇava myth was original and also of overriding importance for the development of later Vaiṣṇava *bhakti* is well recognized by Surendranath Dasgupta:

> . . . the idea that the legend of Kṛṣṇa should have so much influence on the devotees as to infuse them with the characteristic spirits of the legendary personages in such a manner as to transform their lives after their pattern is probably a new thing in the history of devotional development in any religion. It is also probably absent in the cults of other devotional faiths of India. With the Āṟvārs we notice for the first time the coming into prominence of an idea which achieved its culmination in the lives and literature of the devotees of the Gauḍīya school of Bengal, and particularly in the life of Caitanya. . . . The transfusion of the spirits of the legendary personages in the life-history of Kṛṣṇa naturally involved the transfusion of their special emotional attitudes towards Kṛṣṇa into the devotees, who were thus led to imagine themselves as being one with those legendary personalities and to pass through the emotional history of those persons as conceived through imagination.[50]

While the stories about Kṛṣṇa as the beautiful infant and youthful cowherd of Vṛndāvana, and somewhat less so those about Rāma, provided the Āḻvārs with a type of "mythic scenario"[51] for their own devotion, the various modes of

---

why Varadachari implies that riding the *maṭal* entails a type of ritual suicide, although this is not substantiated by the references to the *maṭal* in early Tamil literature.

[50]Surendranath Dasgupta, *A History of Indian Philosophy*. (Cambridge: Cambridge University Press, 1952), Vol. III, pp. 81-82.

[51]I am indebted to Professor Charles White for this term as applied to Kṛṣṇite *bhakti*.

devotional relationship assumed by these Tamil Vaiṣṇavas never approached the degree of formalization and refinement exemplified by some later North Indian *bhakti* sects.[52] There is a greater sense of freedom and dynamism in the devotion of the Āḻvārs than is present in the more scholastic literature of certain of the later Vaiṣṇava devotional cults. Thus, the Āḻvārs, excluding Āṇṭāḷ, feel free to draw upon various mythical precedents at different moments in their relationship with God. One does not get the impression that a particular *bhāva*, i.e., an archetypal mode of devotional emotion and relationship, was chosen and then rigidly adhered to by individual Āḻvārs. Indeed, the systematic elaboration of the various devotional *bhāvas* came later. Rather, the Āḻvārs usually manage to personalize and individualize the relationship within the framework of mythical models. Although the myth offers a return to an *illud tempus*[53] a moment in eternity, a paradigmatic relationship with God, one is aware that this is also the relationship with God of a particular individual with his own peculiar history and needs – of an Āṇṭāḷ, or a Nammāḻvār rather than simply any Vaiṣṇava devotee who has chosen the path of *mādhurya-bhāva-bhakti*. When carried to its final conclusion, the tendency to discover paradigms for devotional expression in myth leads to relationships with the deity that are statically, ideally conceived. But in the hymns of the Āḻvārs the peculiarities of individual personalities are still clearly visible.

---

[52]E.g., on the Bengali Vaiṣṇava cult, see Edward C. Dimock, Jr., "Doctrine and Practice among the Vaiṣṇavas of Bengal," *Krishna: Myths, Rites, and Attitudes*, pp. 41-63, especially pp. 46-51; and Melville T. Kennedy, *The Chaitanya Movement: A Study of the Vaishṇavism of Bengal.* (Calcutta: Association Press, 1925); and on a section of the Bengali Vaiṣṇava cult which came under Tantric influence, see Edward C. Dimock, Jr., *The Place of the Hidden Moon: Erotic Mysticism in the Vaiṣṇava-sahajiyā Cult of Bengal.* (Chicago: University of Chicago Press, 1966).

[53]On this term and for an insightful discussion of the regenerative power of mythical archetypes, see Mircea Eliade, *The Myth of the Eternal Return or, Cosmos and History*. Willard R. Trask, trans., (Princeton: Princeton University Press, 1954).

Conclusion

It is obvious that the different mythologies centering on Śiva and Viṣṇu have evoked different devotional attitudes from their *bhaktas* and, furthermore, have influenced the general flavor of devotional expression in each of the two great Hindu cults. Basically, the Śaiva poets find in myth confirmation of Śiva's greatness, his otherness and uncanniness, and his complete transcendence of ordinary human dimensions. Vaiṣṇava myths, on the other hand, are frequently cited to provide a structure or model, a mythic scenario, for man's relationship with God. That is, they function as paradigms for devotees' attitudes and actions. Vaiṣṇava myths help to shape devotional emotion according to the specifications of certain established patterns of relationship. In a sense, Vaiṣṇava myths and their appropriation by the Āḻvārs emphasize the continuity between the human and the divine, whereas Śaiva myths are often indicative of the differences.

Dynamic relationship between devotee and deity, i.e., relationship subject to change and development, and individuality of religious experience and expression are characteristic of both the Tamil Śaivas and the Āḻvārs. But these elements are more peculiarly attributable to Śaiva *bhakti* than to devotion directed toward Viṣṇu. And while the Tamil Śaiva poets, with rather scant mythical precedent for guidance, occasionally employ erotic imagery in describing their relationship with God, this somehow lacks the utter appropriateness of similar, much stronger currents in Vaiṣṇavism with its finely drawn pictures of a most endearing figure in the Kṛṣṇa of Vṛndāvana. Both traditions may emphasize and indeed seem to thrive on the suffering and anxiety of separation from God, but there is an undercurrent of humor (witness the pranks of Bālakṛṣṇa and Gopāla) and sanguineness in Vaiṣṇava *bhakti* which in Śaivism is largely absent.

One might go so far as to say that the Śaiva relationship with God, with all its unpredictability, is in some ways more ordinary, "realistic," and less exalted – in spite of Śiva's transcendent character – than the idealized, somewhat static relationships enjoyed by Kṛṣṇa and his devotees in an eternal Vṛndāvana of the spirit.[54] But while this might be argued as being true of some forms of later Vaiṣṇava devotion, it does not yet accurately describe Vaiṣṇava *bhakti* at the time of the Āḻvārs. The devotion of both the medieval Tamil Śaivas and Vaiṣṇavas is still too personal, free, and unconfined by convention to admit of such characterization.[55]

Yet there are the differences we have indicated, real differences rooted in the respective myths about Śiva and Viṣṇu; and in view of this divergence of mythical emphasis it is easy to understand why in certain cases Vaiṣṇava *bhakti* became the refined, almost baroque system of devotion which it did and why, on the other hand, *bhakti* never became as absolutely central to Śaiva experience and expression as it did in Vaiṣṇavism. (It should not be surprising that Śaivism has been more productive of ascetical practice than has the cult of Viṣṇu.) For the Tamil Śaivas myths are signs along the way to the goal. They name the whirlwind. They indicate what lies at the end of the road. For the Āḻvārs myths are also paradigms, models to be followed on the path to the goal. Here the myths become the path itself, the means by which the end is reached.

---

[54]For an engaging presentation of the spirit of post-Āḻvār Kṛṣṇite *bhakti*, see David Kinsley, " 'Without Kṛṣṇa There Is No Song,' " *History of Religons* 12, No. 2. (November 1972): 149-180; see especially pp. 165-166 and 178-180 on the nonordinary, playful aspects of the love depicted between Kṛṣṇa and the *gopīs*.

[55]Although the four great Tamil Śaiva poet-saints (Tirunāvukkaracu, Campantar, Cuntarar, and Māṇikkavācakar) later came to be thought of as exemplifying four different types of *bhakti* (respectively, that of servant, son, friend, and supreme wisdom), this schema, which in any case is not based on the mythology of Śiva himself, never came to have the paradigmatic significance for Śaiva devotion that the myths of Kṛṣṇa and Rāma had for the Vaiṣṇavas.

TEN

M. Lucetta Mowry

The Structure of Love in Māṇikkavācakar's *Tiruvācakam*

MĀṆIKKAVĀCAKAR, THE LAST and probably the greatest of the four poet-saints of Southern Śaivism during its formative period, was apparently born to devout Brahmin parents living near Madurai in the early ninth century A. D.[1] Though Śaiva hagiographers have mingled fact with legend in their narratives about this saint, their accounts suggest that he was a very precocious child of an illustrious family whose members served Pāṇṭiyaṉ kings in the capacity of prime ministers. Having mastered Brahamanical learning and the Śaiva Āgamas by the age of sixteen, Māṇikkavācakar came to the attention of the Pāṇṭiyaṉ king, who entrusted him with the responsibility of governing his kingdom and rewarded him handsomely for this administrative ability. Māṇikkavācakar's rapid rise to power had brought him into the cultural life of the court and undoubtedly gave him a knowledge of the intricate literary forms of secular

---

[1]The date for Māṇikkavācakar's life is greatly disputed. K. A. Nilakanta Sastri is inclined to make him a contemporary of the Pāṇṭiyaṉ king Varagunavarmaṉ II, who ruled in Madurai from A. D. 862-885; see *A History of South India*, third ed. (Madras: Oxford University Press, 1966), pp. 175, 425. C. V. Narayana Ayyar, however, argues persuasively for a date in the later half of the seventh century and thus places Māṇikkavācakar before Cuntarar; see *Origin and Early History of Śaivism in South India*. (Madras: University of Madras, 1936), pp. 398-425. See also Mariasusai Dhavamony, *Love of God according to Śaiva Siddhānta*. (Oxford: Clarendon Press, 1971), pp. 158-169.

love poetry.[2] That he mastered this form is demonstrated in his poem *Tirukkōvai*, a work of 400 stanzas which was modelled according to a formalized type of love poetry called *kōvai* (literally meaning that which has sections arranged in sequences). Each of the 400 stanzas deals with a particular aspect of love: the meeting of the lovers, details about their previous births, and events of the youthful hero and heroine in this present birth.

Though this poem discloses Māṇikkavācakar's skilled control of the subject and forms of love poetry, he composed it after he had resolved the conflict between secular and sacred love and intended the *Tirukkōvai* to be understood allegorically in terms of bridal mysticism. The lover is none other than the Lord Śiva and the beloved is the devotee. If Māṇikkavācakar had become knowledgeable about the ways of love and the poetry of love at the Pāṇṭiyaṉ court of Madurai, his earlier training had also made him familiar with the works of the notable Śaiva saint Tirumūlar, whose famous treatise, the *Tirumantiran*, provided the philosophical foundation for Śaiva Siddhanta. From this work the most quoted verse of the 3000 stanzas is that which says:

> The ignorant say, Love and God are different;
> None know that Love and God are the same;
> When they know that Love and God are the same,
> They rest in God as Love.

Other portions of the eighteenth chapter of the first Tantra of this poem are equally instructive for understanding the Śaiva tradition in which Māṇikkavācakar was nurtured.

> My great Love has been directed towards Him (Śiva),
> Whose tiger skin is brighter than gold,
> The Crescent Moon in whose head is luminous and bright
>
> Those with intense love will see God.
> Those with compassion will see His two feet.

---

[2]For a discussion of poetry of this genre, see Kamil Zvelibil, *The Smile of Murugan.* (Leiden: E. J. Brill, 1973), pp. 131-154; and R. Balakrishna Mudaliyar, *The Golden Age of Ancient Tamil Literature*, Vol. I. (Madras: South India Saiva Siddhanta Works Publishing Society, 1959), pp. xxi-xvi.

They do not know my Lord
Who evinced strong love in creating us and opening up the sources of Bliss.
It is He, who with Love, filled this hard life with Love
And filled all space with Love

He (the Lord) is within and without Love,
He forms the body of Love, He is both before and after; . . .
He forms the internal essence of Love . . .
He is the doer, object sought in Love
And He is the help to those who love Him.[3]

In Māṇikkavācakar's earlier work, the *Tiruvācakam*, a collection of fifty-one hymns in praise of Siva, one can sense the magnitude of the struggle within the poet's soul. These poems amply reflect his valiant attempts to flee from the allurements and enticements of secular love which prevented him from realizing perfect union with Siva, the one being worthy of man's complete adoration and love.

The crucial turning point in Māṇikkavācakar's life came when he was sent on a commission by the king to Peruntuṟai, a great harbor town in the Tanjore district, to buy a shipload of fine Arabian steeds. As Māṇikkavācakar approached the town, he saw a humble, yet venerable, guru surrounded by his disciples, who were listening to an exposition of the Śaiva tradition. What Māṇikkavācakar saw was no ordinary guru but Śiva himself, with a galaxy of Śaiva devotees – a great company of saints with whom he longed to be associated. His instantaneous response was to give the guru all his possessions including the king's money for the horses. Neither punishment for his misappropriation of funds nor taunts about his madness could deter him from complete dedication of his life in the service of Śiva and from taking up the life of a wandering ascetic journeying from temple to temple singing the praises of Śiva and pouring out his expressions of desire to be united with Śiva by an unbreaking cord of love. His travels finally took him to the famed temple at Chidambaran where Śiva is worshiped as Naṭarāja, the Performer of the Cosmic Dance. This latter

---

[3]J. M. Somasundaran Pillai, ed. and trans., *Two Thousand Years of Tamil Literature*. (Madras: South India Śaiva Siddhānta Works Publishing Society, 1959), pp. 301-303.

period of his life won for him the epithet, Māṇikkavācakar – "he whose utterances are rubies," – and for his songs, the comment that they have the power to melt hearts of stone.

In his poems Māṇikkavācakar tried repeatedly to express the overwhelmingly powerful yet tenderly gentle experience of the initial manifestation of Śiva's gracious love for him. The experience in itself was elemental and transforming and became the foundation upon which the later structure of love between Śiva and his newly won devotee was to be built. If one is thinking in structural terms with respect to this building, one must use for it the language of the Śaiva mystics of their era. His predecessors had asserted that the building was a spiritual temple not made with hands and mortar. Commenting on this structure, Appar sings in one of his hymns:

> With the body itself as the temple, with a subjugated mind itself as the servants there, with truth itself as purification, with mind as the jewel image, with love itself as the *ghee* and the milk for ablution of the image, with hymn as the food-offering, we have shown the way to conduct the worship of Śiva.

Two of the sixty-three *ṉāyaṉārs* mentioned in Cēkkiḻār's hagiology, *Periya Purāṇam*, devoted their entire efforts to the creating of such a construction. Of Vāyilār, the dumb, poor one of Mylapore, Cēkkiḻār says, "He built the temple of non-forgetfulness in his heart, lit the shining lamp of self-illumination, bathed the Lord in the immortal waters of inner joy and offered him the nectar of his love as *naivedya*." Probably the most famous of such temple-builders was Pūcalār, who day after day built his temple to Śiva. On the same day that the saint had decided to consecrate his temple, the Pallava king Rājasiṃha had also planned a similar celebration for his newly erected Kailāsanātha temple at Kanchipuram. According to the legend, Śiva instructed the king through a dream to delay the dedication of the royal temple so that the Lord might be installed first in the mental temple of his humble devotee.[4] As we turn to examine Māṇikkavācakar's efforts to realize his

[4] V. Raghavan, *The Great Integrators: The Saint-Singers of India*. (New Delhi: Publications Division, Ministry of Information and Broadcasting, 1964), p. 66.

dream of union through love with Śiva, we shall see how the foundation of initial enthusiasm could be built upon only by the painful discipline of love before a mental temple of rapturous bliss could become a reality.

Though Māṇikkavācakar may have had a vague and unformed yearning for Śiva before his conversion, he never believed that he himself had initiated the awakening of his love for Śiva. When Māṇikkavācakar reflected on how this started, he realized that it was not by laborious intellectual striving in the company of erudite philosophers well versed in Vedic literature. In fact, the logicians of every creed imperiled the souls of those who longed for release. In hymn 4 Māṇikkavācakar says:

> Neighbors – close friends all – gathered round
> and talked atheism
> till their tongues became calloused.
>
> Brahmins glibly proved by Vedic texts
> Sectarian disputants
> claiming their respective creeds only as perfect
> clamorously clashed (with each other).
> The tornado called staunch *maaya vaadàm* –
> (the dogma that the world is but an empty dream) –
> swirled and blew and roared,
> the while the conflicting cultural deadly poison
> of Epicurianism – the dazzling doughty snake –
> came and joined forces.[5]

By his gracious condescension in the form of a guru the Lord Śiva interpreted the ancient Vedas and gave to Māṇikkavācakar that illuminating word which even the gods Viṣṇu and Brahmā had searched for but never found.[6]

This experience of awakened love in his heart was a mystery beyond human comprehension. Surely Śiva must have entered his heart in a previous birth and prepared the destiny of his present existence before he had taken shape in the womb and now found his soul encased in a body defiled by impurities and in a state of enslavement to the world. In hymn 31

[5]G. Vanmikanathan, trans., *Pathway to God through Tamil Literature: 1. Through the Thiruvaachakam*. (New Delhi: Delhi Tamil Sangam, 1971), pp. 150-151.

[6]See hymns 48:1, 3:49 and 20:4.

Māṇikkavācakar speaks of himself as enslaved to sin, experiencing a life of anguish and of dense ignorance, and confused by caste, disease, family ties, egotism, delusion, and an existence without aim or purpose. In no way did Māṇikkavācakar feel that he deserved the overwhelming flood of Śiva's love which washed away his impurities. The Lord delivered him not only from death but more importantly from the continuous cycle of rebirth.

> As grass, shrub, worm, tree, as full many a kind of beast, bird, snake, as stone, man, goblin, demons, as mighty giants, ascetics, devas, in the prevalent world of mobiles and immobiles, Oh noble Lord, I have been born in every kind of birth and am wearied! Oh Reality! Your golden feet I saw this day and deliverance from birth gained.[7]

Śiva's unveiling of love evoked from Māṇikkavācakar amazed wonder, wholehearted submission to Śiva, and praise for the greatness of his mercy and kindness manifested in his general governance of the world and mankind and especially in Māṇikkavāckar's own experience of his gracious love. With respect to the seemingly miraculous awakening of love, Māṇikkavācakar beautifully expresses his complete and utter bewilderment in the last stanza of his twenty-second hymn.

> You gave yourself to me and took me in exchange;
> Oh Sankara,
> Who, indeed, is the cleverer one of us two?
> Infinite bliss I gained,
> What did you gain from me?
> Oh Mighty Lord Who has occupied my mind as your shrine,
> O Civan who abides in Tirupperunthurai,
> Oh my Father, Oh Lord of the Universe,
> my body you have taken as Your abode;
> for this I have nothing to offer in return.[8]

In human terms it would be inconceivable that love given to another would not expect something in return. The gift of love bestowed had been a divine light dispelling Māṇikkavācakar's groping in dark and murky ignorance. Overpowering grace had put to flight all that was false, fleeting, and unreal, had routed

---

[7]Vanmikanathan, *Thiruvaachakam*, pp. 108-109.

[8]Ibid., p. 346.

evil desires and stilled the tumult of the mind. The greatest gift of all was Śiva's giving of himself. By coming into the soul of the lowest and meanest of curs, Śiva had taken pity on him and melted his heart of stone so that he lost his body, soul, sense of perception, mind, and ego (hymn 11). The gift of security in Śiva's love had made former years of enslavement to the world seem like a purgatory, or the whirling dance of a puppet show whose dolls now lie exhausted (hymn 50), or like the profitless tilling of a barren field (hymn 40).

In every hymn it is clear that Māṇikkavācakar wishes to be enslaved by Śiva, to recognize him as his true Lord and King, and to give him the only thing he can – unwavering submission. His expression of this desire for a steady, continuous, and supreme dedication of love to Śiva is couched in the traditional phrases of placing himself beneath Śiva's feet, an act of adoration and loyal devotion. Several lines from the first hymn laud Śiva in this manner.

> Hallowed be Namachchivaaya . . .
> Hallowed be the feet of Him Who never departs
> from my heart even for as long as it takes to wink!
> Hallowed be the feet of the precious gem of a Guru,
> Who in Kokazhi assumed lordship over me!
> Hallowed be the feet of Him
> Who in the guise of the Agamaas,
> Stands close . . .
> Hallowed be the feet of the One,
> The Many, the Immanent!
> Let the foot of the King
> Who stilled the tumult (of my mind)
> and assumed lordship over me, prevail!
>
> Obeisance to the feet of the Effulgent One!
> Obeisance to Civan's rosey feet![9]

From the tradition of Śaiva saints, Māṇikkavācakar singles out one, Kaṇṇappaṉ, who had become an outstanding hero of devout and dedicated submission. Of this saint Māṇikkavācakar says:

> Even after finding me lacking in love
> equalling Kannappan's,

[9]Ibid., pp. 104-106.

my Sire, by my own measure
me too graciously accepted,
and ceremoniously commanded me: "Come hither."
To that flood of grace.[10]

The *Periya Purāṇam* has the Lord say that "Kaṇṇappaṉ's very being is an embodiment of love for Us; all his knowledge concerning Us; all his actions are pleasing to Us. Understand his state in this way (and not by external appearances)."[11] Kaṇṇappaṉ was the son of a devout chieftain whose clan lived in the jungles of the hill country, hunting wild beasts roaming in the forests. One day Kaṇṇappaṉ and his companions caught a great boar near a site made sacred by the presence of a *liṅga*, the top of which had been roughly shaped in the form of a head. When Kaṇṇappaṉ saw the holy image he exclaimed, "Ah, wondrous blessedness! To me a slave this divinity has been given! But how is it that the God remains here alone in a wilderness where lions, elephants, tigers, bears, and other wild beasts dwell, as though he were some rude mountaineer like me?" Then noticing that a devotee had already attended to the bathing of the image but had given it no food, Kaṇṇappaṉ gave to the deity the most tender and delicate portions of the roasted boar. The Brahmin priest who regularly performed his worship before the *liṅga* was horrified at this act of pollution. When the Brahmin asked the Lord who had desecrated his image, the Lord replied, "That which thou dost complain of is to me most dear and acceptable! Thy rival ministrant is a chieftain of the rude foresters. He is absolutely ignorant of the Vēdas and the Ҫaiva texts. He knows not the ordinances of worship. But regard not him, regard the *spirit and motive* of his acts. His rough and gigantic frame is instinct with love to me, his whole knowledge – in thine eyes crass ignorance – is summed up in *the knowledge of ME!* His every action is dear to me; the touch of his leathern slipper is pleasant to me as that of the tender hand of my son Skanda. The water with which he besprinkles me from his mouth is holy to me as the water of the

[10]Ibid., p. 262.

[11]Quoted by V. A. Devasenapathi, *Of Human Bondage and Divine Grace*. (Annamalainagar: Annamalai University, 1963), p. 63.

Ganges. The food he offers to me – to thee so abominable – is pure love. He utterly loves me, even as thou dost, but come tomorrow when thou shalt see his worship, and I will give the proof of his devotion to me." The proof of devotion was the saint's healing of the Lord's wounded eye by giving to him his own healthy eye.[12] For Māṇikkavācakar, Kaṇṇappaṉ became the great exemplar of love given totally, unconditionally, spontaneously, and without calculation. Though he admired such dedication, he found it exceedingly difficult to respond in like manner to Śiva's love.

The initial illuminative experience evoked from Māṇikkavācakar not only amazed wonder and avowals of willing submission to the Lord but also words of praise and adoration. In lauding the greatness of Śiva's sovereign power, Māṇikkavācakar draws upon a rich repertoire of stories from Purāṇic and Epic mythology and from legends of Śaiva saints. In hymn 14, for example, the poet recounts the episodes of Śiva's burning the three flying cities of the Asuras, of his punishment of Dakṣa who blatantly ignored Śiva's supremacy, and of his suppression of the evil king Rāvaṇa for attempting to destroy Śiva's abode on Mt. Kailāsa. These stories demonstrate that Śiva acts with justice and love (for he punishes evil but shows mercy to the evil doer) and also that one cannot presume too much upon the Lord's love. In countless ways Śiva has declared his love for his created order and for man. He caught the powerful flow of the heavenly Ganges in his hair so that its descending force did not destroy the earth. He drank the poison skimmed from the nectar that gods and men might live. By his cosmic dance he set the world in motion. He guards his universe and like a monsoon cloud relieves the drought so that the ploughman may sow seeds of love in a field of worship. Thus Māṇikkavācakar writes in hymn 3:

> The globular concourses
> of this section of the Universe

---

[12]G. U. Pope, Ed. and trans., *The Tiruvāçagan or "Sacred Utterances" of the Tamil Poet, Saint, and Sage Māṇikka-vāçagar*. (Oxford: Clarendon Press, 1900), pp. 141-145.

with their immeasurableness and lush appearance
and the way they excel each other in beauty –
if one were to speak of these,
they sprawl a hundred crores and more,
Making them look small like the crowded specks
in a ray of sunlight streaming into a house,
a big one is God.
And if one were to research into it,
the hordes of Brahmaas and multitudes of Vishnus,
emergence, existence,
and the very great cataclysm
associated with the end of all things,
redemption therefrom and reestablishment,
all these microcosms and macrocosms,
like eddies of wind
within the blast of a devastating tornado,
He spins and makes them swirl about –
The eternal Youth.

And as the Ancient One and King of the Universe

The day after day rising sun
He endows with efflugence;
the resplendent moon He endows with coolness;
He creates the heat in the fire of great night.[13]

In a later decad (hymn 19) Māṇikkavācakar composed a verse in praise of each of the ten insignia of a king: (1) Śiva's name and title are Lord and Lord of the gods; (2) his country is the Pāṇṭiyan̲ region; (3) his capital is Uttarakōcamaṅkai; (4) his principal river is that of bliss, which coming down from heaven washes away the impurity of men's minds; (5) his mountain is one of grace, high in the heavens from which emanate rays of light to dispel the darkness of the world and of the soul; (6) his heavenly steed is accompanied by sweet maids; (7) his special weapon is the trident which destroys the three *malas* and liberates his saints; (8) his special drum is a martial one which calls for a war against births; (9) his garland is the creeper grass which wards off karma; and (10) his flag is embroidered with the symbol of the bull which terrifies his enemies.

With great imaginative ability Māṇikkavācakar praises Śiva for his innumerable acts of grace. He praises Śiva not only as one of

[13]G. Vanmikanathan, *Thiruvaachakam*, pp. 133-134.

regal status but also as one who disguises himself in very humble forms and as one who enjoys the playful role of a prankster. In hymn 4, Māṇikkavācakar addresses Śiva as "King of Golden Madurai," "the Dancer in the hall of Tillai." "the one anterior to the never-aging four Vedas," "the Sporter who assumes many forms," among which was that of a sow. Māṇikkavācakar's allusion to this unusual manifestation of the Lord comes from the story about how an ascetic, annoyed by the pranks of twelve mischievous boys, turned them into suckling pigs by his curse. Since the mother sow had been killed by a hunter, Śiva did not hesitate to take on this lowest of forms in order to save the lads. Māṇikkavācakar describes Śiva in his playful form in stanza 8 of the eighth hymn:

> Of the magnificent One
>   Who graciously endowed a prize
>   for the melody-bearing song,
> Of Him with one part (of His body) bearing a woman,
>   of the Lord of Perunthurai,
>   of Eesan of the famed vast spheres
>   borne by the sky,
> of the God with eye-bearing forehead,
>   of the golden Body
>   Which bearing earth (on its back) for wages
>   in buzzing Madurai,
>   was struck by the King (with his cane)
>   and carries (to this day) the scar thereof,
> Of Him let us sing.[14]

According to the legend referred to in the last lines, the city of Madurai was threatened by the flooding of the river Vaigai. To offset this danger the king had commanded the services of one man from each family to raise the river banks. An old widow of the town, who barely subsisted on selling rice cakes, was unable to find anyone who would do her share of the work. In response to her prayer for help, Śiva came in the guise of an ordinary day-laborer to offer his services. Though he built up her area with great speed and ease, he caused considerable consternation by tearing down the work of others, by throwing heaps of mud about, and by lazily lolling while others toiled.

---

[14] Ibid., p. 244.

The king, hearing of his sportive, eccentric behavior, punished the laborer by striking him with a blow of his cane, a blow which made the entire universe shudder. As the laborer mysteriously disappeared, the river receded to its normal level and the town was miraculously saved.

The first disclosure of the Lord's love to which Māṇikkavācakar responded with awe, loyal submission, and gratitude revolutionized his life. Suddenly the man of fame and fortune, prestige, and wealth became aware of the shabbiness of secular love compared with the splendor of divine love. Unknown to Māṇikkavācakar, God had been pursuing him with his love throughout the countless rebirths of his past existence and throughout his present life – during infancy, young manhood when alluring glances of beautiful maidens seemed so enticing, during the years of struggle with poverty and false learning, and more recently with wealth and the honors of court life. In the first encounter Śiva, without calculation and without asking if he was a crook, an evil one, a vile wretch (hymn 10) had entered his mind and being. God had watched over him with his grace until this moment, and now Māṇikkavācakar became aware of how confused by caste, how enslaved to sense, and how aimless in life he had been. In this first flush of coming to know the Lord, Māṇikkavācakar had declared a willing submission of his whole being to Śiva. Yet this first burst of love's ecstasy lacked the full understanding of love itself and of love's commitment.

As Māṇikkavācakar indicates in the majority of his poems, the maturing of love and the discipline of a *bhakta* involves a long, arduous, painful, and torturous pilgrimage. In two of his poems (hymns 5 and 51) he summarizes what this pilgrimage entails. In hymn 5, a poem of 10 decads each of which has 10 stanzas called the Sacred Cento, Māṇikkavācakar takes the reader through the stages of love's journey starting with the first rapture when one begins to comprehend the real and ending with the final overflow of bliss experienced in the consummation of mystic union of the devotee with his Lord. In hymn 51, entitled the lyric of release, the poet, having reached the final stage, reviews the pathway travelled in search of the Supreme. It is as though the poet had charted the course in hymn 5 and in the last hymn of his collected poems had concluded with a song of victory made even more triumphant by viewing in retrospect the intense struggle undertaken in ascending the path, a path which the Lord in his grace had revealed, yet one which had been overcast by gloom, despair, and despondency.

Māṇikkavācakar, as he begins the ascent, is shocked by the realization that he has not been able to sustain his first vows of devotion. Though the Lord has bestowed upon him a secret grace, his heart, like an immature leaf-blade, was witless, foolish, and traitorous. He had intended his body to be a shrine for Śiva. Instead Māṇikkavācakar found that he still lived in the flesh and cherished it, that he catered to the senses as though he were a gluttonous elephant with two trunks, and that he was still attached to his own ego and loved himself and what was his. So he writes of himself:

> Unmindful of the spring-time Cupid's dart piercing me
> and the cool moon scorching (the wound),
> I, becoming whipped up,
> like curd agitated by a churn,
> by the wiles of women with glances like a fawn's,
> would not go forward to enter the city of my Civan
> Who bestowed on me honeyed holy grace;
> but still exist dining and dressing well
> in order to preserve life in the flesh.[15]

Māṇikkavācakar was puzzled by the perversity of his own nature. Having been given so much by the Lord, why was he not able to be single-heartedly devoted to the Lord? Deviation from a steady love for God could only bring about his ruin. Torn by the conflict within his inner soul he pleads with the Lord in hymn 6 not to forsake him. Three stanzas of this hymn (6:11-13) poignantly express the poet's distress:

> Oh magnanimous One,
> See that You do not forsake me
> who, on Your enslaving me,

[15]Ibid., p. 181.

cling to the five senses,
and am bent on deserting You,
Oh Uththarakosamangai's King,
Who is skilled in wielding the spear
to the terror of the enemies!
Oh great Sea of limpid ambrosia
on which, I, of evil nature, feed!

See that You do not forsake me
who, like a dog lapping up the waters of the sea,
am incapable of letting my mind
sink in Your sea of grace,
Oh Utharakosamangai's King
Who lives ever only in the body
of never deserting devotees!
Oh flower-petal Honey! Oh Gem!
Oh Ambrosia! Oh my Flood of nectar!

See that You do not forsake me
who, like tongue getting parched
in the midst of a flood,
though in receipt of Your grace,
am unable to get out of misery.
Oh You who abide in the minds of devotees
who love You!
Oh King of Uththarakosamangai!
To me of crafty mind, do, in your grace, grant
a joy never before enjoyed by me.[16]

The first hard lesson which Māṇikkavācakar was compelled to learn in his quest for rapturous union with Śiva was primarily about himself. He knew that Śiva was Love, and that the pathway to union with Śiva was the way of love. He had utmost confidence in Śiva's faithfulness in continuously supporting and energizing his devotee with his love. Though the Lord was worthy of trust, Māṇikkavācakar had doubts about himself. He was astonished at his own fickleness of heart and lack of singleness of purpose. While Śiva's love was steadfast, powerful, and pure, Māṇikkavācakar had found his own devotion to be weak, impotent, and wavering. For this reason the way of love was fragile and in danger of possible failure. Since union in love with Śiva required the honest intentions and actions of both

[16] Ibid., pp. 209-210.

parties, the major question concerned the action needed for a maturing of Māṇikkavācakar's love for Śiva, making it possible for him to realize his hopes for perfect union with his Lord. Obvious prerequisites for success were patient understanding of the problem and love's way of resolving it. The problem was not an academic matter to be resolved by the mind alone but could be solved only in the experience of life itself.

Of Śiva's five activities – creating, sustaining, destroying, concealing, and favoring – the most effective to be used under the present circumstance was that of concealment. If Māṇikkavācakar's love for Śiva was to grow and be strengthened, he must now earnestly search for the God who had favored him with a revelation of himself in the form of the guru. The poet, according to his hymns, is determined to become engaged in the search and not to give up until he has found the Lord again. It is in this searching that his love, given to Śiva too hastily at the beginning and subsequently dissipated and diminished by uncertainties, became sufficiently firm and resolute to arrive at an understanding of the kind of love needed by the devotee for the desired union with his Lord.

In the *Tiruvācakam* one finds an interesting unit of 16 poems (hymns 7-22) which seems to reflect this period of his life and to have as their models folk games and folk songs. Māṇikkavācakar has apparently adapted this folk lore to express his longing for Śiva along the lines of bridal mysticism. He begins in hymn 7 with the awakening of love within the heart of a young girl who has heard about her bridegroom and closes the section with the consummation of the marriage (hymn 22). The joys and trials of the Lord's devotee are analagous to the fortunes of love so familiar in daily life. A selection of some of these hymns will indicate the nature of Māṇikkavācakar's discipline on the pathway of love.

The inspiration for the first of these hymns, hymn 7, was apparently a festival for Śiva's consort, Pārvatī, upon which occasion daughters accompanied their mothers during the early morning hours to bathe in the river and to make images of Pārvatī. As they walked through the streets, they awakened their friends by singing songs in praise of Śiva and as they made images of Pārvatī, they prayed for a suitable husband. The personal significance of the festival for Māṇikkavācakar was the awakening of a devotee who hoped to be included in the throng of devotees and to be identified in some way with Pārvatī, the Lord's bride. So the poet sings:

> Oh devotion-filled ones!
> Oh Eesan's ancient devotees!
> Oh decorous ones!
> Is it wrong if the Lord enslaves new devotees,
> ridding them of their baseness?
> How great your love is, don't we all know?[17]

Māṇikkavācakar continues by pledging his love to the bridegroom by saying:

> In our fear, we say afresh that (well known) adage:
> "The child in your arms is Your own protege"
> Our great Lord, we will tell you something; listen!
> Let not our breasts join in an embrace
> with the shoulders of anyone but Your devotees.
> Let not our hands do any work except for You.
> Night and day let our eyes not see anything but You.
> If, here and now, this boon You would grant us,
> what does it matter to us where the sun rises?[18]

In hymn 12 the progress of Māṇikkavācakar's discipline of love takes the form of a conversation between a maid in the household and the young girl in love. The maid asks questions hoping that the answers will reveal with whom and why the girl is so obviously in love. The next hymn (hymn 13) has the bride-to-be gathering flowers with her companions to bring them as a gift to her lover.

> Let us pluck the creeper flowers
> for the King of the people of the heavenly land
> Who keeps on dancing
> while I keep on tottering and tottering about
> wailing for Him.[19]

In hymn 15 Māṇikkavācakar shamelessly sings of his love, though many may criticize him for having been filled with a madness of devotion for the Lord. In hymn 17 the young bride

---

[17] Ibid., p. 230. [18] Ibid., p. 239. [19] Ibid., p. 289.

chatters almost incoherently to her mother about her Lover.

> "My eternal Bridegroom is He,
> exceedingly beautiful is He,
> He is ever in my thoughts,
> Oh my Mother!" she would say:
> "He who abides in my thoughts
> is the Southerner,
> the Father in Perunthurai, Bliss incarnate,
> Oh Mother!" she would say.[20]

At the close of that hymn her frenzy is so great that she determines in the following poem (hymn 18) to send the *kuyil* bird to her Lover asking him to come to her. In stanza 3 of hymn 21 the devotee cries out in agony saying that if the Lord does not appear he will perish. He has been like an ownerless bull and like the wearied, yet patiently waiting, crane who stands for hours on one leg waiting for its prey.

Finally in hymn 22 the arduous pilgrimage is finished. The agony of separation, the sense of worthlessness of life without Śiva, the patient hours of hope mingled with despair, and the willingness to declare openly his love for Śiva in spite of uncomprehending critics have had their reward. The Lord has come to claim his bride whose love he can now accept and whom he can take to be his own. The union is rapturous – one of sheer joy.

> You bestowed on me a grace undeserved by me
> and enabled this slave's body and soul
> to joyfully thaw and met with love.
> For this I have nothing to give in requital to You,
> Oh Emancipator pervading the past,
> the future and every thing!
> Oh infinite primal Being!
> Oh Lord of Perunthurai in the south!
> Oh great Lord Civan!
> Oh King of eminent Civapuram![21]

Subsequent poems in the *Tiruvācakam* add details to the poet's description of the pilgrimage. He writes of his weariness of life apart from Siva, of his physical, mental, and spiritual fatigue brought on by long periods of despair, of his inability to

---

[20]Ibid., p. 316. [21]Ibid., p. 342.

find Śiva in any other way than that of love. The pathway has led Māṇikkavācakar to the land of no return where all distinctions of I and mine have been cancelled out and the Lord dwells permanently in his heart, the shrine now fit for the Lord's abode. This final rapturous union, while exultant, brings with it a sense of deep calm, freedom experienced in love, and great joy.

The structure of love in Māṇikkavācakar's *Tiruvācakam* was established on the foundation of Śiva's love. Upon that basis the erection of the temple within Māṇikkavācakar's heart depended upon the work of the Lord and his devotee. Each detail required skillful and patient workmanship. The Lord's supporting and energizing power of love was matched by Māṇikkavācakar's undistracted and single-hearted response of devotion to his Lord. When the structure was complete the merging of love, human and divine, produced a shrine of exquisite beauty in its unity of design – one to be as much admired and a cause for wondering amazement as Rājasiṃha's Kailāsanātha temple at Kanchipuram. This note of mysterious wonder concludes Māṇikkavācakar's poems with the question:

> Who else, indeed, could gain like me the grace
> bestowed on me by the primal Being –
> the Source of everything, my Mother –
> Who, severing my bonds of the three *malams*
> and making even me a thing of worth –
> me who was wandering in the company of dunces
> who did not know the benefits of deliverance –
> made this cur ascend the palanquin?[22]

[22]Ibid., p. 482.

Notes on the Contributors

MARTHA BUSH ASHTON is Coordinator, Humanities Teaching Institute for Bengal Studies, Michigan State University. Her doctorate is in theatre.

SUSAN S. BEAN is Assistant Professor of Anthropology at Yale University.

DAVID BUCK, after having studied for two years in Madurai University, is living in Kentucky.

HARRY M. BUCK is Professor of Religion Studies at Wilson College.

KENNETH A. DAVID is Professor of Anthropology at Michigan State University.

SUZANNE HANCHETT is Assistant Professor of Anthropology at Queens College of the City of New York.

M. LUCETTA MOWRY is Professor of Religion and Biblical Studies at Wellesley College.

M. SHANMUGAM PILLAI is Professor of Tamil at Madurai University.

WALTER SPINK is Professor of Art at the University of Michigan.

CHARLOTTE VAUDEVILLE is a professor at the Université de la Sorbonne Nouvelle.

GLENN E. YOCUM is Instructor of Religion at Whittier College.